THE UNITED STATES AND CANADA

IN 1832, 1833, AND 1834

By CARL DAVID ARFWEDSON

Volume 1

With a New Introduction by
MARVIN FISHER
DEPARTMENT OF ENGLISH
ARIZONA STATE UNIVERSITY

JOHNSON REPRINT CORPORATION

New York and London

1969

The edition reproduced here was originally
published in 1834

Library of Congress Catalog Card Number: 76-79653

Printed in the U. S. A.

INTRODUCTION

Carl David Arfwedson, who was Swedish by birth but wrote in English by choice, was certainly one of the more ambitious and resilient of the thousands of Europeans who in the nineteenth century included America in an extended version of the Grand Tour. Moved far more by curiosity than by the cupidity that possessed some of these visitors, Arfwedson stayed longer, saw more, and endured greater hardships with far less complaint or condescension than most of the hundreds who wrote up their ramblings for the edification of readers back home.

Not yet twenty-six when he arrived in the United States on July 10, 1832, Arfwedson presents a parallel to Alexis de Tocqueville, who, at the same age, had arrived the previous year. But Tocqueville's ostensible purpose (to survey the American prison system) and his far more ambitious underlying motive (to gain an understanding of democratic trends which he saw as the wave of the future) suggest a far more sober personality than Arfwedson's. Although he had written on a phase of American colonial history in a dissertation at the University of Uppsala dealing with the New Sweden settlement on the Delaware River in the seventeenth century, young Arfwedson came to America primarily because his father wanted him temporarily out of sight. Apparently he had created a minor scandal among the more staid elements of Stockholm society, some of whom perhaps recognized caricatures of themselves in a series of farcical playlets which he published between 1827 and 1831. The naughtiness of his *Journey of Three Notorious Young Girls to Immortality* would seem quite innocent today, but the more pointed satirical jibes at a prominent Stockholm businessman in *The Spy in Stockholm's High Society* probably put more pressure on the elder Arfwedson to do something about his irreverent son and his provocative literary bent.

In one sense Arfwedson has an edge on Tocqueville; he undoubtedly got closer to the empirical rather than the conceptual America of Tocqueville, and in several ways he maintained his ties with the United States. For one thing, he found a wife in the New World; he married Elizabeth Alice Ashhurst in Philadelphia in June of 1834, and took her back to Stockholm, where he entered the family wholesale firm. He returned twice more to the United States, in 1839 and 1848, and from 1838 to 1855 he served as American consul in Stockholm. He published two more books drawing upon his American experiences, one of them a guide for emigrants from Sweden and Norway. This series of circumstances probably made him one of the most knowledgeable Europeans on the subject of America. But in the opening pages of *The United States and Canada . . .*, his experience with America was still at second-hand, based on his reading in history and literature and the tales of travelers.

From the movement that he lost sight of the familiar hills of Cornwall and self-consciously bade adieu to Europe, Arfwedson committed himself to recording the "novelties of another world." Like many Europeans, he had first encountered America in the writings of Washington Irving and James Fenimore Cooper. That Arfwedson apprehends them not simply as men of letters but as cultural spokesmen of a much more authoritative sort is an index to their impact on a European audience. Whether prefixed to the opening chapter after his experience in America, or, as is more likely the case, actually shaping Arfwedson's expectation of what he might find, there stands a paragraph from Washington Irving that is rather fitting and illuminating. For quite obviously, Arfwedson agrees with Irving that a long ocean voyage is a proper prelude to experiencing America, that there is a symbolic appropriateness in the vast blank of the Atlantic which erased one's familiar assumptions and signified far greater cultural separation than existed even within the linguistic diversity of Europe. With this in mind, I suspect, Arfwedson proceeded to fill his journal with a record not only of novelties and peculiarities but also of the many attainments and a few discernible defects of democratic ferment.

It was the age of Jackson, whose second administration was about to begin, and, as we understand more fully today, it was also the age of Emerson, who in 1832 resigned his pulpit to extend his ministrations more widely and more vitally. Although Arfwedson never considered himself a poet by temperament or achievement, he looked with intense interest at the very things that Emerson set out as the proper subject matter of the poet in America: "our log-rolling, our stumps and their politics, our fisheries, our Negroes and Indians, our boats and our repudiations, the wrath of rogues and the pusillanimity of honest men, the northern trade, the southern planting, the western clearing."

It was an America where a 50-mile journey could take 12 hours in New England and longer in the South. It was a land devoted to education, whose most venerable university at Cambridge (housed, according to Arfwedson, in undistinguished brick buildings resembling old barracks) had accumulated an impressive 40,000 volumes in its library and an enrollment of 300 students in its halls (already outstripped by the 500 at New Haven). It was a society where the President's soirées were simply announced and no specific invitations sent. Anyone who wished could attend, and Arfwedson describes quite a "mixed company," who came out of curiosity or to pay their respects, and among whom the President moved with ease and affability, shaking hands with all and feeling no danger from strangers nor any distaste for lesser guests.

But some aspects of modern America were already apparent, too. Arfwedson marveled at the efficiency of manufacturing in the United States and the relative prosperity of the workers, whose good wages permitted not only a high standard of living but a savings account as well. At a Massachusetts gun factory he was amazed at the production of 15,000 muskets a year, an accomplishment resulting from substituting "ingenious machinery . . . for manual labour." In northern Europe, by comparison, several persons were needed to turn out gun stocks; in Springfield he saw a single machine doing the job. These New England factory workers had not only a more comfortable life than their European counterparts, they seemed to Arfwedson to have attained a higher moral and intellectual state—due largely, he thought, to the prevalence of temperance societies and savings banks. He also reported the same kind of contrast with Europe present in rural areas. Amid "the general appearance of comfort and prosperity," American farmers were far more fortunate than the peasantry of Scandinavia or England.

Despite a few reservations, Arfwedson was more than sympathetic toward the United States, he was distinctly pro-American. Even on the voyage across the Atlantic, he did not object to being awakened at sunrise by a 24-gun salute on the Fourth of July. Instead, he shared in the admiration for those determined patriots who declared "themselves free and independent, in defiance of the power and fleets of the Mother Country."

He had the misfortune to arrive in New York during a severe cholera epidemic which had upset the normal municipal functions as much as would a simultaneous strike of transportation and sanitation workers today. The disease had claimed several thousand victims; more thousands had fled the city, and there seemed to be more pigs than people in the streets, no doubt thriving on the unusual accumulation of garbage. Arfwedson's first impressions of this American metropolis, quite clearly, were far from favorable. For these reasons, his explorations of inland America began earlier than planned as he embarked on the first of his many river journeys, in this instance by Hudson River steamer.

His descriptions of travel well serve the purposes of those who might be interested in the construction and arrangements of river steamers or railroad coaches in the 1830's. They serve equally well as an almost graphic means of outlining the social characteristics and values of Jacksonian America. Arfwedson was surprised but not shocked to discover that his fellow passengers "were composed of hack-drivers, paviours, lamplighters, masons, carpenters, etc., having all wives and children in Sunday clothes. No distinction of rank between these and the other passengers was perceptible; one is as good as another. The company mixed indiscriminately and the driver considered himself as fine a gentleman as the first dandy on board." Unlike Mrs. Trollope, the tenor of whose work Arfwedson already knew, he found the manners of these plebians quite admirable, especially the manners of young men toward "females of so mediocre a station in life, and to whom nature has besides refused the advantage of beauty."

After a 17-hour trip from Northampton to Boston—very good time, Arfwedson felt—he viewed his second American metropolis. Here he was impressed by the number and variety of mutual improvement associations, some, like the Lyceum, for general audiences, others for more specialized audiences interested in science or religion or world peace. He was pleased also by the public institutions in and around Boston and Philadelphia, particularly the schools, hospitals, and prisons—the latter being the subject of a lengthy chapter in the second volume. He was interested in looking closely at the number and character of religious sects, often distinguished by only marginal differences from one another, a phenomenon he connected with the general atmosphere of freedom and emphasis on voluntary association. To a more bizarre group like the Shakers, he devoted an entire chapter containing a good bit of valuable first-hand observation.

He was fascinated by the outward exuberance and alert to the inner tensions of American political life. Nothing in his previous experience prepared him for the display of high feelings and actual battles which took place in Philadelphia on the day in 1832 that citizens expressed their preference for either Jackson, Clay, or Wirt. Even more astonishing than this heat of political passion was the cool and subdued aftermath. He reported hardly a murmur of displeasure when the statewide results, which were contrary to the wishes of the anti-Jackson majority in the city, were announced.

Arfwedson's own feelings seemed to tally with those of the anti-Jackson segment of the populace, for he, too, feared the rise of undisciplined and ignorant masses. As he saw it, Americans in the earlier years of the Republic expressed understandable fears of "aristocratical ascendancy"; now, however, there seemed more to be feared from "dread of mob rule," as immigrants and poorer classes played a larger part in shaping political decisions and their numbers and power could not possibly be matched by an "equally rapid accession among wealthy and enlightened citizens." In short, he saw a significant difference between Jefferson and Jackson and was not pleased by it.

Further tensions appeared when he explored what was at issue in the Nullification controversy. For an outsider, he was very quick to discern this shoal in the progress of American democracy. He concluded that "the day may yet come, when the progress of the doctrine of State-rights in the Southern parts may attract the serious attention of the Northern." This may be the most prophetic understatement in his entire account.

Central to the relations between North and South was the issue of slavery. No European came to the United States without some strong opinion on this subject, and certainly none returned without giving an account of this peculiar institution and the problems it engendered. Intensely interested in the education and economic status of Negroes, Arfwedson was disappointed to find that even the free Negroes of New York were limited through prejudice and preconception to the most menial occupations and the majority disenfranchised by property qualifications which prospective white voters did not have to meet.

His disappointment gave way to outrage when he witnessed a slave auction in Richmond, Virginia, and at first hand confronted the inhuman attitude that sanctioned separation of a mother from her three-year-old child. He was readily critical of the attitude that kept slaves in ignorance and illiteracy but saw also that such was not universally the case in the South. While condemning slavery, he felt, also, that the well treated slaves of the South were frequently better off than free Negroes in the North. The nub of the problem, as I think he saw it, was that abolition offered no readily applicable solution to a grievous wrong, for in the vast majority of instances the circumstances of servitude had ill-equipped the Negroes for the responsibilities of life as free men and women. It was in every sense a tragic dilemma and ought to impress a sense of the past on even the least historical minded of contemporary Americans.

There was little in America that did not interest Arfwedson. Although he was drawn first to subjects of social and political consequence, he had a concern for architecture and the arts as well. What he had to say was neither flattering nor demeaning, but an honest appraisal of the conditions that underlay Emerson's injunction that Americans had "listened too long to the courtly muses of Europe," that American expression in the arts was "timid, imitative, tame." Thus we have a familiar reference point for Arfwedson's assertion that "the architecture of most public and private buildings in America is, unfortunately copied partly from England, partly from Italy, and even from Greece." Further critical of this apparently mindless eclecticism, he explained that "the Temple of Theseus at Athens, St. Peter's at Rome, and a house in Regent Street, London, are all mixed together; and . . . denominated American architecture."

He was pleased to find Italian opera performed in New York by Italian singers, but he was disappointed at the mediocre performances, which were, understandably, unappreciated and undersupported. Three-fourths of the dramatic offerings in New York, he reported, consisted of plays first acted in England; and, as for native American dramas, "they are, for the most part, wretched productions, often resembling hurried juvenile Christmas farces."

Looking further at the fine arts, he found painting,

sculpture, and literature "still in their infancy." Painters had to support themselves by doing portraits. There seemed to be little demand for landscape or historical scenes, and, generally, if a painting did not represent a Biblical scene, "the majority of spectators invariably object to what they call the impropriety in the dress of the figures." The same genteel strictures compelled sculptors to turn out busts or go abroad to practice their art. And as for literature, the public preferred what stemmed originally from England, or, in the case of an American writer, what had met the canon of English literary taste and been praised abroad, as had Irving, Cooper, Bryant, and a few others. British opinion was, regrettably, the touchstone. But Arfwedson was perceptive enough to note some significant change in process. He saw more hope in the rising, younger generation whose greater confidence and better taste might indicate that "a new era in the arts is at hand," a good observation on the eve of what we have come to call "the American renaissance."

Turning from the traditional attributes of civilization to the wilderness, which was such an omnipresent physical reality as well as mythic and moral force in America, Arfwedson dispelled some of the romantic glamor of the frontier and the Red Indian. Full of romantic expectation, he met what he believed to be a Noble Savage and found him to be a drunken and self-destructive Indian. Curious about the impact of frontier conditions on human character, he was shocked by the lawlessness and degeneracy in a frontier haven for antisocial individuals, a settlement called Sodom, just across the river from Columbus, Georgia. Like Crèvecœur, half a century earlier, he found from experience that the frontier could be a brutifying rather than an ennobling circumstance; and although most of his

European readers might have ignored these de-mythologizing correctives to sentimental excess, they were probably fascinated by his account of living and hunting with Indians on the Southern frontier.

Arfwedson's description of America and the American people is neither impressionistic, pedantic, nor loaded with snobbish preconceptions. There is a nice balance between first-hand observation and intelligent, sometimes very perceptive, conclusion. He cannot rival Alexis de Tocqueville as an analyst of Jacksonian America, but he has done an estimable job of gathering and recording the evidence which underlay Tocqueville's farther ranging, more philosophical, and better known reflections and conjectures.

Marvin Fisher

BIBLIOGRAPHY

Published Works of C. D. Arfwedson

De Colonia Nova Svecia in Americam Borealem Deducta Historiola. Uppsala, 1825.

Min Första Resa till Hufwudstaden. Stockholm, 1827.

Tre Beryktade Flickors Resa till Odödligheten. Stockholm, 1828.

Studenterna i Utscheu eller Zierbenglarnes Historia i China. Stockholm, 1828.

Polymnia. Stockholm, 1828.

Leo XII och Pius VIII, eller Skildring af Rom under Våren 1829. Stockholm, 1830. Republished the following year with a new title: *Den Ondes Visit i Rom Hos Två Regerande Confratres Våren 1829, eller Påfvar, Cardinaler, Mördare och Pack, Betraktade på Deras Rätta Sida.* Stockholm, 1831.

Spionen i Den Förnäma Werlden i Stockholm, eller en och annan Upptäckt om Höga Narrar, Främmande Afventyrerskor och Inhemska Skojare, af En Roturier. Stockholm, 1831.

Femton Månader af en Ung Schweitzares Lefnad, eller Resor i Scottland, England, Irland, Belgien, Rheintrakterna och Schweitz åren 1830 och 1831. Stockholm, 1832.

The United States and Canada in 1832, 1833, and 1834. 2 Vols. London, 1834. Published in Swedish as *Förenta Staterna och Canada, åren 1832, 1833, och 1834.* Stockholm, 1835.

Scener i Nord-Amerika. Ur en Svensk Resandes Minnesbok. Stockholm, 1836.

Minnen från Europa och Amerika. Stockholm, 1837.

Några få Ord till Dem, som Nåsta År Ämna fran Sverige och Norrige, Utflytta till Förenta Staterna, af Eu Opartisk Landsman. Stockholm, 1842.

Konung Carl XI och Hans Gunstlingar. Norrköping, 1845.

Wadstena Kloster. Stockholm, 1848.

1848 och 1868 eller Två År af en Stormig Lefnad. Stockholm, 1871.

Irlandska Folksagor. Trans. by C. D. Arfwedson. Stockholm, 1839.

Secondary Sources

Svenskt Biographiskt Lexikon. Stockholm, 1917——. Vol. II, 167–169.

Svenska Män och Kvinnor. Stockholm, 1942–1955. Vol. I, 126.

Leijonhufvud, K. K:son. *Ny Svensk Släktbok.* Stockholm, 1901 and 1916. Pp. 91–92.

Ollsson, Nils William. *Swedish Passenger Arrivals in New York, 1820–1850.* Chicago, 1968.

Rosman, H., and Munthe A. *Släkten Arfwedson.* Stockholm, 1945.

T. W. Dean, Lithogr.

SOURCE OF THE HUDSON.

THE

UNITED STATES

AND

CANADA,

IN 1832, 1833, AND 1834.

BY C. D. ARFWEDSON, ESQ.

IN TWO VOLUMES.

VOL. I.

LONDON:

RICHARD BENTLEY, NEW BURLINGTON STREET,

Publisher in Ordinary to His Majesty.

1834.

CONTENTS

OF

THE FIRST VOLUME.

CHAPTER I.

Departure from England — Storm during the Voyage — A fine day on the Ocean—The 4th of July—Yankee Doodle—First sight of Land—Dressing for Landing—A News-boat—Unexpected News — The Pilot — Entrance to New York — Manhatta—New Amsterdam, or New York—Indians . 1

CHAPTER II.

The Battery—Negroes — Broadway — City Hall — Private Houses—Hotels—Boarding Houses — Manners and Customs —Population — The Hudson — Hoboken — Cholera in New York—Neglect of Cleanliness—Pigs in the Streets 26

CHAPTER III.

Steamboats — The North American Steamer — Voyage on the Hudson River — Passengers — Attention to Females —

Banks of the Hudson — The Palisades—Sleepy Hollow—The Highlands—A Thunder Storm 46

CHAPTER IV.

Westpoint—Military School—Journey to Catskill — Stage Coaches—Pine Orchard—The Cascades—Remarkable Tree—Rattlesnakes—The Rattlesnake Hunter—Athens . . 60

CHAPTER V.

New Lebanon Springs—Shakers — Ann Lee — Ceremonies of the Shakers—A Modern Miracle—Creed, Rules, and Regulations, of the Shakers—Their Occupations—Schools—Costume — The Shakers' Meeting — Tobacco Smoking Festival—A New Messiah 83

CHAPTER VI.

Journey to Northampton—Soil and Agriculture—Character of the Country — General Appearance of Comfort—Anecdote — Northampton — Villages and Towns in America — Mount Holyoke—Hadley—The Regicides—Springfield—Manufactory of Arms—Comfortable Situation of the Workmen—The Locksmith of Springfield — Journey to Boston — Ware — Worcester 108

CHAPTER VII.

Boston—The Harbour—Public and Private Buildings—The Streets—The Statehouse—Statue of Washington—Neglected Public Walk — Music in the Evening — Faneuil Hall — The Market—Post Office—Banks—Athenæum — The Freemasons' Lodge — American Architecture — Temperance Societies —

Strong Liquors — Crimes from Intemperance — Anecdote — Serenades — Cholera — Panic — Cholera Hospital — Relief Association 129

CHAPTER VIII.

Public Institutions in Boston—The Peace Society—State of Education—Religion — Different Religious Sects—Baptists—Missionaries—Unitarians 157

CHAPTER IX.

Charlestown — Navy Yard — The Constitution Frigate — Breed's Hill and Bunker's Hill—Monument on Bunker's Hill —Lynn—Salem — Beverley—Newbury Port — New Hampshire—Portsmouth — Maine — Breakneck Hill — Curiosity—Female Heroism — Portland — Soil in Maine—Emigrants — Agriculture—Produce—Wages—A Husking Feast . 180

CHAPTER X.

Return to Boston — Environs — Jamaica Pond — Mount Auburn—Cambridge College—John Quincy Adams—Nahant —Balls—Sea Serpent—Cattle Fair at Brighton—A Storm in Boston—Various Uses of Hats — Pawtucket — Providence—Mount Hope — King Philip — Journey to New York — Hell Gate 209

CHAPTER XI.

New York after the Cholera — Brooklyn — Navy Yard—American Navy—Naval Officers—Patterson—Passaic Falls—American Institute and Annual Exhibition of Manufactures—Negro School—The American System of Education — School Agents' Society—American Bible Society . . . 230

CHAPTER XII.

Journey to Philadelphia—Philadelphia — Schuylkill Coal—Literary Societies—Benevolent Institutions—Sunday Schools Association — Pennsylvania Hospital -- House of Refuge — Banks—The Mint—Museum—Mammoth—State House 251

CHAPTER XIII.

Environs of Philadelphia—Waterworks — Franklin's Tomb — Navy Yard — Election of President — Ancient Swedish Colony—Swedish Church 275

CHAPTER XIV.

Baltimore—The Cathedral—Monuments — Charles Carroll —His Death and Funeral—Population of the City—Religion —Slaves and free Servants—Articles of Exportation—Journey to Washington — Washington — Departure for Virginia — District of Columbia — Potomac River — Fort Washington— Fredericksburgh—Roads in the Southern States — Journey to Richmond 295

CHAPTER XV.

Richmond—Public Buildings — Monument for the Persons who perished in the Theatre — Slave Auction — Condition of Slaves in the United States — Dangers attached to an immediate Emancipation — Advantages of the Colonization System 318

CHAPTER XVI.

Tobacco Manufactory at Richmond—Departure for Norfolk —Norfolk — The Dismal Swamp — Journey to Fayetteville—

The Cotton Plant — Fayetteville — Journey to Charleston—Rattlesnakes 353

CHAPTER XVII.

Charleston — Monument to the Memory of Walter Scott—General Hayne—Nullification, its object, progress, and termination 379

CHAPTER XVIII.

Departure for Savannah — Beaufort — Female Slave — Palmetto — Fort constructed of Oyster Shells — Savannah — Journey to Augusta—Augusta — Hamburgh — Casualties attendant on Travelling in the South—Journey to Macon—Land Lottery—Macon—A Negro Shopkeeper—Journey to Columbus —A Gang of Slaves—A Creek Indian 402

THE

UNITED STATES

AND CANADA,

IN 1832, 1833, AND 1834.

CHAPTER I.

The temporary absence of worldly scenes and employments produces a state of mind peculiarly fitted to receive new and vivid impressions. The vast space of water that separates the hemispheres is like a blank page in existence. There is no gradual transition by which, as in Europe, the features and population of one country blend almost imperceptibly with those of another. From the moment you lose sight of the land you have left, all is vacancy, until you step on the opposite shore, and are launched at once into the bustle and novelties of another world.

WASHINGTON IRVING.

THE southern coast of beautiful England insensibly disappeared before my eyes: from the deck of the American packet, I tried in vain to get a last glimpse of the British Isles. The mantle of night enveloped in obscurity the verdant hills of Cornwall. Adieu to Europe.

Our complement on board consisted of two hundred individuals from almost every country in Europe, besides Americans. Among the English and Irish, there was a large proportion of emigrants, who with wives, children, and servants, quitted their native soil, to seek in distant climes a spot, where taxes of a thousand different kinds and denominations might not absorb their little all. When the whole group assembled on deck, it was a truly interesting scene: the bustle of some, who constantly moved about, instilled spirit in others, apparently inclined to despondency. Yes, many were certainly dejected. They left behind, country, friends, relatives; and who could venture to predict whether they would ever see either again, or tread the shore which contained the ashes of their forefathers, and recalled to their minds so many endearing recollections?

The uniformity of a sea-life generally engenders melancholy; the monotony is insupportable: there is no diversity, except in the state of the atmosphere. Whichever way the eye turns, and surveys the circled horizon, no other object is visible but frothing waves, apparently rolling from one side of the blue sky to the other. If a sail heaves in sight at a distance, the event may be compared to a messenger sent from another world. In an instant, the whole deck is covered with people, anxious to behold the strange ship: every spy-glass is put in requisition. But, in our case, curiosity was not satisfied with a bare view of her filled canvass; speculation followed as to the identity of her flag, whence she came, and whither bound. Similar rencontres too often produced violent altercations among individuals of so many different nations, some of whom pretended to be wiser than their neighbours; but they were soon quelled, every one returning to his uniform occupation of contemplating the agitated sea — alternately raising or lowering our little republic — of counting the large shoals of porpoises which faithfully accompanied the ship the whole voyage, or surveying the unchangeable horizon and the swift passing clouds. How often, whilst meditating on the beauty of the immeasurable heavenly arch, have I not fancied I saw a distant shore rising from the deep: the joy, alas! was short-lived: 'twas but a cloud.

One evening, when the moon shone forth in all her splendour, the whole company assembled on deck. Glees and songs, variously executed, formed the amusement: every one appeared happy and contented. It was late before retreat to rest was thought of; melodious sounds, but recently heard above, were now re-echoed from the births below. Before daylight, however, these charming dreams were suddenly converted into gloom. A dreadful storm greeted the convivial companions at break of day. The first glimpse at an enraged element is truly terrific. From a smooth surface — as it had been the preceding night — the sea had risen mountain high; the tops of the waves were as cream-white as the snow-covered Mont Blanc. In the midst of them, our ship was seen dancing, sometimes defying their power, in turn vigorously repulsed by offended masses of water — then hidden between two sea-walls, nearly as elevated as the mainmast — and again almost immersed in the immense deep. The winds — those proud aristocrats of the ocean — whistled in the air, and, with the aid of the rigging, performed a most discordant concert. All the passengers were dejected: paleness overspread the features of the women: silent in a corner, with palpitating hearts, they listened to the roar of the tempest and the waves. Children, seized with fear, clung to their parents, and screamed piteously. Probably, there was no real danger; but a gale in the midst of the ocean is, after all, no joking matter. None, except a person who has actually witnessed a similar scene, can form an idea of the creaking, roaring, and rolling, which incessantly tormented us during four-and-twenty endless hours. The ship rolled the whole time from side to side; and, whenever she changed position, her timbers creaked as when Enceladus turns himself under the weight of Mount Etna. Trunks, carpet-bags, dressing-cases, and desks, were displaced and knocked against each other each time she hove about. Woe to him who happened to be in their way!

Another inconvenience occurred when dinner was announced, which, however, partook a good deal of the ludicrous: the guests were every moment exposed to the danger of receiving in their laps joints of beef and mutton, ducks, hams, potatoes, &c. It was not easy to refrain from laughing on seeing the restless dishes changing situation every instant, sometimes at the top, then at the bottom of the table, and again disappearing altogether under it. But, dinner concluded, mirth also took leave of the company: the storm continued with unabated violence, and gloom once more took possession of all of us. Night came on. None would retire to rest. Around a dismal lamp — sole luminary in the lonely cabin — assembled a group of passengers; who, by way of pastime, related a variety of anecdotes, clearly showing what subject was uppermost in their minds: they all had reference to shipwrecks. At sea, tales of this description may be compared to ghost-stories on shore, for no one ever heard of ghosts on board a ship—probably from antipathy to the watery element.

Morning soon broke in upon our company — still excited by the recitals of the preceding night. The sunbeams, spread over the surface of the sea, gradually dispersed the clouds, and seemed to insinuate to the winds their wrath at the continuance of the storm.

Prostrate lay the towering waves — on the smooth surface played the sun — the ship was stationary—her canvass, drooping and heavy, clung to the masts; the exhausted tars betook themselves to rest: in dancing groups appeared multitudes of fish, and in their centre stretched forth a monstrous whale, desirous to behold the majesty of light. Aloft, in circles round the masts, harmonious concerts were performed by aquatic birds. The day was fine: every thing appeared to have acquired new life. No comparison can be drawn between a beautiful day at sea and one on shore: there is something so delightful and reviving in the former, that its influence is irresistible. The 4th of July was just one of this description. Who is the American that does not rejoice at the recollection of what occurred on that day, 1776? Who is ignorant of the memorable act then signed by the boldest men in the colonies? Who has forgotten the determined step adopted by these patriots to declare themselves free and independent, in defiance of the power and fleets of the Mother Country. An American is justly proud of the result of this revolution, when comparing the past with the present.

The anniversary, however, is associated with so many interesting events, that it is invariably celebrated with great solemnity. Wherever an American happens to be on that day, whether in the midst of the ocean, or in the forests of the Western Country, the 4th of July must be observed. Our packet, as I have before observed, was American: the captain therefore made the necessary arrangements for its celebration. At sun-rise the passengers were awoke by the firing of twenty-four guns — being one for every State in the Republic. The handsome American flag, now waving in every sea, and admired in all parts of the globe, was hoisted with demonstrations of joy. The numerous stars seemed delighted at the roar of the cannon, while the sunbeams gave them a light red die, approaching to nature. All the Americans on board hastened on deck as soon as the first gun had been fired : the fineness of the morning, added to the remembrance of former times, made them feel a degree of ecstasy, which soon communicated itself to the strangers on board. Every one recollected some noble deed, some heroic action, performed during the national contest for liberty ; and all emulated to raise to the skies America's beau-ideal—Washington.

By this time, the whole company had assembled on deck, listening to the speakers. Among the steerage passengers, there was a short, thick-set man, almost seized with delirium on hearing recorded many acts of valour and intrepidity attached to the names of a number of revolutionary men. Long did he try to suppress his feelings : he touched his hat, or turned upon his heel, with a view to check his emotions; but, when one of the orators happened to mention the words—*Independence, Equality,* and *Liberty,* he had no more command over himself: he vociferated "*Yankee Doodle.*" This national song is, properly speaking, an old Italian melody: obsolete or forgotten in the Old World, it all at once got in vogue in the New, and has in later times become so popular that there is hardly a child who cannot hum it. When sung by several persons, any one may put whatever words he pleases to the music; by this means, many ludicrous and appropriate, and some very indifferent and vulgar, verses are introduced; but, either way, they are always approved by the company, which, to signify its acquiescence, repeats the two last verses. Upon the present occasion, no individual ventured to give an impromptu: the old words, in praise of Washington, Franklin, Liberty, Equality, &c. were preserved.

Hilarity presided at dinner. Of toasts and speeches there was an ample supply. One of the latter, in particular, was an eulogium on the President of the United States. Toasts were also given in honour of the respective sovereigns of Sweden, France, and England. The entertainment concluded with a general dance on deck, composed of old and young, poor and rich, love-sick and sea-sick, sober and drunk; in short, of nearly two hundred persons. The band consisted of four inebriated individuals, with their hats cocked up on one side. The violins were certainly not of the Cremonese fabric; they appeared to have weathered many a gale, and would unquestionably have baffled even Paganini's skill. Their inefficiency, however, did not interrupt the conviviality for a moment, the performers beating time so loud as nearly to drown the music. The dancers, too, were so animated, that harmony was almost unnecessary. A couple of corpulent Irishmen, especially, continued dancing long after the music had ceased, as if it required a certain time to stop their evolutions when once put in motion. One of them, whose capers were truly dangerous to the bystanders, on being informed that the music had ceased, and that dancing was consequently over, answered very laconically, "What about music?" and proceeded to twist about his fair damsel for at least ten minutes, to the great hazard and danger of the surrounding party, every moment exposed to a summerset into the sea. No accident, however, happened; and, when dancing had been kept up to a late hour, in the midst of the finest moonlight the company retired, apparently delighted with the amusements of the day.

At length, on the 9th of July, in the forenoon, I heard the magic sound, "Land!" pronounced from the top of the mast-head by a sailor, sent on the look-out by the captain, who was as anxious as any passenger to set foot on *terra firma*, after a voyage of thirty-nine days. The joyful intelligence passed from mouth to mouth, with the rapidity of lightning, until every one on board had repeated—"Land!" Every eye sparkled with joy. Fancy already landed the whole company on the American shore; they thought they saw trees, houses, fields, and cities. The men began to talk about good hits and speculations; the elderly women about housekeeping; the girls blushed at the idea of being so near their lovers! The young men formed a thousand projects of amusement by way of indemnity for privations endured during a long and tedious voyage. All were in a most happy state of mind; even those who had experienced the effects of sea-sickness, and had been quite indifferent as to the future, now raised their heads, and hurried, like the rest, to put their things in order, adjust their toilette, and indulge in a promenade on deck, for the benefit of fresh air. Bustle and confusion were every where visible. None would be behind-hand in dress; costumes, which, for more than a month past, had enjoyed uninterrupted tranquillity in carefully packed trunks, were now sported. Bond Street hats saw light again, and were substituted for the few remaining caps, many of these having deserted their owners during the late gale, to take a view of the coast of Labrador or Nova Scotia. One of the passengers, and his family in particular, had, in the course of ten minutes, undergone so perfect a metamorphosis, that it was next to impossible to recognize either him, his wife, or two little children, to whom we were greatly indebted for infantine concerts all the time we were at sea. The husband appeared in a new snuff-coloured frock-coat, a sugar-loaf hat, and a neatly-plaited frill, which, however, upon closer examination, turned out to form a mere exterior appendix to a very dirty shirt; laced wristbands covered his fingers, in part adorned with rings, and a fashionable cane in the right hand completed the *tout ensemble*. The attire of the lady was proportionably elegant: she eclipsed all that approached her. Her costly Parisian bonnet had nevertheless met with a sad accident, which not only damped her spirits most sensibly, but called forth a shower of abuse, and a succession of oaths on the part of the disappointed husband. A clumsy sailor had unfortunately thrust his foot through the bandbox which contained the treasure, and, by the pressure, so completely discomfited shape and plumary ornaments that no traces of its original beauty could be distinguished. Recourse was had to repairs; or, to use a sea phrase, to jury-masts; but, such was the demolition produced, that the impression of the sailor's foot could never be effectually removed; the bonnet, after all, preserved the appearance of an old ruin, to the great mortification of the fair owner. Straw-coloured kid gloves covered a pair of blood-red hands, and transparent silk stockings decorated a couple of feet of uncommon size. Thus attired, the handsome couple took shelter under a large umbrella—for the rain fell in torrents—consulting how they were to spend the evening. The husband proposed a walk in Broadway, as the most fashionable place of resort; but this was overruled by the lady, who insisted on going to the play.

Whilst the party were thus discussing the point, the other passengers had already made up their minds as to the mode of celebrating their landing on the American soil. Some flattered their palates with the prospect of fresh vegetables, particularly new green peas; others were exclusively bent on strawberries and pineapples. Two young Americans made a long harangue on the superior flavour of American apples. In the midst of these important deliberations, our packet was hailed by one of those fine fast-sailing boats belonging to the newspaper establishments in New York, which, in spite of the worst possible weather, invariably put to sea to meet the European packets, for the purpose of getting the earliest intelligence. We were all anxious to get a sight of the first American; and, although much occupied with plans for the evening, could not refrain from gathering round the messenger the moment he put his foot on deck. The captain shook him heartily by the hand, gave him the London journals, and asked, with a kind of *nonchalance*, "Every thing is well in this part of the world, I suppose?"

"No, quite the contrary," answered the boatman, casting a look which paralysed us all.

"What is then the matter?" exclaimed the captain, struck with amazement, and impatient. "Is New York in flames—or is the President dead?"

"The cholera is among us, and causes the most dreadful havock," was the answer.

"What! cholera in America!" uttered every one, and the paleness of death spread over countenances but lately tinged with the colour of the rose. Looks were exchanged, as if to derive consolation from one another; half sentences were muttered by some on the nature of the disease; others expressed surprise how it could possibly have crossed the Atlantic, and cursed their unlucky star for having deceived their expectations. Adieu theatre, pleasures, promenade in Broadway, vegetables, green peas, and high-flavoured apples!

The packet, however, neared the shore, until every object was perfectly discernible; a little country church and Sandy Hook Lighthouse were clearly visible to the naked eye. We now took the pilot on board. An original like him I had seen in no country in Europe. Once on board, he moved fore and aft with the rapidity of lightning, from larboard to starboard; then, climbing up the rigging and the gangways, commanded aloud, and in a tone of voice indicating his own self-importance. It appeared impossible for him to be quiet a single moment. "Quiet to quick bosoms is a hell," says Lord Byron very justly. He might be compared to a *perpetuum mobile:* every thing that stood in his way was kicked about. Respect for the fair sex was entirely out of the question: *Duty above all* was his motto; and to this he strictly adhered. His exterior was a true personification of his character. His brown summer trowsers, by being too often ingulphed in the washing-tub, had shrunk to such a size that the knees filled the space allotted to the calves; these were, in turn, covered by a pair of white and blue stockings. Many were the button vacancies in his sky-blue coat; and the knot of a coloured neckhandkerchief had fixed its abode on one of his ears. His brown hat also had received so many knocks, that its appearance resembled that of agitated waves. The whole personage presented a singular *coup d'œil.* But, if the exterior denoted his character, so did also his countenance. None was ever more striking. It has been contended that the soul of man is pictured on his forehead—that the eyes are spectacles for him who chooses to read the heart. In him this proved correct. The first aspect convinced us what a little d—l we had got on board (this was the title given him by the sailors); and his figure, I am well satisfied, is still fresh in the memory of many of the passengers.

We were now close in shore, passing a sound called "The Narrows," a mile in breadth. Inside this, a most beautiful bay opened to our view, intersected by several islands, amongst which was Governor's Island, with a kind of Martello tower on it, built of brick. This bay, formed on one side by the New Jersey shore, and on the other by Long Island, is about twenty miles in circumference, and every where so deep that the largest ship can ride at anchor. At a distance appeared a point with a small castle on it, surrounded by trees planted with great regularity and taste; and, behind, steeples rose in infinite number. This was the city of New York. On the left of Castle Garden, the beautiful Hudson showed itself; and on the right flowed the East River, properly speaking an arm of the sea, dividing the city from Long Island. Thousands of ships, steamers, and boats, passed each other in various directions;

and flags of Europe and America waved peaceably together. Country seats and trees covered the opposite shores; the verdant foliage charmed our eyes, not yet accustomed to this novel sight. The scene was truly magnificent, and can only be justly appreciated by those who, having been long at sea, suddenly enter a beautiful port.

"The temporary absence of worldly scenes and employments," says Washington Irving, "produces a state of mind peculiarly fitted to receive new and vivid impressions."*

It is probable, had we landed at another place at first, and only gradually been prepared for the beauties of the port of New York, we should not have enjoyed it so much. Certain it is, however, that the entrance to it, the extensive bay that opens to the view, and the two magnificent rivers that present themselves to the right and left, form a *coup d'œil* which can barely be matched in the whole world. When I surveyed this fine scene, and the city surrounded by water, I could easily conceive the admiration with which honest Hudson must have been struck when he beheld these natural beauties for the first time. Juet, his travelling companion,

* The Sketch Book.

called the island on which New York is situated *Manna-hata*, which means the island of manna — in other words, a country where milk and honey flow.* And an old Indian tradition furnishes another proof how, in the remotest times, these parts were admired. "The name Manhattoes is said to be derived from the great Indian god Manetho, who is stated to have made this island his favourite place of residence, on account of its peculiar attractions. Indian traditions say further, that the bay was formerly a large lake, filled with silver and gold fish, in the middle of which was this fine island, abounding in every species of fruit and flowers; but that a sudden inundation of the River Hudson destroyed every vestige of these beauties, and that Manetho fled in consequence behind the extensive waters of Ontario."† To me it appears, therefore, not unlikely that the first Europeans — a handful of Dutchmen — who, a few years after Hudson's return to Holland, set sail in the celebrated bark, Goede Vrouw, under the particular protection of St. Nicholas, should settle in this neighbourhood, and found a city, where, for a period of fifty years, they enjoyed all the advantages of a real old-

* Knickerbocker's New York, v. i. † Ibid.

fashioned Dutch life. The immortal Knickerbocker gives an account of the situation of New Amsterdam, the name of the city at that time, in the following manner:—

"It was fortunate for New Amsterdam that the words learning, education, taste, and talents, were perfectly unknown there: a genius was a strange animal, and a learned woman would have been as great a piece of curiosity as a frog with horns, or a burning dragon. None, in fact, knew more than his neighbour, nor did any body wish to know more than an honest man ought to know, who attends only to his own business: the clergyman and the notary were the only two who knew how to write, and the wise Governor Twiller always signed his name with a X. The houses were of wood, and the large gate only opened upon the occasion of some marriages, funerals, new-year's days, St. Nicholas' day, or other great festivities. The families lived in the kitchen. The fireplace was of real aristocratic size, where all the members of the household, old and young, master and servant, black and white, even cat and dog, partook of the general privilege, and had a corner allotted to themselves. Here sat the old burgher, for hours together, in deep meditation, smoking his pipe, and looking at the fire with half-closed eyes, without thinking of any thing. The good wife opposite was busily employed in spinning or knitting stockings. They had a great aversion to giving dinners, but kept up the spirit of society by occasional tea-parties. The company used to assemble about three o'clock, and returned home at six: in winter time, the fashionable hours were a little earlier, to enable the ladies to get home before dark. In the middle of the tea-table was placed a large earthenware dish, with fat pork cut in slices, and tea was served out of a very large coarse porcelain tea-pot, painted with figures, representing little, thick Dutch shepherds and shepherdesses, watching swine — boats sailing in the air, and houses built in the sky. To sweeten the beverage, a bit of sugar was placed by the side of each cup, and the company helped themselves with much decorum, sometimes to a bit of sugar, sometimes to a drink of tea — until an old, cunning, and economical mistress invented an improvement, which consisted in having a bit of sugar attached to a string suspended to the ceiling, and hanging perpendicularly over the table, so that it might pass from mouth to mouth. The young girls never opened their lips, except to say *Yah Mynheer*, or *Yah, ya Vrouw*, to every question put to them, and behaved in every respect as well educated housemaids. The passion of a lover was greater or less in proportion to the size or breadth of the object; and a stout girl, with a dozen petticoats, was declared by a Dutch poet from the interior to be as brilliant as a primrose, and as voluptuous as a full grown cabbage-head. Certain it is, that, in those times, the heart of a lover could only be fixed upon one fair lady at a time; our modern youths may, on the contrary, have half a dozen. Attired in half a score of inexpressibles, and shoes with a pair of tremendous brass buckles, a low broad-brimmed hat, and the hair, hanging down his back, in the shape of a queue, enveloped in an eelskin, the lover, thus equipped, stepped manfully forward, with pipe in mouth, to court some *belle*. Seldom or ever did he miscarry in his attack, but generally, after having thoroughly smoked his fair damsel for some time, took the fortress by assault on honourable terms."

Whilst recalling to my memory the many remarkable circumstances, which, from former times up to the present, are associated with the parts that now appeared before me, and while comparing the manners of New Amsterdam, when "the honest burghers were sitting for hours together smoking, and slumbering over the affairs of the State, without once breaking the silence, so essential for deep meditation," with modern New York, where every one complains of the shortness of time, and none appears to have a moment to spare—under these various contemplations I landed, and trod for the first time the American soil —that soil whose early inhabitants and legitimate masters were persuaded through the agency of money, words, the sword, and blood, to believe that white strangers had a greater claim to it than themselves, and that a Holy Father in another country, called the Pope, had distinctly declared, that the Red men were infidels, who ought to be thankful to the Whites for their religious zeal in crossing the Atlantic Ocean to improve the condition of these savages, preach a new and only half-understood doctrine, and, finally, despatch them either to heaven or to some deserted spots in the western parts of the country, as a reward for their faith. Where are now these unhappy heathens, who were butchered by the Christians without commiseration? Where are the descendants of Massasoit, of Philip of Pokanoket, of Norridgewock — these Indian heroes? Where shall we find a trace of these valiant and patriotic men, who fell in defence of country and liberty? Not a solitary ruin of their huts has been left behind by the inhuman strangers — all has been levelled to the ground — every vestige is obliterated from civilized America. No canoe is seen on the majestic rivers — no fires kindled on the tops of mountains, as a rallying post for the warriors: nothing remains of all this, except, perhaps, the fragments of some blanched bones sometimes brought to light by the plough of the Whites. They have set with the sun — even there they are persecuted; and from the forests of the West, Black Hawk and the Prophet* have lately been brought in triumph round the country. Unfortunate people, whom Fate has condemned to disappear from the face of the earth without leaving the least trace of their existence! In a short time, the Indian will lay down his bow, and slumber in eternity, without a mournful glance from child or friend. Solitary on this beautiful earth, among men who ought to be

* Two celebrated Indian chiefs who were taken prisoners during the war 1832, and brought in chains to St. Louis.

his brethren instead of his murderers, he casts his looks towards the West, where his God has promised him the bliss of Paradise, and sings a hymn, like the heroic female — the last of Norridgewock's race — who performed her own requiem. When the sun sets, he will be in Paradise.

CHAPTER II.

In the deep umbrage of a green hill's shade,
Which shows a distant prospect far away
Of busy cities, now in vain display'd,
For they can lure no further; and the ray
Of a bright sun can make sufficient holiday.

BYRON.

I WAS now at length in America. The steamboat, which brought the passengers from the packet, landed us near a fashionable promenade, called the Battery, formerly a fortified place. Even during the Dutch occupation, this was considered a favourite spot, although surrounded by walls: in later times, when New York, by an increasing trade and wealth, and an easy communication with an extensive and cultivated back country, has become the first city in the United States, the Battery has less of a warlike appearance. Pleasant walks between rows of trees have been substituted for walls. From the extremity of the city, where the North and East Rivers form a junction, the most agreeable *allées* are laid out, commanding one of the most extensive and beautiful views that can well be imagined. Towards the north end is a kind of bastion, formerly known by the name of Castle Clinton, now called Castle Garden, being no more used as a military post, but merely as a place of recreation. On Sundays this public walk is filled with people of all classes, particularly those of the sable cast, making a profuse exhibition of their finery. To the negroes, this place of resort is, something like Hyde Park, near London, a place for show. Their dress, in general, borders on extravagance: the women wear bonnets decorated with ribbons, plumes, and flowers, of a thousand different colours, and their dresses are of the most showy description: the men are attired like real French *petits-maîtres manqués,* the coats so open that the shirt sticks out under the arm-pits; the waistcoats are of all colours of the rainbow; the hat is carelessly put on one side; the gloves are yellow, and every sable dandy carries a smart cane. At first, it was with difficulty I could refrain from laughing, on seeing these black *beaux* (the name by which they generally go) doing homage to the black housemaids or cooks, known as *belles.* One group in particular attracted my notice: their conversation appeared very animated, and the dark gentlemen, as well as the dark ladies, indulged in it with a liveliness and amiability which would not have disgraced even the first saloons in Paris. The former had chains round their necks (I will not vouch they were of gold) and canes in their hands — two indispensable things. The ladies made a fine exhibition of parasols, although no sun had been perceptible since the preceding day. A great deal of flirtation and display of wit seemed to be among the gentlemen, for the ladies were delighted and showed continually their white teeth. One of the beaux — a flat-nosed indívidual, with curly hair, extending at least four inches on each side his hat—excelled in civility and *bons-mots*. Whenever he uttered a sentence, the ladies were so convulsed with laughter that the plumes and other ornamental parts of their bonnets were actually displaced. His eyes, if I mistake not, were invariably fixed upon a lusty, ordinary, Donna, a great admirer of his repeated witticisms. Sometimes he addressed to her a word or two privately, and, when this occurred, she looked down abashed, and had recourse to her pocket-handkerchief. These symptoms of modesty threw the lover in raptures, and his eloquence became as flowing as the North River. His gestures partook of the theatrical, and his feet followed the action of the hands. I expected every moment to see an attitude *à la Taglioni*, and anticipated the pleasure of witnessing a love-declaration from this African, as the result of so many tender looks, such classic effusion of wit, so many fatiguing evolutions. In the midst of these expectations, however, I felt a drop or two of rain, and, looking up, perceived a dark cloud which threatened us with a heavy shower. The speaker began also to be uneasy, having already seen the effect on his straw-coloured gloves; and, abruptly concluding his harangue, prosaically addressed the fair: "Had we not better retreat?— we shall be deluged with rain." He then politely offered his arm to the object of his affection, and, followed by the rest of the company, they all wandered up Broadway in the midst of one of those sudden and drenching showers so frequent in America.

Broadway is the principal street in New York: it runs through the City in a parallel direction, about three miles in length, bordered by hotels, houses, and churches, and embellished with shops of every description, tastefully arranged. The street is neatly paved with wide side-walks, filled with carriages, omnibuses, and pedestrians without number, and patronised by the all-powerful goddess, Fashion. This thoroughfare is, without exception, one of the finest that can be seen, and deserves the honour of comparison with Regent's Street in London, the Corso in Rome, and the Strado Toledo at Naples. It commences at the Battery, or more properly runs from a small square called the Bowling Green; in the middle of this place was formerly a statue erected to the honour of one of the kings of England (George III.): but during the revolution it was demolished, and the metal of which it was composed converted into cannon. The spot is now only surrounded by an iron railing and a few scattered trees. Further up in Broadway is another square or opening called the Park, in which is City Hall — an edifice appropriated to public offices. It is of white marble, and produces a fine effect at a distance. The defects in the architecture, which is rather upon a confined scale, cannot then be perceived: it is only upon closer inspection that they become striking.

The houses in New York are generally small, and resemble the English a good deal. The new ones, now building in the upper part of the City, are intended to be upon a larger scale. Wooden houses are prohibited, on account of the frequency of fires; few are seen built of this material, and they are generally in by-streets. The buildings are of brick, three stories high. The exterior of many is neither whitewashed nor painted, but coloured red and white, which gives them the appearance of being plastered. A low iron railing leads from the steps round the house, about one yard from the wall; and many of these steps are of white marble. The interior is chiefly in the English style, both floors and staircases being covered with that agreeable article of luxury—carpets. The kitchens are in the basement, below the level of the streets. In most streets I found houses in course of building, so that the exterior of New York has at least a new appearance, although in the opinion of a European it may not be so handsome as if the buildings were painted white. Poor dwellings, such as are so frequently seen in the principal cities in Europe, and of which Stockholm can furnish its quota, I did not perceive; the rising prosperity of the town, and the constant conflagrations, gradually diminish their number. The singular locality of New York, between two rivers, obliges a large portion of her population, annually on the increase, to remove in the only direction that is left. The upper part is gradually becoming the place of residence of the wealthier classes, and may not inaptly be termed the west end of New York.

Cooper, in his work, "*Notions of the Americans*," says, "I have been told, and think it not improbable, that the city of New York does not contain five hundred buildings which can date their origin before the peace of 1783;"* and this statement is, in my opinion, far from being exaggerated.

The principal hotels, situated in Broadway, are, as far as the exterior is concerned, not unlike the celebrated establishments of a similar description at Francfort on the Main. The comforts are, however, inferior to those in Europe; in all I found a defect which, in a climate so warm as this at times, is as disagreeable as it is pernicious to the health — the bed-rooms are invariably too small. They are often so diminutive, that from his bed the tenant may step out of the window.

* Notions of the Americans, by a Travelling Bachelor, vol. i.

Had Sir John Falstaff lived in our times, his bulky frame would, unquestionably, have got entangled between the wall and the bed. The walls of the sleeping rooms are in most cases only whitewashed, and the furniture consists of a few rattan chairs and a table ; but they are always carpeted. An American seldom complains of the want of additional furniture, being hardly ever in the room, except at night ; most of the hours of the day he either attends to business or passes his time in a parlour, simply but tastefully furnished, something like the drawing-rooms in England.

It is a common practice in America to live in what is called boarding houses, or private families, where a certain sum is paid for meals, &c., whether you dine there or not. The breakfast is at seven, half-past seven, and eight o'clock ; dinner from two to five. I often wondered how families could find any comfort in living in this way the greatest part of their time, when the interchange of strangers is so continual, and the society so varied. In Europe, a similar existence would be considered intolerable. To a lady it must nevertheless have its attractions. She passes her whole life without once giving herself the trouble of thinking of the concerns of her house. Even some of the first and wealthiest families in New York spend occasionally many weeks, or months, at an hotel, whenever their own house is undergoing repairs, or, as was the case now, when driven from their homes by the approach of the cholera. Few people have country seats : rather than hire one, and enjoy the benefit of tranquillity and a free and unshackled life, a family, with children and servants, prefer taking up temporary quarters at some hotel or tavern in a neighbouring small town or village. A person arriving from the Old World cannot help wondering at this strange, and, in his opinion, highly dependent way of living. I can account for it in no other manner than that it must be a saving of expense to the husband, and of trouble to the wife. Be this as it may, each country has its customs, which must be respected by every foreigner, however opposed to his notions and habits, and however singular and absurd. In France, John Bull's comfortable practice of taking wine after dinner is ridiculed, while Englishmen consider a Frenchman, with all his vivacity, a foolish being. An Italian exclaims with astonishment, "*Corpo di Bacco!*" whenever he sees an inhabitant of the north take a drop of brandy before dinner; and the latter is not less surprised at the sight of the numerous *cavalieri serventi* which surround the wife of the former. Is it then to be wondered at if a European finds many strange things in the United States? But, to criticise or censure all these indiscriminately, as late travellers have done, merely because they are not in harmony with the customs of London, Paris, or Vienna, is as unreasonable as the expectations of a certain foreigner, who thought it very extraordinary not to find the very best Lafitte or Château Margot at every petty ale-house in the remotest part of England.

The situation of this large town, which, within the memory of man, has trebled its population, promises a greater increase of trade than any other city in the Union. In the year 1831, there arrived from foreign parts no less than one thousand six hundred and thirty-four vessels; in 1833, the number had augmented to one thousand nine hundred and twenty-five, of which one thousand three hundred and eighty-four were American, three hundred and seventy-one English, forty-one Swedish, and thirty-five Spanish, consequently, an accession in two years of two hundred and forty-one vessels. The number of passengers, which in the course of 1833 arrived at New York, was forty-one thousand seven hundred and fifty-two; the greatest number landed in June, July, and August; and the smallest in January, February, and March. This exhibits a great increase: from the 1st of October, 1821, to the same period, 1822, no more than eight thousand four hundred and eighty-two passengers in all came to the ports of the United States.

One of the first evenings, after landing, I spent on the banks of the majestic Hudson. There is something attractive and inspiring in this stream. From Broadway, which, as I have before observed, commences at the Battery, and traverses the whole city, there is a road leading to a small hamlet called Manhattanville. On proceeding in this direction, several places present themselves, from which the romantic scenery of the North River is viewed in all its perfection. From one hotel in particular, whence a footpath has been traced which takes the visiter to a rock close to the shore, the prospect is truly enchanting. But, from no place did the Hudson appear to me to greater advantage than from Hoboken, a delightful spot on the New Jersey side, opposite to New York, between which and the city steamboats are continually plying. The proprietor of this beautiful retreat, emphatically called the Elysian Fields, Mr. Stephens, with a liberality worthy of his high standing in society, has thrown open the whole range of extensive park to the public; and it is in the summer season, to the inhabitants of New York, one of the greatest recreations that can well be imagined, and for which they must ever remain greatly indebted to this high-spirited gentleman. Nothing can exceed the taste — the matchless taste — with which the gardens and walks, aided by the hand of Nature, are laid out. The perspective view of Staten Island, of Long Island, of the Bay of New York, of the City itself, with all its steeples, of New Jersey City, of all the shipping, on one side; and of the River Hudson, and all its tributary beauties, intermingled with steamers, sloops, and pleasure-boats on the other, presents to the delighted and astonished eye a panorama of such unparalleled and variegated splendour, that it baffles all description. The noise inseparable from large cities could at times be heard across the stream. I listened, and recollected these beautiful lines of Horace:—

> Beatus ille qui, procul negotiis,
> Ut prisca gens mortalium,
> Paterna rura bobus exercet suis,
> Solutus omni fœnore.

But, as soon as the sun had set, and the moon began to rise in all her brightness, the scene became still more beautiful. From elevated chimneys, attached to numerous glass and iron manufactories on the opposite shores, issued columns of fire, which illuminated the whole range of contiguous buildings; great masses of flakes also burst forth from the passing steamers, and accompanied them on their swift course, like the appendage to a comet. The whole had the appearance of the commencement of a great conflagration; the City and stream seemed threatened with being suddenly enveloped in flames and smoke. This dream of imagination chilled me for a moment, and I turned my eyes away from the sight; but, once more looking up, I beheld the silent moon calmly glittering on the surface of the Hudson, and I continued to enjoy the happiness of contemplating a picture to which nothing could be compared. The freshness of the evening, the stillness of the leaves, the beauty of dormant Nature surrounding me on every side, and, lastly, my own state of mind, all contributed to fix me for a long while as a silent spectator. At length I was overtaken by the lateness of night, and unwillingly left a spot combining so many attractions. With lively emotion, I still remember the richly overshadowed tree, whose wide-spread branches sheltered me during my deep meditation; and also the mossy rock on which I rested, in full admiration of the scene before me. It seemed as if I heard a voice softly whispering the following lines of Bryant, one of America's poetical sons:—

> River! in this still hour thou hast
> Too much of heaven, on earth to last;
> Nor long may thy still waters lie,
> An image of the glorious sky:
> Thy fate and mine are not repose,
> And, ere another evening close,
> Thou to thy tide shalt turn again,
> And I to seek the crowd of men.

The cholera raged in the meanwhile with dreadful violence in New York. This epidemic had been brought over to America by an English ship, which landed a number of emigrants at Quebec. A few days after their arrival, the disease broke out, and shortly afterwards made its appearance in New

York. It is contended that some of the passengers, having relatives in the latter city, quitted Quebec immediately on a visit to them. This is the manner in which the sudden breaking out of the cholera at New York has been accounted for. The physicians were all the time divided in opinion as to the nature of the disorder, whether it was contagious or not: all insisted on the correctness of their conclusions — the advocates of non-contagion by contact, but possibly by inhaling the breath, seemed finally to preponderate.

When it is considered that more than half the population of the city left it under the influence of fear, it may indeed be said that this visitation caused the greatest havock and consternation. From the 26th June, the day when the first bulletin was issued by the Medical Board, up to the 29th August following, when the official reports were discontinued, the number of cases were no less than five thousand nine hundred and twenty-eight, and deaths two thousand nine hundred and fifty-one. On my arrival at New York, the cholera was greatly on the increase; and, on the 21st July, there were one hundred and four victims, and three hundred and eleven new cases. Accounts from unquestionable authority stated, however, that the majority of persons who sunk under this alarming disease were generally individuals of debilitated constitutions, who had indulged in the vice of intemperance and its concomitants; but, nevertheless, it not unfrequently occurred that even men of regular and exemplary habits were snatched away by its baneful effects.

New York could not boast of any particular cleanliness during the prevalence of the afflicting disorder; and, as it is well known that the want of it materially contributes to its duration, this neglect gave, perhaps, additional vigour to the virulence. I certainly do not mean to infer that New York is inferior in point of cleanliness to places that meet the eye of a traveller in Italy, Ireland, and other countries: even Paris and London, in some of the obscure purlieus, exhibit sometimes a filthy appearance. I cannot, however, refrain from remarking that, when I saw a variety of uncleanly matter thrown from the houses into the street, (recalling almost to mind a *sèjour* at Lisbon) and this too during the worst time of the cholera, I could not but make melancholy anticipations of its ravages. "Experience has proved," was the answer made to my observation of its impropriety, "that hogs always keep the streets of a town in a state of perfect cleanliness." And, upon the strength of this argument, the unseemly animals enjoy, in this rising city, a free and independent life — at perfect liberty to perambulate the thoroughfares and indulge in hearty repasts on offals of every description thrown in, and streaming down the gutters in offensive abundance, and this too in the midst of coaches, horses, and pedestrians. The following ludicrous paragraph, illustrative of this nuisance, and addressed to one of the editors of a New York newspaper, appeared during my residence in that city.

To the Editor of ————————

SIR,—Permit me to inquire, through the medium of your columns, whether the worthy corporation of this city has, in its wisdom, lately granted any particular license to the proprietors of certain animals, the name of which I feel hesitation in mentioning, for daily exhibitions in the principal streets of New York.

Groups of these unseemly quadrupeds congregate, as if by appointment, at all hours in various directions, but more particularly in the immediate vicinity of the City Hall; and, by their unceasing grunting, seem to vociferate the high sense of gratitude they feel towards the constituted and ever-watchful authorities for the unrestrained liberty they enjoy under a free and happy constitution, in being allowed, without interruption, to perambulate every avenue in defiance of the wishes of the well-organised citizens; and in being able, moreover, by the aid of their natural perfume, effectually to counteract and *nullify* all the chlorides and other disinfecting matters — so absolutely necessary upon the present calamitous occasion.

Shall it be said of the western metropolis—as this city is emphatically called—that by the side of a handsome American lady—attired in all the elegance and variety of London and Parisian fashions—or in the suite of an exquisite dandy, calculated to eclipse even a finished beau of Bond Street or Regent Street—shall it be said, I ask, that in this assemblage is seen a group of animals of the filthiest order, unceremoniously splashing the elegant costume of the one, and as unconcernedly discomposing, by friction, the well adjusted garments of the other. The idea is monstrous. For Heaven's sake, Mr. Editor, spare no pains to have the evil removed instanter, or rest assured Mrs. Trollope will wet her quiil, and prepare another chapter to her work.

SPECTATOR.

In Boston, the cleanliness of the streets is properly attended to: they might serve as a pattern to any city in the world.

The cholera had converted bustling and animated New York into a place of gloom and dulness, the effect of which was seriously felt by those who, from some reason or other, had to remain behind, and could not follow the multitude that fled from the pestiferous air to contiguous villages near the sea. A dark cloud appeared to overhang the city—every countenance bore the stamp of fear. Broadway, invariably crowded, was now deserted, like the streets in Pompeii; and the few individuals that were visible passed each other with a singular rapidity, as if afraid of infection by contact. Numerous houses were entirely shut up, and rows of shops not opened for several days. Closed doors and shutters indicated that the tenants had fled, and, but for the name still fresh on the former, it might have been inferred that the occupants had been dead long ago. The silence which pervaded every avenue was dismal in the extreme: it was only occasionally interrupted by a discordant concert from perambulating quadrupeds of the race just mentioned. No living being ever appeared in the windows of houses, still occupied in part; and if by chance the head of a Negro ventured to show itself out of a cellar, it was generally under a strong apprehension that contagion might possibly follow. No workshops were in activity — all the steam-engines were standing still: no trade, no bustle. Every thing was dead. Here and there a few individuals were seen, engaged in an animated conversation: if the question was asked, "what subject?" *The Cholera.* At another place might be seen a silent, solid-looking man, leaning against an iron railing, apparently engaged in serious thought about some extensive commercial operations, or banking speculations. If asked, "what occupied his mind?" he would answer, "*The cholera.*" Again, a woman might be discovered, carrying a child in her arms, and evidently in a hurry to attend to some important business : turning round at every step, and pressing the infant to her breast, pale as death. If asked, "what she was afraid of?" she would answer, "*The cholera.*" Every newspaper treated of no other subject than the *cholera.* If a miserable object was lying in the street, suffering under the double calamity of poverty and disease, instead of lending him assistance, people would run away and leave him to his fate. Why? *Because he had got the cholera.* If the driver of a simple and unattended hearse was seen accelerating the speed of his horses, the question was asked, "Why does he go so fast?" *Because the hearse contains a number of dead, victims to the cholera ; they must immediately go to the burying ground, without ceremony and without friends.*

CHAPTER III.

> Could the ceaseless vultures cease to prey,
> On self-condemning bosoms, it were here,
> Where Nature, nor too sombre, nor too gay,
> Wild but not rude, awful yet not austere,
> Is to the mellow Earth as Autumn to the year.
>
> BYRON.

I SOON left the ill-fated city, and took my departure in one of the numerous steamboats which are daily plying on the Hudson. Nothing can exceed the elegance of these boats; those we have in Europe are as inferior to them as a gun-brig to a frigate. But the steamers that run from New York are much smaller than those on the Mississippi and Ohio. The largest of the former are the *President* of above 170, and the *North America* of 150, horse power. The trips of the first are to New Providence, whither she proceeds during night-time: births for several hundred passengers are arranged on each side of the dining-room, which extends nearly the whole length of the boat. The latter again only runs in the day-time, and is fitted up with every degree of taste and elegance. Both have double decks, that is, a small one built above the other, covered with awnings, on which the passengers may walk in the cool air. The ladies' cabin is generally on a level with the lower deck, but in some boats it is on the other side of the dining-room. The saloon, in the North America, is peculiar for its magnificence. Mahogany, and a variety of other beautiful wood, in imitation of marble, is displayed in every direction, and between each window are pictures painted by good artists.

Most of the steamers have two boilers, one on each side the lower deck. The machinery is generally above deck; and the large walking-beam moves up and down, in the open air, between the two chimneys, which rise to a considerable height on each side of the boat.

The trip of the North America is generally to Albany, a distance of about one hundred and forty-seven English miles, which she performs in ten hours and a half, including stoppages at landing places. She has even done it in ten.

Punctuality on board these boats is observed in the highest degree. The clock had hardly finished striking five, before the paddles were in motion, and the boat slipped out of the harbour with the same ease as when a ship is launched. No indulgence, no favour, was shown to persons who had the misfortune to come half a minute too late; they were left behind without mercy, and had the mortification of admiring the swiftness of the boat, and her fine appearance, at a distance. It was a truly ludicrous scene to behold all these gentry, "who were just in time to be too late," with bundles, carpet-bags, and bandboxes, remaining stationary on shore, faintly hoping that the captain, out of pity, might stop the machinery and take them on board. Vain were their hopes: the captain threw the blame on the clock, which, it is well known, waits for none. Perspiring, and puffing under the weight of their loads, they at length returned to their homes, and had at least the satisfaction of meeting, on the way, a number of others in the same predicament, hastening to the spot in hopes of catching the boat.

I was now on board with several hundred passengers, of every station, age, and sex. The apprehension of the cholera had already driven a great many from the city; and such was the terror still prevailing, that I feel satisfied at least two thirds of the persons present had no idea of leaving New York but for this untoward occurrence. In this opinion I was the more confirmed, when I took a review of the numberless trunks and bags which rose on deck in the shape of a pyramid. The major part of these travelling appendages had reached a comfortable age, and might, without fear of misrepresentation, be supposed to have accompanied some of the first settlers who landed on the American coast from England. Assuredly, these antiquities would never have seen the light, but for the general consternation. Many a trunk, if the name may be applied, might be seen, whose decayed bottom had severely suffered by the destructive hand of Time, and was only attached to the sides by being strongly corded ; but, maugre this precaution, not a few white dresses and Merino shawls were peeping out at the corners. Cobwebs and mildew were still perceptible, the hurry of departure not having permitted their removal. The locks, too, were of the simplest make, and to all appearance manufactured at a time when the spirit of invention had not arrived at its climax ; they were, besides, so rusty and filled with dirt, that it was a matter of surprise to me how the keys could possibly fit.

The owners of these precious relics were equally objects of curiosity ; they were composed of hack-drivers, paviours, lamplighters, masons, carpenters, &c., having all wives and children in Sunday clothes. No distinction of rank between these and the other passengers was perceptible ; one is as good as another. The company mixed indiscriminately, and the driver considered himself as fine a gentleman as the first dandy on board. This equality was particularly observable at the tea-table. A young American, with whom I had been in company a few days before in one of the first houses in New York, was seated at the long table between two females, one the wife of a driver, the other that of a lamplighter, both past the age when young men are generally flattered at being near the elbow of a belle. I saw him, with perfect attention, serve both his fair neighbours before he thought of himself, and, during the whole repast, continue his civilities with so much grace, that the example might serve as a salutary lesson to many a European coxcomb, who certainly will not put himself to inconvenience for the sake of being attentive to females of so mediocre a station in life, and to whom nature has besides refused the advantage of beauty. A young Frenchman, who came to America about the same time I did, could not help remarking to the American, that he was surprised at seeing a man of birth, of *blood*, condescend so far as to enter into conversation with a couple of vulgar women. The American answered, that it appeared to him equally extraordinary how a man of birth could ever forget the respect due to every female by a person of education, let her rank be what it will in society. "Civility to all women," added he, "is considered in America as a distinctive proof of a well-bred man." The Frenchman retired confused, without saying a word, only shrugging his shoulders, as if to say that he by no means admitted the propriety of a similar condescension.

The Hudson continues wide for a considerable distance; its breadth, until near the Highlands, may be said to be about one English mile, or more. The eastern shore is well cultivated, and presents to the eye a succession of smiling landscapes. Most of the hills are covered with verdure and fruit trees; and, from the remotest woods down to the river, nothing is seen but corn-fields, pastures, and gardens, in the midst of which beautiful country seats are situated. Villages, embowered among trees, are now and then visible; and the reflection of the setting sun on their pointed steeples makes them appear as if rising from the midst of a forest. Rivulets meander in various directions, and fertilize the fields. The prospect on the western shore of the river is, however, quite different: there, a chain of perpendicular rocks, about five hundred feet high, follows the direction of the stream for nearly twenty miles. They are not unlike artificial breastworks, and are therefore called Palisades. They stretch sometimes downright into the river, sometimes retire a few paces, leaving only sufficient place for the residence of a few scattered stonecutters. Some of their houses are built against the rock, so that one of the walls is formed thereof. A few huts are visible here and there; and, to complete the picturesque view, cattle are sometimes seen at a small distance, seeking a scanty subsistence between the crevices; or children, joyfully jumping from one rock to another. A habitation like the one just described must naturally appear very confined and uncomfortable to a traveller viewing it from the steamboat; but, if the healthy and strong inmate is asked whether he is happy there, he will undoubtedly answer that, as long as he is permitted to behold the majestic Hudson flowing below his retreat, all his wishes are realized.

Yes, majestic indeed is this river; nor does it in the least surprise me that the Indians had so high an opinion of it, since, according to their own traditions, their god Manetho betook himself to flight, when the river, like a supernatural being, descended from the rocks with frightful noise, and took possession of the dales and fields below. The poetical part in these old traditions of the Highlands, of which I propose speaking hereafter, shows what power they granted to the God of Waters; and this respect, which they invariably observed, was, after he had conquered all the country round Manhattan, and governed his kingdom in peace and quiet, changed into a majestic veneration: to this circumstance may probably be attributed the surname *Majestic,* now synonymous with the river Hudson.

On my right, I observed the four square walls of Sing Sing prison, and not far from them the village of Sparta; further on, the Sleepy Hollow, where the spirit of Ichabod Cranes* is still haunted by the headless spectre of a Hessian dragoon. I fancied I saw the tall slim schoolmaster, with narrow shoulders, long arms and legs, hands which hung a mile below the sleeves, feet which might be used as spades, with a head uncommonly small and flat, a pair of enormous ears, large green shining eyes, and a long parrot nose, resembling a weathercock on a high pole, showing which way the wind blows. I fancied I saw this gaunt figure haunted by the headless unknown, and working with hands and feet to preserve his equilibrium on a horse after the saddle had been lost; sometimes slipping on one side, then on another, again leaning over the horse's head, then shook to pieces against the thin knots of his hind legs. Washington Irving's excellent description appeared so natural when I passed this place, that I could not refrain from indulging in a hearty laugh. A few serious Quakers and Quakeresses, who happened to be close to me on deck, seemingly contemplating the beautiful picture before them, were suddenly roused by my unexpected fit of laughter; and gave

* Vide the account of Washington Irving, in his Sketch Book, vol. ii.

me looks perfectly indicative of what they thought. They concluded, probably, that I was a maniac; for they exchanged signs, shook their heads as if expressing pity, and then resumed their former attitudes. My first idea was to say a few words by way of explanation, but I checked my intention upon a second reflection. "These people," said I, "care very little about the fate of Ichabod: they are probably so religious that they never read a word about him; explanation is therefore unnecessary." I let the matter rest, but could not help thinking once more of the haunted schoolmaster.

The steamboat neared the Highlands. The river is here contracted between the rugged heights. I do not doubt but some violent revolution in former times has caused this narrow passage, leaving a small opening to the stream to discharge itself in the sea. Tradition relates as follows: — "These high rocks were in ancient times used by King Manetho as prisons for rebellious spirits, dissatisfied with his mild rule. For several centuries, they were left to repine under the weight of the heavy rocks. But Hudson proved their friend; he destroyed by the roar of thunder these dreadful prisons. Since that period, they have enjoyed unrestrained liberty, but still tremble whenever the elements are agitated, fearful that Manetho might return, and renew their imprisonment in their dark dungeons. The echoes incessantly heard between the mountains are nothing but expressions of lamentation and fear on the part of the spirits at the most trifling noise."

These mountainous parts are not unlike the shores on the Rhine from Bonn to Coblentz. Mountains follow in succession: between them are sheltered dales. Bushes and trees cover the walls of the rocks almost to the tops. From some of the woods may be seen the ruins of small fortifications, which were used during the revolutionary war. At another point in the river is a simple monument, to the memory of some fallen warrior; (almost every spot in these Highlands recalls some deed of valour during the struggle for liberty). Further on, a loosened piece of rock overhangs the river, ready to attempt once more to close the passage.

Darkness overtook us, as soon as we came between the mountains. The sun had set long ago, and in the western horizon rose a mass of clouds, which announced the approach of a storm. Gradually, the lightning became more vivid, and a threatening black sky spread in a few minutes over forests and mountains. All Nature trembled at the awful perspective, and all that had life on shore hastened to take shelter in grottoes and crevices. Fireflies, which shone and disappeared more rapidly than thought could follow them, ceased to show their brilliancy against the green trees; even these trifling insects, which lightning could hardly strike, felt awe at the storm, and went to rest. Every animal seemed to take shelter in some hiding place: to man alone it was reserved to defy the united attacks of the elements, and to venture a look towards the agitated heavens. Several steamers passed me: their lamps in the stern, ahead, and in the mast, appeared in the dark as magic lights. Our steamboat also had similar lamps, which produced on the nearest objects a feeble and gloomy light. From both chimneys issued millions of sparks in an irregular dance; like gold dust, they spread over the stream, and expired the moment they reached the surface of the water. Thunder was heard above our heads, and lightning seen in every direction proceeding from the heavy clouds; forests and rocks, and valleys and streams, grew pale every time the Western Deity shook the heavenly lights out of his mighty hand. But in the East a storm was also gathering. Jealous of the conquests of the West, it rose from a long rest, to dispute the ascendancy assumed by the latter. A few unexpected flashes from the opposite shore announced the commencement of hostilities; the West, offended at the temerity of its antagonist, advanced at once with its whole artillery, determined to crush, by a few effectual discharges, its slowly advancing adversary. The conflict was dreadful: each minute added to its obstinacy and fury. Often did I presume that preliminaries of peace had been concluded between the contending parties, but the next moment I was convinced to the contrary. From summit to summit — from rock to rock — the thunder roared, and each stone seemed to re-echo it. It was a concert; an accompaniment of various instruments, like a complete orchestra, which I could fain attempt to describe. Rain fell in torrents; the whole was awful and imposing in the extreme, and characteristic of those sudden tempests or storms which so often visit the Western hemisphere. It was only after two hours' hard fighting that the contest ceased between the belligerents above; and victory declared in favour of the West, by the appearance of a beautiful blue sky, and a few stars glittering over the field of battle. The beaten legions of the East retreated in haste, pursued by the elated victors, who put them in confusion. Their triumphant shouts gradually gave way, and, when I shortly afterwards looked up, not a cloud could be seen; the whole firmament was covered with brilliant stars.

"Passengers for West Point!" was now heard from one end of the boat to the other. I hastened on deck, collected my baggage, and went on shore.

CHAPTER IV.

Can you so watch
The sunrise which may be our last?
It is
Therefore that I so watch it, and reproach
Those eyes which never may behold it more
For having look'd upon it oft, too oft,
Without the reverence and the rapture due
To that which keeps all earth from being as fragile
As I am in this form.

BYRON.

THE Academy of Cadets is situated on this spot, and occupies a tolerably extensive plain, a few hundred yards above the river, at the foot of a mountain, intersected with wood. A number of brick houses have been built for this purpose, and in front is a spacious piece of ground, adopted for drilling and other military exercises. A few tents were pitched for the Cadets, then going through various evolutions; and not far from this spot is the "*corps de garde*," before which some of them, in grey uniforms, were seen walking, guarding the avenue to the camp.

Captain Hall, in his published Travels in North America, 1827 and 1828, criticises, perhaps not altogether without foundation, their deficiency in "*tenue militaire.*" They wear a kind of military cap, so small in size, that, in order not to lose it, they are obliged to let the fore part rest on the nose, thus leaving the whole neck bare. This objectionable fashion has not been found so useful as was expected; the greatest part of the Cadets appeared to me to have narrow chests and were rather round-shouldered: two defects which among European officers are strongly objected to. This Academy is the only one of its kind in the United States, and is maintained at the expense of the government. The avowed object is not only to give young men, destined for military service, a perfect education in various branches, but to keep up and disseminate all over the country a correct and sound knowledge of this science. Captain Hall seems to question whether America will ever derive any real advantage from this institution, and endeavours to show, in the usual laboured way, his reasons for so thinking. I am far from being of his opinion, and cannot see why the community should fail being benefited by an Academy, conducted with so much care and attention, and the professors of which are men of first-rate talents, chosen and esteemed by their countrymen.

The number of Cadets is limited to two hundred and fifty. None can be received unless he has attained his fourteenth year. The President of the United States reserves to himself the right of granting admissions to this Academy, and generally endeavours to divide an equal number of candidates for each State. They attend to their studies for a period of four years, during which time they are instructed in mathematics, geography, history, philosophy, chemistry, and mineralogy; the French language, drawing, the art of fortification, &c. If any one belonging to either of the four classes cannot pass his examination, notice is given to his relations to remove him from the Academy, where it is considered he can be of no use. If again he goes regularly through the ordeal, he is entitled to employment by government. Stored with the knowledge he has acquired, he is now sent to places where it can be made available. Not only is he commanded to proceed to the peopled and cultivated Eastern States, but, like productive corn, is scattered over the whole range of country, and often obliged to settle in the remotest parts, among woodcutters in Michigan and Missouri. It would indeed be singular, if, in this manner, no good result should follow; it must be the case, although I cannot help thinking that the maximum of two hundred and fifty cadets is too inconsiderable for such a country as the United States, to effect all the good that might be derived, if the number were two thousand five hundred instead of two hundred and fifty. Time will probably change this system, when America finds that the hopes she entertained of this useful national institution have not been disappointed.

The scenery round West Point is extremely romantic. The mountain, at the foot of which the Academy is situated, is covered with wood, in the midst of which the ruins of Fort Putnam may be seen; this was an important post during the war with the English, but has since been abandoned. The prospect from this fort is very extensive, but cannot, in my opinion, be compared to the one from the balcony of the hotel. This hotel is recently built over a projecting cliff near the river, on a level with the Academy. From this balcony is a fine view of the Hudson, confined between the two walls of the Highlands; and at a distance the little town of Newburgh. A few white sails were visible spread over the smooth surface, now and then agitated by numberless steamers, passing in that direction. On the opposite shore, I saw elevated chimneys belonging to an extensive iron-foundry for casting cannon; and the report of the guns which underwent trial resembled that of the thunder-storm I had witnessed during my trip to West Point. As the noise re-echoed through the surrounding mountains, I thought I heard the frightened cries of the emancipated spirits, who, at the least alarm, trembled in fear that Manetho would once more return and load them with chains. At a little distance is Antony's Nose, a projecting rock, so called from a remarkable circumstance which is reported to have occurred here, namely, that the trumpeter, Antony Van Corlear, by means of the reflexion of the sunbeams on his shining nose, killed a large sturgeon, who happened to be in the neighbourhood.* On this side of the river is also a simple monument erected to the memory of Kosciusko: the noble and gallant Pole lived here several years, remote

* Vide Knickerbocker's New York, vol. ii.

from his own unhappy country, and afterwards recrossed the Atlantic, and took up his residence at Soleure, in Switzerland, where he closed a glorious career in the year 1817, enjoying at last in death that repose, the sweets of which he could not taste while alive, and seeing his beloved country subjugated, mutilated, reduced to slavery.

I spent a few days delightfully at this charming place, more and more pleased with the beautiful prospect. The steamboat, however, arriving from New York, I was obliged to take my leave. I quitted West Point most unwillingly, and went again on board for the purpose of continuing my journey up the Hudson. All the small places, villages, hamlets, and towns, situated on the banks of the river, have, more or less, owing to the great facility of communication, risen in a very short time to a state of prosperity ; and, with few exceptions, appeared flourishing. Among the number I may mention a few which are between West Point and Catskill: Newburgh, Tishkill, Poughkeepsie, Kingston, Rhinebeck, &c. Time did not permit me to visit them in person ; but, from what I could judge from the deck of the steamer, coupled with the accounts I received from respectable people, I am led to conclude that they have to thank the increased navigation of the Hudson, and the large market at New York, for their present prosperous condition.

It was at Catskill I, for the first time, entered an American stage coach. It was not unlike the French *Diligence*, although not near so large or heavy. Carriages in the United States are generally built very light, and the springs are made equally so; which leads you to fear they will break at every moment. The stage coaches in the Northern States have mostly leather thongs, instead of springs. I often wondered how they could possibly resist the numberless hard knocks which we encountered in passing over a road, in many places full of deep holes and broken stones; but the thongs are tough, and proof against any shocks. There are three rows of seats inside, for three persons on each: on the coach-box beside the driver is also room for one or two. The middle row is between the two doors, of which one is seldom made to open. Leather curtains are used on the sides, so arranged as to roll up or let down at pleasure. Every thing indicates that they are built for the summer season, when a free circulation of air is so necessary in a warm climate; but, in winter time, our European carriages, I must confess, are preferable. The *tout ensemble* has somewhat of an old fashioned appearance, particularly to a person coming directly from England.

The distance from Catskill to Pine Orchard, an hotel between the mountains, is about twelve miles. The road is in some places steep, and twists itself from right to left along the sides of the mountain through a thick wood of various trees, such as cedar, fir, locust, white oak, maple, birch, ash, mountain-ash, walnut, chesnut, hazle, cherry, wild apple, &c. all growing close to each other, as if of the same species. The wild vine, twisted round the trunks of different trees, appeared endeavouring to unite those which in our hemisphere grow far asunder, like irreconcileable enemies. This mixture of trees is a peculiarity characteristic of American woods, and gives to the landscape a variegated appearance.

About half way from the foot of the mountain to Pine Orchard, where the road suddenly takes another direction, the traveller arrives at a kind of amphitheatre, formed of steep and woody rocks, the straight side of which descends to a precipice, whence a few trees

F 2

shoot their crowns; and, with an extra-ordinary temerity, strive to extend their wide branches so far, that no eye from above can perceive the depth of the precipice. On this spot, where a rivulet now rattles between bushes and green meadows, Rip Van Winkle passed twenty years in sleep; here it was that, awaking from a long fairy slumber, he found every thing changed: trees grown up where formerly stood only bushes, rivulets rattling where formerly was a footpath, precipices opening where formerly was a long descent. But the worst of all was, he found himself changed, stiff all over his body, with a long grey beard and spread hair, and, into the bargain, a free citizen of the United States instead of an humble subject of George III. This occurrence so admirably described is now so generally known, that I need only allude to it; but, if any traveller, intending to visit the Catskill Mountains, has not read Washington Irving's history of Rip Van Winkle,* I recommend him by all means to do so. He will then derive infinitely more pleasure from his tour, and Sleepy Hollow will become so interesting,

* Vide Sketch Book of Washington Irving, vol. i.

that it cannot easily be obliterated from his memory.

The appearance of Pine Orchard Hotel (the Mountain House) is that of a palace. It is situated on the declivity of a rock, two thousand two hundred and fourteen feet above the level of the river. During the summer months, it is much frequented by the first families in the neighbourhood, and pic-nic parties take place very often by people from New York and Albany. But this year many were deterred taking up their residence here, on account of the cholera, and the difficulty of obtaining medical aid, in case of necessity. I was nearly alone in this large establishment.

When, on the following morning, I got up, and looked around me, it appeared as if I was hovering in the air, above the clouds. These, as it often happens in elevated situations, were lower than the point of the mountains on which I stood, and entirely obscured the country below. This scene recalled to my memory the snow-mountains in Switzerland, the different forms of valleys and heights in the snow regions, the white mountain-tops, the reflexion of the sunbeams on the masses of snow, contrasting with the dark and desolate appearance of the valleys beneath. The winds were whistling between the clouds, and kept them in constant motion, as when the northern breeze stirs up the light snow, and forces it to rise in whirls from the earth. The sun had at last sufficient power to dissipate these cloudy landscapes, and gave me an opportunity of beholding, not an imaginary but a most extensive and enchanting view. No sudden change of stage scenery or magic metamorphosis has ever produced a similar effect upon me as the one I now experienced. I could hardly believe my eyes. I was absolutely struck with astonishment: every one present seemed to feel the same impulse. In deep meditation, we all contemplated beautiful Nature, hardly venturing to raise our eyes for fear of destroying the illusion. It was too fine to be lost sight of; I dreaded the next minute would make it disappear like a vapour, as quickly as it had presented itself to my view. But it was no enchantment. The Hudson was as immoveable as a silver streak drawn on green canvass; the mountains, hills, forests, fields, and houses, remained the same. The whole picture bore a strong resemblance to views in Switzerland, which so justly excite the admiration of travellers, and are the boast of the inhabitants. A dim chain of mountains is seen in the back ground, which cuts through Massachusetts, Vermont, and Connecticut; in the foreground again, nothing but fertile fields are observed, intersected with woods and green hills, close to neat and comfortable villages.

At a distance of two miles from the hotel are the Cascades: although told in New York that these waterfalls are very insignificant, and hardly worth seeing, particularly in a state in which Niagara is situated, I nevertheless determined to visit them, conceiving there is nothing in nature so fine, so magnificent, and majestic, as a cataract.

A vehicle, something like a Swedish country waggon—

> A cursed sort of carriage without springs,
> Which in rough roads leaves scarcely a whole bone—
>
> BYRON.

brought me across a most abominable road, along the banks of two small lakes, to the Cascades in question. A stream flows from these lakes, which, like a stranger in the neighbourhood, unacquainted with footpaths and roads, seeks an issue through a maze of wood, twisting to the right and left, and finally arrives at an unexpected precipice, down which it dashes itself almost unconsciously. The waterfall formed by this stream is over a perpendicular rock, one hundred and seventy-five feet high. The mass of water is precipitated down between dark rocks into a pit or basin, where it collects for a few minutes; and, with an additional quantity, rushes over another rock, eighty feet high, into a valley so thickly wooded, that the water disappears between stones and roots of trees the moment it reaches the bottom.

The pit in which the water collects after the first fall has a strong resemblance to a theatre. The walls, almost perpendicular, form a perfect semicircle, cut off in a straight line (similar to the fore-scene in a theatre, or the row of lamps which divides the orchestra from the scene), over which the water falls a second time. Imagination may also fancy scenery and curtain, for Nature has been pleased to represent the whole as a *coup d'œil de theatre.* The trees, too, are grouped together in such an effective manner, that one would suppose the grand Master had copied some forest scene from the theatres in Paris or London; and the mountains which raise their heads at a distance are a true representation of the finest curtain that could possibly be painted by a first-rate artist.

The walls in the pit are, as I have before observed, nearly straight, and incline rather in an inward direction in nearing the foundation: there the water moistens and sweeps away the soft matter, so that it is possible, as under a vault, to walk round the foot of the mountain, sheltered by a roof.

I seated myself for a long while on a small rock, and eyed with great attention the mass of water, which came thundering down from above me, apparently not touching the walls of the rocks, but throwing a mist on all the objects around. Trees and bushes grew on the cliffs that surrounded me; but my attention was particularly directed to an old tree, the roots of which were perfectly bare, hanging almost unsupported along the sides of the stones. Nevertheless, it not only had life, but appeared to possess full vigour. I was lost in conjecture how a tall tree could possibly exist, and be able to withstand storms, to which it was continually exposed, without any solid support, and destitute as it was of nearly any earth for its subsistence. Yet, it seemed full of life, and now and then bent its luxuriant crown, whose leaves playfully chatted with the summer breezes. I took a great fancy to this tree, and for a long time admired its temerity and joyfulness. But a strange, singular sound suddenly reached my ears, and broke off the link of my meditations. Unconscious of what I did, I happened to look at my guide, who had heard it before I did, and who was resting on his wandering staff, with both eyes and ears attentively fixed. I am ignorant whether his attention was merely to listen or to excite my curiosity; but he could not be persuaded to utter a single word. Another moment, and he still remained immoveable—the next he had retired far from me. Jumping from stone to stone, creeping between bushes and roots, he sometimes was visible, sometimes out of sight. At one time he stopped, then he advanced, again he raised himself on his toes, and then listened to the incessant rushing. At length he reached a rock, round which the mysterious tree had loosely thrown its root. He seized with one hand the thickest part of the root, turned round on the rock, and commenced beating boldly against the trunk of the tree. The strokes followed in rapid succession; and leaves, bark, briars, and branches, flew in every direction, as when the woodcutter fells with his axe a leafy tree.

Repeated blows against the trunk, and violent shaking, caused, however, the weak root—sole support of the tree—to yield. It fell suddenly with a dreadful crash into the water, and followed it down the second fall. It has since been condemned, probably, for some years, to lie with the crown towards the earth, at the foot of a venerable oak, boasting of its age and rank. The water, arrested in its progress by the fallen hero, foams with rage, and covers its body continually with froth.

I visited this place some time afterwards; the tree remained on the same spot. The leaves had disappeared, and green turfs were growing here and there on the bark, but the trunk seemed still fresh. A few frogs had taken up their abode underneath, and were then in serious deliberation about the affairs of their kingdom.

As soon as the tree had quitted the rocky spot on which it had spent its youth, I could clearly see something glittering and moving in the nearest bushes. My daring guide did not discontinue his blows till the rattlesnake (for so it turned out to be,) had ceased to live. Triumphantly he seized the venomous animal, threw it down before me, and exclaimed, "Look what a fellow I have caught!"

The animal was one of those dangerous snakes which, during the summer months, are so full of venom, that they become blind with it. I had often, since my arrival in America, heard of the bewitching power these animals possess, of which many people seem thoroughly convinced, and which has probably obtained credence with the first colonists in very remote times. My guide was one of those who entertained no doubt on the subject. I availed myself of the opportunity to put a few questions, and gave him to understand I doubted the truth of it. He could not forbear relating to me the following narrative, well known in the Northern States:

"Among the first colonists in the vicinity of the green mountains in Vermont, there was a man who, prepossessed in favour of the fertility of the country, took up his residence there with his young and handsome wife. They lived in that part about a year, and all difficulties incidental to new settlers had nearly been removed. They now began to enjoy themselves, and found their abode tolerable. The Indians were no more dreaded; the wild animals in the forests were kept aloof by the never-failing gun of man. The only danger to which they were exposed was that of being stung by rattlesnakes, of which there were great numbers. Several persons had had the misfortune to be stung, and expired in the most dreadful agony.

"One day, the husband, accompanied by his wife, went into the woods to hunt. The weather was fine — the sun almost scorched their heads. The young wife, after wandering some time among bushes and stones, at length became tired, and sat down to rest herself on the branch of a tree, in expectation of the return of her husband. He followed in the meanwhile the traces of a deer, climbing from rock to rock, with a view to enter a green plain at the foot of a mountain. All at once he observed, lying before him, a rattlesnake of uncommon size. Surprised at the sight, he stopped, and attentively considered the dangerous animal, which, only a few paces from him, seemed to deliberate whether it should venture to take a leap down the precipice. It suddenly formed a plan, bent its long body, and, as if imploring mercy, fixed upon the husband a pair of eyes which, far from expressing hatred towards mankind, spoke only the accents of mildness and friendship. There was something so extraordinary and so touching in the movements of the animal, that the husband remained silent and motionless on the spot. The snake displayed the finest colours, which the burning sun changed, as it approached, from green to purple and gold. Imperceptibly it rolled onwards; a strange music was heard, not unlike the melting tones of the honey-bird, and the animal disappeared, without his perceiving what direction it took. He thought at first he was in the midst of a world of mysterious colours, which cleared up, darkened, and again revived with a magic light. Harmony continued to enchant his ears. Perspiration covered his brow; his frame shook, as if attacked by ague; his legs refused their office. 'Is it a dream?' exclaimed he; 'what retains me at this place?' He made an effort to get away, but his feet were almost benumbed, and he felt as if fastened to the rock. The unfortunate man was bewitched.

"Another sound reached his ears; it was the voice of man, dismal and plaintive. Twice he heard it, but could not move. A white female eagerly seized his arm, and her breath roused him at once from the dream of enchantment. Music and colours disappeared at once. Round his feet twined the rattlesnake, with fiery eyes and extended sting. His frightened wife clung to his breast. Within a second they were attacked by the snake. The woman was the first victim. The venom spread with the rapidity of thought, and her lamentations soon informed the unhappy husband of the dreadful scene that awaited him.

"Half crazy, he rushed forward, and trampled under his feet the snake, which now endeavoured to steal away. Vengeance was not satisfied till the animal was crushed, and torn piecemeal against the sharp and pointed rocks.

"The sufferings of the expiring wife called him to her side. Terrified, he examined the blueish black wound, which every minute grew darker and darker. They were far from home or from any human habitation; still they wandered for a while, hand in hand, till excruciating pains stretched the female senseless on the ground. Although greatly exhausted, the husband took her in his arms, carried her to a neighbouring rivulet, and refreshed her by means of cool water. She recovered a little, but had no strength to raise her head, which rested motionless on his breast. Hours passed in this way, and no human being appeared to assist the unhappy couple. Solitary, in an endless forest, he watched the progress of death, joined his prayers to hers, and saw her expire."

These last words my guide expressed with so much emotion, that I clearly perceived he was deeply affected by the tragic narrative. My curiosity was in the mean time excited to know the fate of the husband, and the particulars of his after life. My guide gave me the following account:

" From that moment the unhappy widower thought of nothing but revenge, and made the most sacred vow to consecrate the remainder of his life to the extermination of that curse of man, the rattlesnake. This oath he strictly observed till his death, and thousands of snakes fell continually under his vindictive blows. For this reason he was generally known under the name of the Rattlesnake Hunter. Not many years ago, I saw the old grey-haired man; and never shall I forget the tears he shed at the recollection of his young consort, and his solemn and piercing look in expressing these words—'Yes, by G—d! these bewitching d—ls shall soon cease to plague the earth! Do not believe that these animals are only snakes—creeping snakes: they are servants of fallen angels—the immediate agents and spirits of Hell.'"

Here my guide ended his narrative. We returned to Pine Orchard in deep silence. The tale of the unfortunate snake-hunter remained a long while impressed on my mind; and when subsequently, in the Southern States, I had frequent occasions of seeing snakes of different kinds, I always remembered this anecdote.

From Catskill Mountains I proceeded to a small village, five miles up the river, to which the classical name of Athens has been given. It was the first place I arrived at in America, bearing an old European name. This, however, is very customary: in my subsequent travels in the country, I found several places called Sparta, Rome, Utica, Syracuse, &c. These names have been adopted without any attention being paid as to whether the situation of the village or hamlet bore any resemblance to the old city after which it was baptized: whim or chance have determined the appellation.

American Athens, for example, is situated on a plain, without a single hill, and on the banks of a river; whereas ancient Athens was surrounded by eminences. At first, it appeared singular to me to see a place, which, since my youth, I had pictured to myself filled with venerable relics, and ruins of temples and palaces, only consist of a few wooden houses of modern architecture, unpaved streets, showing no other ruins but those of abandoned blacksmiths' shops, or the walls of houses destroyed by fire. It was also a peculiar feature in Athens to behold hogs and other quadrupeds occupy the thoroughfares and squares, instead of having the ears delighted with speeches from eloquent orators.

From hence I crossed the river to Hudson, a small hamlet on the opposite side, and continued my journey to Lebanon Springs, in company with one of the most amiable American families I ever met with, and the recollection of which will follow me through life.

CHAPTER V.

"I joined myself to the people. It is now thirty years since, I believe, and," added she, raising her hands and eyes, and speaking with more energy than she had yet spoken, "I say the truth before God, and lie not: I have not repented for a moment—I have been heartily thankful that I have borne my testimony. I have purchased a peace that cannot be taken away, and cheaply purchased it."

MISS SEDGEWICK.

THESE Springs are among the most fashionable in the Northern States; in the summer season they are filled with the first and best company. They are situated on the declivity of a mountain, from whence, for miles round, Nature appears in her finest mantle. The water is lukewarm and perfectly harmless. The greatest part of individuals visiting this place do it less from a desire to taste the waters than to see and acquire a knowledge of the remarkable religious sect, whose head-quarters are in this vicinity, and the members of which are called Shakers.

Several branches of this sect are spread over various parts of America; but the principal place — the central union — is at a village about two miles from the Springs, exclusively inhabited by Shakers, and built by them. Every stranger, visiting it for the first time, cannot help remarking the peculiar cleanliness and neatness everywhere prevailing. On both sides of a wide street are houses two or three stories high. One row is built at the foot of a mountain, which shelters it against the north-easterly winds, and furnishes, besides, to the inhabitants sufficiency of water to carry on saw-mills, flour-mills, and workshops of various descriptions. The other row, again, is surrounded by gardens, abounding in every kind of vegetables; and extensive meadows are seen at a distance, where the finest cattle are fed on the most luxuriant herbs. On this side of the street, also, is the meeting-house, erected in the year 1825, by zealous members. It is of wood, eighty feet long, and sixty-five wide, with a vaulted roof, covered with tin plates. The interior and exterior is painted white. The inside is destitute of ornaments — no pillars, no painted windows, no tasteful pulpit. The floor is the only part with which they seem to have taken any pains. It is of American fir, of a brown colour, and so shining and clean, that one is almost unwilling to walk upon it. The whole appearance of this church bears the stamp of simplicity and cleanliness.

The United Society of Shakers had its origin in England. The first founder was a female of the name of Ann Lee, born at Manchester, in the year 1736. Her father was a poor blacksmith, who could not afford to give his eight children any education.

Ann commenced her career in a cotton-factory: afterwards she engaged with a hatter; then as a cook in an hospital; and finally married, at the age of eighteen, a smith of the name of Stanley, who treated her in the most cruel and barbarous manner. This produced a depression of spirits, and she was observed invariably seeking solitude.

From a hypochondriac she soon became a religious fanatic. She ardently sought and got admission into a Quaker company. Here her fanatical ravings gained additional strength, and she began at length to preach and proclaim her own creed about the year 1770. She pretended to be the second Christ, sent on earth to make revelations; and added that the kingdom of a thousand years was at hand, and that she was immortal. Many believed her, and thought she actually was what she represented herself to be. From that time she was called Mother, and was subsequently worshipped as the Redeemer. One of their hymns establishes this point:

> Glory give unto the Son,
> For he has redemption won;
> Glory unto Mother give,
> For the Saints through her do live.

I heard one of her adherents declare: "Mother Ann Lee was the temple of the Holy Ghost. We know she was Christ in his second revelation on earth, and that Her gospel has saved us from perdition."

In one of their hymns they again say:

> I do believe that God and Christ his Son,
> The Holy Ghost, and Mother joined in one,
> Will soon complete the work which they began,
> And will redeem the fallen race of man.

This is a kind of confession, showing pretty clearly that they make Divinity consist of four persons, and that Ann Lee is one of them.

The cruel treatment she experienced from her husband induced her to relinquish all idea of matrimony, and to propagate the doctrine that it was only the work of Satan. She endeavoured to prove this by asserting that the Redeemer was never married, nor the Apostles; and that neither he nor any of them ever urged a state of marriage. She further advanced, that as Jesus Christ was a second Adam, so she was the second Eve, and that she had come on earth to restore the female part of mankind to that celestial purity and innocence which distinguished our first mother before her fall. This induced her to introduce in the worship of the new sect a ceremony which has been so much and so justly censured, that of dancing without any garments. She supported her command in this respect by a quotation from the Bible, Genesis ii. 25, and was perfectly convinced that man could not be innocent, and free from crime, without following, in every thing, the example of our forefathers before their fall.

The following verses from a hymn, bearing the title, "*Restoration*," show that the sect to this very day believe in the truth of it:

How great is the myst'ry which God has made known!
He's come in the Daughter as well as the Son;
Now Satan's dark works he will fully defeat,
And final redemption will soon be complete.

The first Eve was tempted, and led into sin;
The second, more faithful, has led out again;
With a firm resolution (her word was a sword)
She fought her way through, and creation restored.

A full restoration has now taken place,
For all who believe of the first Adam's race;
The male and the female made free from the curse,
And Adam's probation is brought down to us.

Another of her commands was, that the members should confess their sins, at least once a week, to some of the Elders, who made a report of these confessions to her. By this politic measure, she obtained a despotic rule over the Society, and could imperceptibly do what she pleased with her enthusiastic followers. They were not only commanded to reveal their own sins and thoughts, but to state what they knew of the other brethren and sisters — every thing that passed between them, conversations, &c.

In this manner she acquired a perfect knowledge of every circumstance, and took an opportunity of reproving them, long before they had been confessed, for acts which they endeavoured to conceal. It was therefore natural that ignorant people, witnessing what appeared to be her omniscience, would believe that God revealed to her every thing that was to happen on earth.

Among the many singular ceremonies in their worship, the observance of which she insisted upon, those of dancing, clapping hands, jumping, stamping, shaking, jogging, and crying, were particularly remarkable. "God has commanded it," exclaimed she; and the audience, composed of persons of the lowest order, without any instruction, passed from belief to blind enthusiasm, and from that almost to madness.

The idea that they were the only men who worshipped the Creator as he ought to be, and that he loved them like a father, made them frantic victims of fanaticism. They never ceased to dance and jump (which, according to their ideas, is absolutely necessary to subdue the body and expel all sensual appetites) till, completely fatigued, they fall down, like Turkish Dervishes. The world, in their eyes, has lost all charm, and no joy or consolation remains for them, except in the certainty that the kingdom of a thousand years is near at hand, and that the purity and innocence of Paradise awaits them. They often fancy themselves inspired; and many pretend to give a description of God Almighty, seated on his throne — of the dress of Lucifer, &c.

It was in the company of such followers that Ann Lee embarked, in the year 1774, for America. She told them that a divine revelation enjoined her to proceed thither; but in reality it was to elude the persecutions to which the sect was continually exposed in England.

The following miracle is stated to have occurred during the voyage—let who will believe it! The ship sprung a leak during a heavy storm. The water rushed in so quickly and in so great an abundance, that, although all pumps were going, the vessel soon filled. The captain declared that there was no hope of salvation, and that all the passengers would, in the course of a few hours, inevitably perish. But Ann assured him this should not happen. She added, with a determined accent, "We shall all arrive in safety in America. I saw just now two angels near the main-mast; they showed me the coast of the New World."

She encouraged the sailors, and begged them to persevere: she even assisted in working the pumps. A few minutes afterwards the ship was struck by a heavy sea, and behold! the loosened plank was replaced!

On arriving in America, they first settled in a small town called Waterobet, but removed their head-quarters, in the year 1788, to New Lebanon, their present residence, where I visited them. The Holy Mother had, in the mean while, contrary to the expectation of every one, departed this life in the year 1784, although, in the whole course of her existence, she never ceased to preach about her immortality. If any Shaker is asked how this happened, he will answer: "She meant in a spiritual sense not to die."

Notwithstanding this reply, I continued insinuating my doubts: an elderly member of the sect heard this, and appeared rather displeased: he angrily asked, "If Ann Lee had not been inspired, would she have proclaimed to the world a doctrine, apparently so unnatural, as that of celibacy?"

After her demise, the Pontificate devolved on J. Whitaker, her confidant, who died two years afterwards, in the year 1786. He was succeeded by Joseph Meacham, a man who had sense enough to see that many ceremonies of the sect were useless, and that a reform was absolutely necessary. He, very properly, waved the hope of a celestial innocence on earth, and undertook seriously to alter the rules and rites of the Society. The Elysian dance, and some other ridiculous and even indecent customs, were abolished: his regulations are strictly observed to this very day. He died in 1796, and was succeeded by Lucy Wright, who governed the sect till 1821, when she also expired; and the direction was given to Ebenezar Bishop, who is still alive. This individual is not destitute of talents, but rather illiterate and uncivilized. His exterior is pleasing, and inspires respect among the fraternity.

The creed of this remarkable religious sect, such as professed at this time, was stated to me as follows:

Christ has discovered himself a second time on earth in the person of Ann Lee.

God is only with them, and there is no spiritual salvation without them.

The day of judgment is now. God judges the world through his daughter Ann Lee.

Those who marry do not know Christ, and do not belong to his kingdom.

Without confessing, none can be blessed.

Every one must submit to purgatory after death; and all those who have died after Mother Ann must, in the first instance, listen to a discourse delivered by her in the world of spirits, before they are permitted to leave the purifying fire.

Numerous rules and regulations are prescribed to them, all supposed to have emanated direct from God. None are given in writing, "for"—the Shakers observe—"leave every thing to memory—this great gift of God." I will here mention a few of the most striking:

No man is permitted to live with a female, or to be in the same room with her, without the attendance of a third person.

Brothers and sisters cannot visit each other in their respective rooms after the evening prayer is over, nor whilst they are occupied in making beds.

No brother is allowed to meet a sister on the staircase, or enter her room without first knocking, and *vice versâ.*

No sister can go alone to the store of a brother, nor can brothers or sisters take each other by the hand, or touch each others' clothes, or milk cows at the same time.

No person is allowed to shake another by the hand who does not belong to the Society, or discover any thing relative to it.

It is not permitted to say that he or she lies, or use epithets, or quarrel among each other.

It is not permitted to write or receive letters without the consent of the Elders, or to read any thing without their sanction.

It is not permitted to borrow money from any person, or to have private money transactions.

It is not permitted to be absent from divine service, nor to attend it without having previously been confessed.

It is not permitted to read newspapers or any worldly books on a Sunday; neither must the members cut hair or nails, wash feet, clean boots, or shave, on the Sabbath day.

It is not permitted to attend church in boots, or snap the right thumb over the left, while praying.

It is not permitted to kneel down on the left knee first, or have the pockethandkerchief in the hand, while praying.

It is not permitted to use watches, umbrellas, and spurs, or hats of any other shape than the usual one, or right and left shoes.

It is not permitted to play with dogs and cats, or to kick or ill-use any animal, &c.

Each of their villages is divided into lots, and each lot is occupied by a family. Whenever a person is admitted into the sect, he becomes a member of one of these families, lives in the same house, boards at their table, and is clothed from the same store. The females are the whole day occupied, partly with work necessary for the common good, such as knitting stockings, making clothes, washing, weaving, baking, preparing food, &c. partly in manufacturing articles, which are afterwards disposed of for the benefit of the community. The men again are employed in the cultivation of fields, in cutting wood, attending to gardening, or pursuing different professions.

When I saw these people, working hard from morning to night, some even beyond their strength, and obliged sometimes to follow it up on Sundays, and all this not for their own individual benefit, but merely with a view to increase the common stock, I could not help comparing them to culprits confined in a house of correction, and condemned to hard labour for the sake of improving their morals. All those with whom I conversed seemed, nevertheless, perfect enthusiasts, and attended to their business with apparent satisfaction, bearing, I must add, a strong resemblance to real pleasure.

But, if we admit that many of them, from weariness of the world, from ignorance of a better and happier life, from motives of repentance only for past trespasses, fulfil their severe task with cheerfulness and without repining — if we admit, I say, that many are contented with their situation, what is the cause that so many pale faces, so many sunken eyes, so many parched lips, are invariably seen among them? What is the cause that they become old men and women, before they arrive at the age of manhood? What is the cause that, out of about one hundred women I had an opportunity of seeing, not one was even passable in point of appearance? And yet some were pointed out to me, whose age was not twenty-four, and who ought at least to have exhibited some indications of freshness. What is the cause that girls, known to have been handsome and agreeable at the period of their admission into the Society, after a short time become pale, ugly, and melancholy, resembling spectres more than living beings? I can only pity the unhappy and deluded objects of an erroneous and fanatical doctrine.

But, if travellers are disgusted with the principles of this absurd creed and its ceremonies, none, without departing from justice, can deny them a certain portion of admiration for the order, industry, economy, prudence, and frugality, so peculiar to their sect. Every description of goods manufactured by them is of the very best quality. Their cattle are far superior to those of their neighbours, and can only be compared to that fine breed so often seen in Switzerland. The schools also, particularly those for the girls, have been carefully attended to. Marriages being contrary to their tenets, in order to preserve and uphold the sect, they are obliged to admit orphans, or poor children, handed over by destitute parents. These children are instructed in reading, writing, grammar, arithmetic, and a superficial knowledge of geography and astronomy. By the observance of a severe discipline, to which they are immediately subjected, they acquire a certain degree of seriousness in walk and look, which, according to our worldly notions of things, does not harmonize with the vivacity of a child, whose disposition is generally lively and active. A genius, except in the mechanical art, is seldom found in any youth brought up under their care; and, if any one should happen to show an inclination to study more than another, he generally leaves the sect as soon as he arrives at the age of maturity.

The Shakers have often been suspected of attempts to seduce rich people to become members of their sect, merely with a view to get possession of their property; which is always vested in the general fund on entering the society, and never redeemable if the party should wish to retire. This accusation would, if proved, be an ineffaceable stain on their reputation; but I have no reason to think it is the case: I am on the contrary persuaded that this peaceable people are incapable of such baseness, and, therefore, unless the statement be clearly established, it must be considered a calumny. The common fund is administered by a few select brethren and sisters, who account for every thing in a regular way. Those who quit the sect can lay no claim to any part of this fund; those again who remain have the satisfaction to know that the capital is always accumulating, and that they are sure of being provided for to the end of their existence.

The dress of the men consists of long old-fashioned brown coats, with pockets in the sides, blue or brown small-clothes, shoes or short boots, white cravats, tied close round the neck, with collars turned down, and the hair hanging loose down the back. The females, on working days, are dressed like German peasant women; but on Sundays they are attired in short-waisted white dresses with tight sleeves, white neckhandkerchief, and a thin, white, transparent bonnet; the hair is turned up under the cap, so that none of it is seen; the stockings are white, the shoes have high heels, and a white pocket-handkerchief with a black border hangs on the arm. Their hats are of an oval form, white, yellow, or grey. Those of the men are large and broad-brimmed, like the usual Quaker hats.

Divine service, or what is called "meeting," was just going to begin. The brethren had entered through one door, and the sisters through another, all in a row, in regular military order. Several strangers were beside me outside the church, curious and anxious to be admitted. One of the Elders opened at length the door through which the men had passed: the whole crowd rushed in at the same time with anxious eyes. The places given to us were on the same side with the principal entrances, and opposite was the whole congregation seated, consisting of nearly two hundred and fifty persons of both sexes, separated, but facing each other, and turning their sides to the strangers. On surveying all these white-dressed female spectres, which, mummy-like, remained immoveable and close to each other, it struck me as if I had entered a vaulted tomb. The first impression was indeed solemn: why was this so soon to vanish when service commenced? At a given signal they all rose from their seats, and placed themselves in the form of a sugarloaf, the Elders at their head, and the men and women remaining separated the whole time. They began singing several psalms and hymns, the melody of which was the most uniform I ever heard. Every one exerted himself to the utmost of his lungs, so that I even entertained some apprehension for the tympanum of my ears. To understand a single word of what they said, I found at once impossible; but one of my companions pretended afterwards that he heard them say: "Blessed Mother, Divine Mother Ann!" The music, however, did not appear deafening to the singers. They seemed pleased with it, hardly ever looked up, and accompanied the melody with a continual stamping of their feet. At the end of every psalm, they opened their closed hands, and let them fall by their sides; after which those brethren and sisters who felt inspired delivered a short discourse extempore, which, to my great surprise, was addressed to the strangers present. At the conclusion, the whole being merely phrases without meaning, and repeated with many pauses, singing was resumed. When three psalms had been gone through, the members changed their position by turning their backs to the spectators. They were then placed in rows, the men on one side, the women on the other, with their faces towards the Elders, who stood along the opposite wall near the strangers. All the men had, in the meanwhile, taken off their coats, and stood in their shirt sleeves; the women laid aside their pocket-handkerchiefs, to be ready for the ceremony. In the midst of a shrill and singular cry, they now began to dance, advancing three paces and retreating one, and continued in this way for a long while, now and then turning round on their heels. Many appeared to labour so hard that perspiration ran down their cheeks in great profusion; they pretend in this way to subdue carnal appetites, and to express their joy at the victory gained over the power of lust. The noise attending this ceremony they defend by quotations from the Bible, of which I happen to recollect one: Isaiah xii, vi. "Cry out and shout, thou inhabitant of Zion: for great is the Holy One of Israel in the midst of thee."

As soon as this unpleasant music was over, they commenced jogging round the room: the men first, three abreast, and the women afterwards, in the same manner. This jogging is neither walking nor running; they take their steps in regular time, and move about with crooked knees. During this operation, they stretch out and wave their hands incessantly, not unlike the motion of a dog splashing with his fore-feet when thrown into water. A few members of both sexes stopped in the centre of the room, singing some very discordant hymns, the others jogged round them, accompanying the song. At the end of each hymn, a few admonishing words to the strangers were generally uttered by one of the party, as he happened to be inspired, after which the dancing continued for some time, with the only exception that they formed at last *two* rings, one inside the other, and each going round in an opposite direction to the other.

I was anxious to know what might be meant by this circular dance, and inquired of one of them on the following day. "This circle," answered he, "means sin on earth, and our evolutions round it show our abhorrence, as well as the powerful effect of the Holy Ghost on us." A foreigner, who, like myself, visited this place for the second time, to acquire a more perfect knowledge of the principles of the sect, happened to hear this reply, and observed, in a nearly audible tone, "I pity them. They give themselves a great deal of unnecessary trouble, and submit to an infinity of privations for the sake of a few absurd and ridiculous maxims." The holy brother heard this remark. "We know very well," retorted he, whilst lowering his sharp brown eyes, "that conformity to these principles requires a large portion of self-denial. But, in truth, if we believe in the assertion of our Redeemer, this does not amount to a positive proof that they are not the true principles of the Christian faith. Approved or disapproved by the world, pleasing or disagreeable to the weak part of mankind, none can reasonably complain, or oppose them, when every one is at liberty to follow them or not." Neither of us made any remark to this observation; the individual retired apparently satisfied, conceiving doubtless that he had triumphed, by irresistible arguments, over two worldly, and in his eyes lost, sinners.

But I must return to the service. Dancing was now over, and the brothers and sisters resumed their former places. One of the Elders advanced between the rows, and delivered a kind of sermon, exclusively directed, as before, to the strangers, in which he endeavoured to explain and justify the singular ceremony observed upon the occasion. The sermon was extremely dry, and without any pretence to sense. Every one of the auditors complained of its length, and seemed excessively delighted when the orator resumed his place. Psalms and hymns concluded the whole; and one of the members, in a loud voice, informed the congregation that the service was over. The men very silently put on their hats and coats, the women their bonnets, and all departed through different doors, as they had arrived, in perfect military order.

Before I take leave of the Shakers — these peaceable, industrious, and unhappy religious victims — I will relate an anecdote, which I heard from a person in the neighbourhood of New Lebanon, relative to them:

" A few years ago," said he, " the Shakers signified an intention of celebrating the debarkation of Mother Ann Lee on the American shore. It was determined that the ceremony should be observed by a profuse and general tobacco-smoking fête. A "bull," or edict, was issued, directed to the scattered members of the Society in every part of America, enjoining them to assemble on a certain day in the month of August, for this important purpose.

"I did not neglect to attend upon this solemn occasion. When I entered the church, I found that the order and regularity, which had hitherto distinguished the sisters, were entirely gone. Their natural and unpretending manners — their attention to discipline — all had vanished; in its place, I discovered an unusual degree of negligence in their walk, a wildness in their looks, a strange confusion altogether, which unquestionably surprised me at first, but which I endeavoured to explain by the extraordinary sublimity of the ceremony.

"All sat down in deep silence. Ebenezar Bishop occupied the principal seat, and uttered a few half-broken sentences in allusion to the divine solemnity now to be performed, which, according to his notions, was ordained by God. He then turned to one of the younger sisters, and ordered her to procure fire, which she did. He lighted his pipe, drew a long puff, and afterwards slowly blew out what he called the first victim of the day. In a dignified manner he withdrew the pipe from his mouth, raised his eyes towards heaven, and said, 'Brethren and sisters, unite.'

"All now lighted their respective pipes, and, like novices in the art of smoking, lost no time in blowing out the smoke, which in the course of ten minutes so completely obscured the room that no object could be distinguished. The Elders looked upon these clouds of smoke, which surrounded their heads, with religious awe.

"The ceremony was ordered to last one hour. A quarter of that time had hardly elapsed, before a number of smoking individuals found the atmosphere altogether intolerable. Several, particularly the young women, who had hitherto looked to the Elders for protection, now directed their looks towards the door, with faces as pale as death. Every one was more or less unwell; and never did I witness so strong a desire to depart. But only when the clock announced the termination of the hour was the meeting dissolved ; and, believe me, no one was behindhand in effecting a retreat for the purpose of breathing fresh air."

Would any one think such fanatical scenes possible in the nineteenth century — in enlightened times like ours? The religious toleration generally observed in the United States prevents government from putting an end to a sect whose creed is as unreasonable as its ceremonies are ridiculous ; and, as long as the Shakers continue peaceable, and abstain from violation of the laws, no American President can compel them to discontinue dancing, or reject their belief in Mother Ann's equal divinity with that of the Redeemer.

This liberty of conscience, every where prevalent in North America, and on which I will touch more hereafter, gives rise naturally to a number of sects, many of which are as extraordinary as the one just mentioned. In the year 1832, for instance, a man in New York assumed the garb of a Jew, and preached that he was nothing less than the Messiah himself. A great many persons flocked to the room where he delivered his discourses, curious to see and hear this modern prophet ; and all returned perfectly disgusted with the individual and his doctrines. As long as his sermons had a peaceable tendency, he was left undisturbed; but at length his follies and absurdities went beyond the limits of endurance, and he was not permitted to continue his ravings. The end of his prophetical career was — a residence in a madhouse.

CHAPTER VI.

Glens which might have made even exile dear.
BYRON.

FROM Lebanon I directed my course through the heart of the flourishing state of Massachusetts. My first day's journey terminated at Northampton, a distance of about fifty miles, which it took nearly twelve hours to complete. The roads were certainly very rough; in some places so bad, that travellers ran a risk of coming in collision with each other's heads, and breaking their limbs; but, upon the whole, they may be called tolerable, particularly when compared to the roads in the Southern and Western States.

Our slow progress was not to be attributed either to the badness of the roads, or to the horses, which had an appearance of strength, but entirely to the drivers. They were changed several times in the course of the day; but, to the regret of all present, little was gained by the alteration. One, in particular, was excessively slow in his motions, and rather abusive. I do not know if I was the unfortunate cause of it; my companions pretended I was, for having inadvertently—and certainly without intending, or even supposing, it would give offence—addressed him by the disreputable title of "Coachman," always used in England, and which I thought was also applicable here. Enough; I discontinued the word from that hour as long as I remained in America; and never forgot, upon subsequent occasions, to call republican coachmen "drivers."

The part of the country I now traversed was very rich and fertile. Wheat, rye, and Indian corn, were growing abundantly in every direction. Fields, intermixed with sand, were seen here and there; and in these places the crop appeared rather indifferent. Large tracts of land, particularly in the neighbourhood of Northampton, lay waste and uncultivated, although some are considered good. This I can only explain by supposing that the farmers are either satisfied with what they already possess, or that they cannot extend their agricultural pursuits for want of sufficient hands. They are, however, all in easy circumstances.

The eastern part of Massachusetts cannot boast of so many substantial farmers as the western; the soil is not near so rich; and many of the natives are, therefore, obliged to abandon farming, and take to manufacturing.

The country presents, upon the whole, a very variegated aspect. Hills and mountains succeed dales, woods, and fields. The former delight the traveller with the finest prospects. From the top of a mountain not far from Lebanon, the beautiful foliage of the trees, grouped together in the midst of luxuriant fields, formed a rich picture.

The country houses are generally two stories high; the walls are built differently from those in Sweden; the planks are laid on the top of each other along the ground, and not raised vertically, as with us. They are mostly painted white, with green blinds fixed outside, giving them an appearance of cleanliness and neatness seldom witnessed in Europe. The interior arrangements, if not costly, are invariably tasteful. I often saw houses of farmers so comfortably fitted up, that they might be taken for the residence of a Governor of the State. Gardens, filled with every description of vegetables and fruit-trees, particularly apple-trees, are every where seen; and, with a view to make these habitations still more agreeable and cool, trees are planted all around, the leafy branches of which afford ample shade to the inmates. The rearing of cattle is also particularly attended to. Cows and oxen are of the very best breed; their immense size and strength often recalled to my mind those seen in enchanting Switzerland.

A European, travelling in this direction, cannot help admiring the general appearance of comfort and prosperity so singularly striking. To an inhabitant of the Scandinavian Peninsula, accustomed to different scenes, it is peculiarly gratifying to witness, instead of gorgeous palaces by the side of poor huts, a row of neat country houses, inhabited by independent farmers.

A Swedish servant, lately arrived in America, on looking round and perceiving the happy state so generally diffused, exclaimed, with surprise and characteristic simplicity, "Sir, have the goodness to inform me where the peasantry live in this country."

Northampton is a small town, so clean, neat, and agreeably situated, that it richly deserves the name of "Massachusetts' favourite doll." It may be called a village, rather than a town. The streets are few; and the whole is not unlike a group of country seats, surrounded with gardens, and built in a row close to each other, for the inspection and admiration of spectators.

The houses, chiefly of wood, are painted white, with green blinds. Trees are planted in all the streets, or rather roads, for they are not paved; and shrubberies, with a thousand different flowers, greet the passengers with their beautiful fragrance.

Northampton carries on a considerable trade with the neighbouring country. Connecticut River, distant about a mile and a half, and Farmington and Hampshire Canal, which commences here, and directs its course to New Haven, a distance of seventy-eight miles, contribute in no small degree to its flourishing state. But it is not its commerce, industry, or manufactures, which attract numbers of strangers to this spot every year. It is to view the handsome plan in which the village is laid out that thousands visit it. Few things have given me greater pleasure than the sight of this spot in Massachusetts and the villages Canandaigua and Geneva in the State of New York, which are equally attractive. It was something so cheering and new to find myself in the heart of a village, without being obliged to attach to it the idea of dirt and uncleanliness — to see, in its stead, neat churches, a bank, printing-offices, &c., with a population of nearly three thousand seven hundred souls, that I remained several days longer than I originally intended.

It may be remarked that villages, properly so called, are hardly found in the United States: spots that spring up from nothing do not become in the first instance villages or hamlets. They take a leap from insignificance to the rank of towns; the rise is so rapid that in a very short time they are able to maintain a bank and a printing-office — two establishments which Europeans only think of in regular towns. The timber is hardly cut for the purpose of laying the foundation for houses before it is publicly announced that a newspaper is published in such and such a town, that a bank is in full operation, that canals are cut, railroads planned, and steamboats being built, to facilitate the communication with the new city, sprung up, as it were, by magic. I will resume this subject in a future chapter.

Not far from Northampton is a mountain called Mount Holyoke, the summit of which is, or ought to be, visited by every traveller passing through this part of the country who wishes to enjoy a remarkably fine prospect. I proceeded thither on horseback, and arrived at the foot of the mountain, after having crossed the stream in a ferry-boat propelled by horses. The road towards the top was at first both steep and stony; but my horse, accustomed no doubt to the rough and irregular track, did not stumble. At length, however, the poor animal became so completely exhausted, that he could not advance another step: traces of a road disappeared, and in its stead a few steps made of loose stones proved to me the necessity of leaving the horse behind till I returned. I continued climbing up the hill. Whoever has weak nerves, a delicate constitution, or is subject to giddiness, I would particularly recommend to abstain from visiting the summit of Mount Holyoke. Not only is a person obliged at certain places to take giant-steps from tree to branch, and from branch to tree, but to tread on stones without any solid foundation whatever! These, very unceremoniously, slip away under the weight; and, if particular attention be not paid, the visiter is apt to take a leap down the precipice in company with the fragments of the rock.

I reached, however, the top, a distance of nine hundred and ninety feet, in company with several friends, without any accident, and our pains were then richly repaid. It was not a Swiss panorama, the icebergs being wanted, but a prospect which, once beheld, cannot easily be effaced from memory. The whole landscape beneath resembled a circle-bound picture, viewed from the centre. On one side appeared Connecticut river, serpentining in various directions, sometimes disappearing, then showing itself again, forming, to the south-west, a peninsula, three and a quarter miles in circumference, and only about two hundred and twenty fathoms across the isthmus; at last, towards the south, at the foot of Mount Tom, it is entirely lost to the sight: here, the smoke arising from the cataracts at South Hadley is perceivable. But, both from far and near, valleys, hills, mountains, fields, meadows, and forests, were seen, all dressed in the mantle of the richest vegetation. Corn-fields, covered with abundant and ripe crops, remunerated the labours of the husbandmen, and farmers were seen occupied in cutting golden harvests: others again, sown with oats and Indian corn, had not yet changed the garb of spring for that of autumn. Flocks of cattle crowded the valleys: they were feeding on the most luxuriant herbs, whilst teams of oxen carried from the fields loads of new-cut hay. In the midst of this picture of industry, and among a variety of colours, private dwellings of farmers were visible, equally pleasing to the eye by their whiteness and lofty green blinds; and also small towns (Northampton, Hadley, Amherst, &c.,) surrounded by rows of full grown trees; and last of all, as if strewed over the ground, a number of handsome churches, of which I counted at least thirty.

The day was far advanced when I quitted this eminence, and the descent required as much precaution as the ascent. We rejoined with pleasure our horses at the place we left them, and returned to Northampton extremely fatigued, but delighted with our excursion.

On the following morning I started for Springfield, a small town on the banks of the same river, where a musket factory, upon a large scale, is carried on upon account of government. The road leading to it passes through a wild country, following the direction of the river. In South Hadley, there are two waterfalls, one thirty-two, the other fifty-two feet high, both, as is customary in America, made available for working mills. Another little town called Hadley, also situated on the road, fixed my attention, as being one of the oldest in the State. It was here the two regicides and Judges Whalley and Goffe, during the reign of Charles II., sought an asylum to evade persecution. During their short residence at Hadley, it happened that the Indians, then in open warfare with the Colonists, attacked the town. Soldiers were not wanted to defend it, but there were no leaders. In this emergency, a stranger presented himself, whose appearance inspired respect, and whose counsels and example instilled courage to the desponding inhabitants. Personal bravery, added to a great fund of military acquirements, insured a complete victory; and, after a short struggle, the Indians owed their safety only to flight. Their warwhoop had hardly ceased, and the fugitives had only just quitted the neighbouring woods, before the stranger disappeared. This gave rise, in these superstitious times, to a general belief that the individual must have been the protecting patron of the town, or rather its guardian angel. But who was this stranger? The fugitive, persecuted, unfortunate Goffe, who, at the risk of being himself taken, quitted his place of concealment to rescue a town from danger, in which he did not dare to show himself publicly, and where his head would unquestionably have fallen under the axe of the executioner had his person been recognized.

The gun-factory at Springfield deserves to be visited by every traveller. More than ten thousand muskets are manufactured here every year: I was even assured, that fifteen thousand have been turned out in that time. To judge by the quantity, it may be inferred that all the inhabitants are occupied in this branch; but this is not the case: the simplest and most ingenious machinery is used as a substitute for manual labour. This manufactory has, in consequence, acquired a high degree of perfection, both in point of economy and solidity. If the great wages paid to the working people, and to able locksmiths, for instance, from one and a quarter to two dollars a day is taken into consideration, it cannot be wondered at if a ready-made musket costs about ten dollars. This prime cost, looked upon as cheap in America, would be considerably higher if manual labour was exclusively employed to carry on the works. The stock-making, which in the North of Europe is done by several persons, and forms the most expensive part of this species of manufacture, is here prepared by a single machine. The annual expences of this establishment are upon an average one hundred and ninety thousand dollars.

The work is done in different houses: there are only a few factory buildings in which the people work together in large rooms or halls, occupying nearly the whole range of the building; the other houses are converted into small workshops, scattered over the whole town, in which particular branches of the trade are carried on. Every thing is worked by water, of which there is great abundance.

The muskets, when finished, have a very fine appearance, though rather heavy, attributable in a great measure, I should suppose, to the size and clumsiness of the locks. The barrels and bayonets, formerly made of Swedish iron only, but now of American also, are painted brown for the purpose of preserving them from rust. The stock is of walnut, a very strong and hard species of wood. The mode of trying the strength of the spring under the touchhole is by means of a balance, extremely simple in its construction, but which very effectually puts the spring to the test, in making it support a weight of one hundred and twenty pounds. All the component parts of the musket are, besides, so made, that they fit any musket manufactured there, and may be taken from one to another.

The factory is under the direction of a superintendent appointed by government, whose business is to receive from the workmen different parts of the musket, examine them, and pay the people according to a fixed rate for their work: he afterwards deposits the ready-made muskets in an arsenal close by, lately erected in lieu of the old one consumed by fire.

The workmen are under no control of the manager, further than merely delivering their work and receiving pay. Their number is about two hundred and eighty: they have, for the most part, their own houses and a piece of ground adjoining. Poverty is seldom discovered among them, nor are they addicted to indolence, drunkenness, or any other vice. Those not possessed of sufficient property to have their own houses, live at a cheap rate with their companions, till, by dint of industry and economy, they are able to become proprietors themselves. What particularly contributes to this happy state of things among the workmen may be traced to the following causes: First, Temperance Societies, and, second, Saving Banks, two establishments which both here and in other manufacturing towns in America have really done wonders among the labouring classes, and not a little contributed to their improvement. Not only have they increased the stock of the labouring man, but they have effected another good, superior to all the rest—a moral and intellectual amelioration. The time generally spent in conviviality and inebriety, and in conversations destitute of all interest and utility, is now employed in reading instructive books, from which they derive many useful acquirements, confirming them in the belief that nothing but a regular life can make them happy and prosperous, and which they are equally anxious to inculcate into the minds of their children. This establishes, in a satisfactory manner, the otherwise questionable fact, that I found, among these smiths and stockmakers, individuals who were "Gentlemen," in the true acceptation of the word, with whom I could converse on subjects which would have appeared something like hieroglyphics to other factory men; they were not only acquainted with every improvement lately introduced in their particular trade, the correctness of which they were able to canvass, but had also invented several things themselves, and could prove their utility. They were, moreover, civil, hospitable, and had good manners. Some laid by their work when I entered the workshops, and insisted on going round and showing me every thing that might be interesting: I met no one who did not immediately discontinue his occupation, in order to give the stranger an opportunity of examining every thing, and this, too, as long as he pleased. To offer the slightest remuneration is considered an insult, and to receive it would be equally degrading.

One of these hospitable men went even as far as to insist on my going home to his house, although in the busiest part of the day, with a view, as he expressed himself, "to see how neatly and comfortably he lived." I accompanied him, accordingly, to a small but clean one-story frame house, the outside painted white, and the inside as neat as a *boudoir*. Two rooms and a kitchen formed the whole establishment; and, although small, was extremely pleasant. Every thing bore the stamp of being regulated by a steady and industrious mistress; and in this I was by no means deceived, for she was indeed an unexceptionable wife. The husband extolled her merits in a manner which reflected the greatest honour on him: she entered the room shortly afterwards, leading a boy and a girl by the hand, simply but neatly dressed, and bowing to the stranger; the whole ceremony was performed in a manner seldom witnessed in Europe by a woman in her situation in life. If domestic felicity exists on earth, it certainly might be traced to this unostentatious dwelling; both wife and husband cast a glance at each other and at their children, truly indicative of happiness.

My landlord, justly proud of his comfortable home, and anxious to show me every thing, from the garret to the cellar, now requested me to accompany him to the garden adjoining the house, also his property, and tastefully laid out by his own hands.

"This small enclosure," said he, "has been made by myself, the same year I married. All the flowers, vegetables, shrubberies, and fruit-trees, that you see have been planted and nursed by this hand."

The garden bore evident marks of having been greatly taken care of the trees almost sunk under the weight of various fruits. I also discovered vines, of which more than ten were crowded with grapes. On returning to the house, I was not a little surprised — I may add, agreeably surprised — to find that the mistress had, during our temporary absence, prepared a cold collation, of which no landlady need have been ashamed. The table-cloth partook of the whiteness of snow; and, although the knives and forks could not lay claim to extraordinary beauty, yet the whole arrangement was so inviting, that it was truly delightful to sit down to the frugal and hospitable board.

My landlord knew I came from Europe, though not from what part; but, on being apprized of the country that gave me birth, he exclaimed with joy, whilst emptying a glass of cider, "From Sweden! From the land of the honest and the brave! I should amazingly like to get better acquainted with that country. The inhabitants of the Scandinavian Peninsula, they say, are a hardy race. In this opinion I fully coincide; for a country producing such excellent iron as Sweden must also necessarily be the abode of good people. Tell me what is the name of your actual President?" I acquainted him with our form of government.

"Well," rejoined he, "every nation has its own opinions in similar matters; what suits one country and one people does not suit another. For my part, I am not fitted to live under the rule of royalty; let us therefore drop the subject, and drink to the health of our absent friends." This was done. Who could possibly have thought that this individual was a mere locksmith, brought up to the trade from infancy, and who had never emigrated further than a few miles from Springfield?

On my return to Northampton, I lost no time in continuing my journey to Boston. The distance is about ninety-one miles, which is performed in seventeen hours.

The road is sandy, hilly, and uniform, leading through a country destitute of interest, which made the journey doubly toilsome and fatiguing. The drivers, besides, were in the habit of watering their horses every quarter of a mile; and this circumstance, added to the frequency of changing coaches, and the accompanying inconvenience of removing luggage, at least five times during our progress, completely exhausted my patience. The country appeared poor and indifferent. In the midst of a real desert, fit only for the growth of pines, my eyes were all of a sudden gratified with the sight of a flourishing manufacturing place called Ware; so named from the river that runs through it. Few villages have had so rapid a rise as this. The children employed in the manufactories remember still the time when not a house was found on the spot where the great cotton-factories are now erected. They are the joint property of particular companies, who bought lots of land around the place on speculation, for the purpose of establishing these factories. That they have proved successful beyond expectation is easily seen by their present prosperous condition.

A little further on, I passed through another small place, having also the appearance of being constantly whitewashed, called Worcester, larger in size than any of those I had hitherto visited in the New England States, and built, perhaps, upon a more elegant scale. The houses all look new, adorned with colonnades of the Doric and Corinthian order, and surrounded by gardens and trees, which give them alike the appearance of rural and town residences. A railroad was then being constructed from this town to Boston, a distance of forty-three miles, which is to be completed in the course of a few years, and from which the greatest results are anticipated. "Blackstone Canal," as it is called, goes from this place to New Providence, in Rhode Island, opening a communication from the interior of the country with the East River and New York.

The country between Worcester and Boston appears more fertile: the nearer one approaches the latter city, the more gratified is the eye with the sight of cultivated tracts of land, and delightful country seats. The houses follow each other in more rapid succession; and one village hardly disappears before the next is visible. More cottages, in the English style, are seen on this road, and in the vicinity of Boston, than I have discovered in my subsequent journey through nearly all the States of the Union. They are generally of wood, painted white, with open porticoes on every side of the house, thus giving a delightful shade and coolness to the rooms. These cottages were mostly built on an elevated grass mound, about four feet high on one side, above a close-cut field, not unlike the smooth surface of a green billiard-table; and on the other side inclosed by gardens and parks.

The churches are also of wood, and painted white. The windows, as well as those of the dwelling houses, have all green blinds, tastefully ornamented, which gives to these country churches the neatest and most becoming appearance I have ever seen. They invariably occupied the most prominent situation in the villages. Such was the aspect of the rural spots, which by degrees prepared me for the sight of Boston. When yet ten miles distant, every object announced the approach to a large city. The road became wider, hard, and well kept; the country assumed a cultivated and snug appearance; country residences were more frequent; gigs and landaus passed each other. In the midst of all this appeared a city, crowned with an elevated cupola. A long bridge led me into it; and I was now in the midst of Boston.

CHAPTER VII.

Cet air si froid, qui congéle le souffle de la respiration, fait rentrer la chaleur dans l'âme; et la nature dans ces climats ne parait faite que pour repousser l'homme en lui-même.

DE STAEL HOLSTEIN.

Boston is the capital of Massachusetts, and is one of the oldest cities in the Union. Its advantageous situation for commerce, added to the circumstance of its possessing within its precincts a community wholly devoted to the occupation of trade and navigation, places Boston in the rank of the second town in the United States with regard to shipping. The city is situated on a peninsula which joins the main land by means of an isthmus, extending to a small delightful village called Roxburg. The original name of Boston was Trimountain, derived from its situation on three eminences: the present one, if I mistake not, was given after a town of that name in Lincolnshire, England, being the birth-place of the first preacher in Boston, in commemoration of whom the city was called.

The harbour is very spacious and safe: five hundred ships, it is said, may safely and without difficulty ride at anchor, the bay being very extensive. The inlet, however, is rather narrow, admitting barely two ships abreast: whilst about eighty small islands, partly inhabited, partly uninhabited, but more or less covered with verdure, are interspersed in every direction. Two forts for the defence of the port have been erected on those nearest the sea.

The exterior of Boston is striking. On approaching it, either from the sea-side or by some of the numerous bridges which connect it, the stranger receives an impression which is fully realized by a nearer acquaintance with the different objects. The State-house, situate on the most elevated point in the city, forms, as it were, the extremity of a pyramid rising out of the sea. Whichever way one goes, the high cupola is always visible. The number of other public buildings is also considerable, and some are distinguished by good taste. Private dwellings are built partly of granite, partly of brick, but mostly of the latter, and then seldom painted: a few, however, are white. Their exterior appearance has nothing striking in point of architecture, but the interior arrangements are extremely commodious. The rooms are not so spacious as those in Europe, but they appeared to me very comfortable. Simplicity was every where apparent.

The streets are narrow: not one can be compared to Broadway in New York. In the old part of the town particularly, there are some so confined and crooked, that it is nearly impossible to distinguish an object fifty yards ahead. The new part, however, is very different, but still I cannot say that there is any street particularly fine.

I lost no time in visiting the Statehouse, the boast of the city. It is a brick building, with a double row of pillars forming the front. From the cupola, which rises above all other buildings, the view is justly admired by every stranger. The beautiful and comfortable city presents itself in all its charm. The cleanliness of the streets—the numerous churches, with their high steeples—the extensive walks—the long bridges—the wharfs, covered with goods, and built in the form of basins, in which the vessels conveniently load and unload—the amphitheatre-like harbour, filled with boats, sloops, ships, and steamers — further, Charlestown with part of the navy — Bunker's Hill with the half finished monument — the heights of Dorchester, memorable in the annals of the revolution as being occupied by Washington the night preceding the 4th of March, 1776 — Cambridge, with its University — the new Cemetery of Mount Auburn — numerous country-seats in every direction — Brighton, Roxburg, and other neat villages in the vicinity — and, finally, the great Atlantic Ocean, rolling its bottomless waves to the shores of Europe — all these different views form a panorama hardly to be excelled in beauty.

It is in the Statehouse that the Legislature of Massachusetts generally hold their sittings. The Senate, consisting of forty members, besides the President, has its own separate hall, in which their annual assemblies are kept. This is also the case with the Second Chamber, whose members in 1832 amounted to four hundred and seventy-nine; it has likewise a separate hall in the same building. Neither Chamber was sitting during my residence in Boston.

On the ground floor, opposite the principal entrance, in a niche made for that purpose, may be seen Chantrey's celebrated statue of Washington. The great English sculptor has upon this occasion displayed an unusual degree of ability and genius. The very first glance is striking; it develops something so lofty and noble, that even the most indifferent spectator is seized with awe and admiration. Washington is represented in a standing attitude, covered with a mantle, carelessly yet tastefully thrown around him, which he raises with one hand, resting it on his bosom. The head is bare, and the features perfectly resemble those of the original. His powdered hair, his high forehead, his expressive eyes — to these and to every lineament has the chisel of the artist given life. I was informed that for this *chef d'œuvre* of the last of the Romans, America's great Saint, the sculptor received the sum of ten thousand dollars.

Opposite this edifice is a public walk, which by the caprice of fashion has become the most private of all. Seldom or ever is any lady to be seen here, the whimsical goddess of fashion having in her wisdom shown symptoms of indifference to this promenade; and the consequence is, that this place, formerly frequented by the Bostonians in great numbers, is now nearly deserted; for who would venture to disobey the decrees of such an omnipotent Deity? This revolution in taste has been a source of great regret to many individuals, as the walk had always been patronised by the respectable part of the community, but particularly by the fair sex.

I remember having one day had a conversation with a young lady of Boston on this head, when I took the liberty of making some free allusions to the deserted walk. Her reply was of an entirely opposite character: she made the most poetical panegyric with regard to the pastoral beauty of the place, the venerable age of the trees, the free and delightful prospect. In all these observations I joined heartily, but proposed nevertheless an alteration, namely, that the straight rows of trees, with the open green space in the middle, should be converted into an English park, with winding walks, and planted with shrubberies. The lady here suddenly interrupted the thread of my conversation, by drily observing: "We are perfectly satisfied with what we have got; we don't want any alteration!" In this place is a little pond, in which children amuse themselves in navigating men-of-war half a yard long, and firing broadsides on the shoals of singing frogs who have here taken up their residence. I ventured to christen this pond, which now goes by the name of the Frog Pond.

This park or walk is on three sides surrounded by houses, unquestionably the best in the city. The season was still very warm, (in August) and all the windows were open; in almost every mansion, it was customary to have music in the evening. These melodious sounds attracted a number of passers-by, and many a delightful evening have I spent in this way. Proceeding from house to house, I listened with rapture to very fine music and many excellent voices. More than once was I caught whilst indulging in this amusement, leaning over the iron railing fronting the windows: more than one glance did I receive from venerable parents seated behind the blinds; but nothing, so long as the singing or playing continued, could divert my attention. I mention this circumstance merely in case this book should by chance happen to find its way to any family in hospitable Boston, that I may be allowed to take this opportunity of testifying my gratitude to the unknown fair singers for the fine entertainment they afforded me.

Among the public buildings generally shown to strangers are the following: Faneuil Hall, the Market, the Post Office, the different Banks, the Athenæum, and the Freemasons' Lodge. In the first-mentioned, where all public meetings are held, there is a hall in which the first deliberations took place during the revolutionary war, and which had subsequently so great an influence on the result of the struggle for independence. This hall is rather large, and fitted up with seats along the two sides. Above the two entrances are written in large characters the immortal names of Washington, Kosciusko, Lafayette. On the opposite wall several portraits are hung, among which those of Washington, Lafayette, and Hancock (the first President), are conspicuous; and around these were placed the names of the warriors who had distinguished themselves by sea or by land during the contest for liberty. These names were entwined in wreaths of laurel, to show that they were imperishable in the memory of grateful countrymen.

The market is the largest of its kind in the United States: it is built of granite, five hundred and thirty-six feet in length, and is two stories high. Pillars, also of granite, are at each end; and on both sides, the length of the building, neat shops are fitted up. I was curious to visit this place one morning, during the market hour. The approach was almost impossible from the concourse of people; but, by degrees, as the bargains were concluded, I obtained admittance. Each kind of trade had a separate stand; butchers were not mixed with fishmongers, nor these with fruitmen. Every thing bore the stamp of convenience and cleanliness. The butchers' stalls did not inspire that distaste too often produced on visiting similar places in Europe, nor was there any offensive smell perceptible where fish was vended; and with regard to the fruit shops, though not supplied with great variety, they were well kept.

I had often heard that married men in America are in the habit of attending market themselves in the morning, to provide the necessary articles for their families; a custom which with us on the other side of the Atlantic exclusively belongs to the department of the cook. Mrs. Trollope mentioned the same in her history of "Domestic Manners of the Americans;" but, on that very account, I considered the statement an exaggeration, and rather inclined to the contrary opinion.

But a few minutes' stay in the market soon undeceived me. Several of the married gentlemen, whose acquaintance I had made on the preceding day, I met here, occupied in purchasing and sending home meat, fish, vegetables, and fruit; in short, all the wants for the day. Although I cannot easily be persuaded that this occupation necessarily belongs to a man, yet it may be tolerated perhaps in a country where the manner of living is unostentatious, and where one solid joint, upon ordinary occasions, forms alone the whole repast. It may moreover be a pleasing sight to visit a place where the tasteful and cleanly exhibition of different articles almost invites the visiter to become a purchaser. But to adopt this method in towns where established custom requires a variety of dishes, differently dressed, and of various kinds, would be rather a troublesome task; to acquit himself satisfactorily, a man must indeed be a confirmed *gourmand*.

During my stay in Boston I had frequent opportunities of witnessing the prevalence of this custom, and found that almost all the married men perform this morning walk. At first it appeared strange to me how they could so correctly know the exact market prices of the most trifling article; but it was soon explained. At a dinner, at which I happened to be present, the lady of the house showed perfect ignorance of the cost of vegetables and fruit, and was obliged to apply to the husband for information, which she did in these words: "My dear, what is the price of sweet potatoes? Grapes and peaches, what are they worth?" But each country has its customs; I shall therefore abstain from all comment, merely mentioning the circumstance.

The Freemasons' Lodge is a poor imitation of Gothic architecture: there is always something sublime and lofty attached to this mode of building. I have never yet contemplated a Gothic structure, without thinking that I ought to kneel down and worship the Deity, who speaks so clearly and distinctly to our sensitive hearts in the splendour of the whole fabric, and in the beauty of the minutest part of it. Far from exciting this sensation, the Freemasons' Lodge appeared to me as if built upon a small scale, and sketched by a master of ordinary talents. I do not pretend to say that the dimensions were incorrect, but certainly tasteless. The ornamental part seemed out of place; and where there were no ornaments, the nakedness was obvious. The architecture of most public and private buildings in America is, unfortunately, copied partly from England, partly from Italy, and even from Greece; but is seldom preserved in its original taste. The temple of Theseus at Athens, St. Peter's at Rome, and a house in Regent Street, London, are all mixed together; and out of this variety a whole is produced, which is denominated American architecture. "The genius of architecture," says Jefferson, this acute and experienced judge of the fine arts, "seems to have shed her maledictions over this land."

During the whole of my journey through the United States, I never saw a house that could be compared to any of the palaces in the Old World; nor did I, in fact, expect it; but the recollection of Athens and Rome had, since my youth, so strongly impressed upon my mind the idea that no Republics could exist without a forum, decorated with statues, temples, triumphal arches, and palaces, that it was not without difficulty I changed my opinion, and began to conceive that liberty, glory, and patriotism, may even thrive in common dwellings, without statues, without temples, without triumphal arches, without palaces. But America is still a young Republic; the time may yet come when forums and arches will be raised.

"A Republican Government can in no manner more appropriately exhibit its magnificence than by the grandeur or beauty of its public structures. A noble hall, for the purposes of legislation or justice, or a grand pile of buildings for the uses of learning, is the immediate property of the people, and forms a portion of the inheritance of the humblest citizen. An enlightened patriotism should, indeed, rest upon much more solid ground; but no man, who knows and feels that, even in our best and wisest moments, we can never become wholly creatures of reason, will object to the aid of local pride and natural association, to strengthen and animate his love of country. The ancient legislators understood the force of such principles well. In the mind of an ancient Greek, the history of his country, her solemn festivals, her national rites, her legislation, her justice, were indissolubly combined with the images of every thing that was beautiful or sublime in art." Thus speaks one of America's greatest statesmen and orators, when alluding to the architecture of his own country. I mention this as a proof that my opinion in regard to American architecture is corroborated by one of her own sons,* and that this art, which approaches nearest Nature's greatness and sublimity, now forms a subject of deep contemplation with thinking men in America. May then the curse, which Mr. Jefferson asserts has been heaped over the country by an angry genius, soon be converted into tenderness, and this art not fail to overtake her sisters, who have already considerably distanced her!

The Freemasons erected this building at their own expence; but, suspicions having shortly afterwards gained ground that they had clandestinely made away with an individual who suddenly disappeared, this event produced so great an effect on the State government, that a law was promulgated, enacting that no more lodges would be tolerated in Massachusetts. Under these circumstances, they were obliged to let the hall for public meetings, &c; and it was at one of these I was for the first time introduced into this building. One of the Temperance Societies, so numerous in America, had there

---

* G. C. Verplanck, member of Congress for the State of New York in 1833. Vide his masterly speech, delivered in May, 1824, on "The Fine Arts in America."

a public meeting. I lost no time in attending it, curious to know what progress these associations had made in the country in which they had at first originated.

The baneful and dangerous influence which intemperance has every where exerted on the moral and physical condition of man is a subject seriously occupying the attention of every Christian and philanthropist. Instances of suicides, committed under the effect of inebriety, are of common occurrence in America as well as in England. The ocean checks not this killing propensity. Once addicted to the demoralizing habit, the votary is precisely the same, whether he be an inhabitant of the shores of Albion, of the mountains of Scandinavia, or a backwoodsman in North America. Ardent spirit is an idol, equally worshipped under the starry sky of the north and the burning sun of the tropics: every where the pernicious effects are the same. Considerable quantities of rum and whisky, both of execrable quality, are consumed in the United States, particularly in the western parts, where they are continually in requisition. Spirituous liquors are sold in all directions. In the towns it is next to impossible to proceed fifty yards without meeting what is called a "grog shop," where bottles filled with the tempting liquid adorn the windows. Again, in the country, there is scarcely a house where whisky is not sold, and a kind of drinking room established. When travelling by the mail or stage, passengers generally get out every time the coach stops to change or water horses, in order to moisten their palates. On board steamboats there is, if I may be allowed the expression, a kind of *perpetuum mobile* of circulating tankards, filled with brandy and water, punch, sangarie, and other compounds.

Of such a variety are the different mixtures composed, that it requires a long time and no ordinary degree of acuteness to get acquainted with their denomination. I remember once, in one of the larger towns west of the Alleghany Mountains, overhearing a conversation between two respectable individuals, as to the best place of taking a sip in the morning; when one of the parties affirmed, on the salvation of his soul, that none could make a better mint-julep than Mr. A.; whilst his opponent called heaven and earth to witness that no living being had as yet excelled Mr. B. in the art of concocting whisky-punch.

From all this one is apt to infer that inebriated persons are every where to be seen; but this is far from being the case. In no country I have hitherto visited have I seen so few drunken people in the streets as in America; and, during a whole winter's residence in New York, the largest city in the Union, I can safely assert that I only saw a few intoxicated stragglers, and they were mostly foreigners. This general addiction to hard drinking is, however, more conspicuous in the States most remote from the Atlantic Ocean, although pretty prevalent in the eastern ones also. The majority of crimes are fostered and committed under the influence of this vice; in the prisons, the proportion of criminals addicted to this propensity to those who are not is as three and a half or four to one. In the State prison at Auburn, for instance, there was, according to the report for 1833, of the former number five hundred and eight, whilst of the latter, only one hundred and seventy-five.

"Four-fifths of all crimes committed in the United States," says Mr. Grundy, senator for Tennessee, a gentleman whose legal experience is of thirty years' standing, "may be traced to drunkenness as the prime cause."

"Were it possible," remarks Mr. Wirt, another profound American lawyer, to "obtain statistical details of unfortunate families and individuals, and at the same time ascertain the real cause of their misery, I feel persuaded that, in nine cases out of ten, perhaps even a larger proportion, the use of ardent spirits would materially have contributed to this state of things." "Of seventy-seven persons," says the fifth report of the American Temperance Society for 1832, "found dead in various places in the country, sixty-seven were declared by the coroner's inquest to have perished from excessive drinking."

With similar and many other facts before us, it is no wonder that a radical reform, as far as it could be effected, was seriously contemplated; and the first Temperance Society was in consequence instituted in Massachusetts. It is, in truth, a subject of strange contemplation that, in the nineteenth century, we Christians, who consider ourselves so superior to all other religious sects on the face of the earth, should endeavour to abolish drunkenness, a vice which already in the seventh century ceased to exist among the uncivilized adherents of Mahomet. But better late than never. America has given the first impulse: Europe listens with attention to the result.

In the State of New York alone, there were already in 1832 one thousand one hundred and forty-five Temperance Societies, and in the whole Union, about the same time, more than five thousand similar associations. One million five hundred thousand persons had left off the use of strong liquors, and bound themselves not to procure any for other people. That these societies make incredible progress, and do much public good, is daily perceived by the diminished quantity of ardent spirits distilled in the country, and by the lessened importation from foreign parts. Great quantities of this article were formerly made in the New England States; many of these distilleries are now discontinued. In Boston, there was a general outcry among the sellers of spirits, against the ruinous tendency of the Temperance Societies; they went even so far as to give vent to their displeasure in the public prints. But this did not prevent the success of the good cause.

The importation of spirits into the United States, in the year 1824, amounted to five millions, two hundred and eighty-five thousand gallons; and in 1830, only to one million, one hundred and ninety-five thousand, showing a difference in consumption of four millions, ninety thousand gallons in the course of six years, whilst the home distilleries declined in the same proportion. According to the first report of the American Temperance Society, the cost of ardent spirits consumed in the country exceeded forty millions of dollars per annum. The number of individuals who, by indulgence in this vice, descend to a premature grave, was calculated, according to the same authority, to be no less than about thirty thousand every year. Both these amounts are now upon the decline; and the numerous humane friends attached to these useful and praiseworthy associations anticipate with confidence the period when drunken scenes will be as seldom witnessed as they are now of common occurrence.

On leaving the meeting in question, in company with a clergyman from one of the Southern States, this gentleman related to me an anecdote, illustrative of the difficulty of converting a person once addicted to drunkenness. "If it be true," said he, "that man carries with him his passions and vices into the other world, it may reasonably be inferred that a drunkard continues the same there, if it be in his power to gratify his desires. A very respectable individual in Virginia," added he, "indulged in this propensity, and was continually in a state of intoxication, although his friends incessantly warned him of the danger he incurred of suddenly ending his life under the influence of liquor. This friendly advice, however, was totally disregarded; he apostrophised, and called them fanatics, whose only object was to deprive him of his sole earthly enjoyment; and he continued his indulgence. One day, being as usual overloaded with spirits, and unconscious of what he did, his friends determined to try an experiment, namely, whether fear would make any impression upon him. They accordingly procured a coffin, wrapped him up in a winding sheet, and lowered it into one of the deepest pits of a neighbouring coal-mine. Darkness and silence dwelt in this frightful abode. After a while the drunkard recovered his senses. A few minutes' reflexion induced him to believe that he was actually dead, and that his friends were in the right. 'Well! is it at length come so far?' exclaimed he; 'I am then no more! But am I really dead?' The friends who stood near him unseen answered with an impressive voice: 'Yes, you are unquestionably dead, and buried too.' Shortly afterwards they appeared before him in disguise, with tapers in their hands, and raised the trembling man in order to inflict, by way of punishment, a sound bastinado. He now fancied himself in a real purgatory, and pitifully implored forgiveness for past trespasses; but they appeared inexorable, and continued the chastisement until perfectly exhausted; they then retired, after having again inclosed the unfortunate man in the coffin. On hearing them take leave, he called out lustily, and in a supplicating tone: 'Halloo! Halloo! Mr. D—l, wouldn't you be so kind as to procure me something to drink?'"

A custom very prevalent in Boston is to perform serenades at night time, for the edification of the fair sex. A young American proposed to me one evening to accompany him on a similar excursion. I accepted the offer, and repaired to the spot agreed upon, where four or five young men were already in attendance. Provided with a guitar and a flute, we started about midnight, and proceeded, in the first instance, to a house in the lower part of the town, the residence of one of the belles of the city. In full imitation of the Italian fashion, we were wrapped up in cloaks, and formed a group exactly under the window stated to belong to the bed-chamber of the lady. The first piece performed was a duo between the two instruments; subsequently followed songs, with accompaniments. Within a few moments our attention was arrested by the noise of a window softly opening. I tried in vain to recognise some of the listeners ; the darkness of the room, however, prevented me from distinguishing any object within. Our persons must, however, have been easily discernible in the bright moonlight ; for, a few days afterwards, the same ladies told me unhesitatingly that I had formed one of the party. It may be easily imagined how sentimental were the tones which pierced the ears of the listening fair ones, enhanced as they were by a beautiful moon — an invariable friend to serenades — and in what a delightful mood the young gentlemen must have been, after singing and playing a dozen difficult airs. How the ladies in the window felt when the music ceased is not within my province to determine. The whole company, actors and audience, appeared, nevertheless, to part under visible feelings of melancholy; and I hastened, half frozen, to my hotel, to dream of finding myself once more in *la bella Italia,* listening to her nightly serenades.

During all this time the cholera raged with the utmost virulence in New York and its vicinity. The dreadful epidemic had, on the 21st July, reached its climax. But, though it was on the decline in August, and had entirely ceased about the middle of September, still the panic prevailed every where in the country: so great indeed was the apprehension, that people were afraid of their own shadows, and abandoned friends and relatives, if either had the misfortune to be attacked by this frightful scourge.

The following occurrence took place about this period, and illustrates unequivocally the terror generally experienced: an old man, of the name of Ballow, above fourscore, was suddenly seized with the disorder, whilst travelling in the stage between New York and Providence. The other passengers in the coach, fearful of infection, positively refused to allow him to remain inside, insisting that the driver should take him on the coach-box. The unhappy man was obliged to yield, although so reduced by weakness as hardly to be able to hold fast. Neither money nor entreaties could induce any of them to allow him a place inside; and, as there happened to be a public hospital in the town through which they passed for the reception of cholera patients, the old man was left in the open street. No one dared to approach him: when it was absolutely necessary to pass that way, persons hastened by at as great a distance from him as possible.

At length one individual, prompted by a large reward, was prevailed upon to convey him in a cart to a place called Cumberland, the very spot to which, in the first instance, he intended to proceed. On the following morning the poor patient was found lying on the steps of a neighbouring house. When he arrived at Cumberland, his place of nativity, where his brother was residing, he ordered the driver to set him down at the house of the latter; but — would this act of cruelty and barbarity be believed? — even here the doors were shut against him. A barn, an uninhabited outhouse, was assigned to him as a lodging. And in this very barn, belonging to a brother, the helpless old man was suffered to expire alone and abandoned by the whole world; his lips parched with thirst, and crawling under an accumulation of the most excruciating sufferings, which never quitted him till life was extinct. A doctor, it is true, was called in; but the pulse had already ceased to beat. He found only a lifeless corpse stretched on the straw. Is there a heart that can help feeling the deepest sympathy for an old man of eighty-five, who had travelled a distance of several hundred miles from Ohio, solely with a view of once more beholding the place that gave him birth, and of embracing, for the last time, his only remaining brother, and who, on arriving at the spot where he first saw the light, finds every avenue closed, and the same brother turning him adrift to end his sufferings in a desolate barn?

This was indeed a subject that could not escape the attention of the philanthropic and public-spirited inhabitants of Boston. A cholera hospital was immediately established, which, though not very large, proved in the sequel sufficiently spacious for the city. A society was also formed under the denomination of "Relief Association," whose object was to assist and relieve all those who happened to be attacked with the disease. Every class took part in it. Not only young and old bachelors became members; elderly and married people, with wives and children, also enlisted. With the latter the risk was naturally greater, as they might possibly, after attending their duty, bring contagion into their families; but, despite all this, rich and poor added their names to the list. Enthusiasm spread with the utmost rapidity; all were hearty in the cause. Animated by the impulse of example, the citizens waited with perfect resignation the approach of the disorder. They formed themselves into a kind of humane fraternity, determined to devote their lives to the cause of suffering fellow-creatures. The dreaded foe, however, made no serious attack: a few isolated cases only occurred. Thus did Boston, by the protecting hand of Providence, and by the firmness, prudence, and timely arrangements, of its citizens, escape a visitation, which proved so fatal in many places.

The following rules were adopted by this benevolent Association:

Whereas a number of citizens, resident in districts where cholera has made its appearance, have been seized with panic, and under its influence abandoned the sick without aid or attention, by which neglect many fatal cases have occurred, it has been deemed expedient, with a view to restore public confidence, and to check the calamity as far as possible, to form an Association, the members of which hereby bind themselves to succour and assist the sick, and take especial care that proper attention be paid to them.

1st. This Society to be called "Relief Association."

2nd. The members are divided into sixteen Committees, according to the different wards in the city; the duties are limited to their own ward — they have no connexion with each other.

3rd. Each Committee has the right to elect its own President, or Vice President.

4th. The Presidents of these Committees form collectively a Central Committee, which meets for mutual deliberations, and is empowered to vary the appointments of the Ward Committees, by exchanging the members, so as to make the duties and labours fall equally on every one.

5th. As soon as a member is called upon to assist a patient, he must immediately either repair in person to the sick bed, or without delay procure the attendance of a doctor, and see that every care be taken of the patient.

6th. The President of each Ward Committee must state to the Secretary of the Central Committee the name and place of residence of each member. He is also bound to make a regular report to said Secretary, in case any of the members are prevented from attending to their duty, or wish to leave the city.

7th. All funds, collected by subscriptions, to promote the object of this Association, are to be distributed by the Central Committee among the Ward Committees, and all accounts are afterwards to be examined by the former.

CHAPTER VIII.

J'aime à me peindre un vrai citoyen meditant dans son cabinet solitaire: la patrie est à ses côtés, la justice et l'humanité sont devant lui, les fantômes des malheureux l'environnent, la pitié l'agite, et des larmes coulent de ses yeux.

THOMAS.

No city in the whole Union has so many public institutions, having more or less benevolence and instruction for their object, as Boston. I shall only mention a few of the principal ones, as their number does not permit me to enlarge so fully on their merits as I could wish.

Among these, the Lyceum of Boston unquestionably occupies a prominent place. It was founded, if I mistake not, about the year 1829, and has ever since met with great success. This excellent institution is divided in classes, devoted to different sciences, such as mathematics, natural philosophy, astronomy, &c. The annual lectures have been numerously attended, and justly appreciated by visiters. The Lyceum has several branch establishments, some in Massachusetts, some in other States, and thereby materially contributes to the propagation of general knowledge.

The Mechanics' Lyceum is not exactly on the same plan as the former, but has, nevertheless, done a great deal of good among that class of citizens whose name it bears. I was confidently assured that many of its members are men of no ordinary information. The society publishes a periodical, called "The Young Mechanic," which possesses merit, and gains an increased circulation.

The Mechanics' Association and the Mechanics' Institution are two other societies, totally distinct from each other, but having also the advancement of knowledge for their aim. The first-mentioned is the oldest of its kind in Boston, composed exclusively of masters. Lectures are delivered here weekly in the winter season, and alms distributed with a liberal hand to distressed fellow-mechanics. The other, again, is accessible to all classes of mechanics; lectures are here also delivered. It possesses a small collection of implements suitable for the different wants of the members.

The Association of Mechanics' Apprentices is one of the most remarkable institutions in the city. Apprentices here deliver lectures every week, which, at times, are so sensible and well turned that they would not disgrace even literary men. A speech, made by one of these individuals, at a late annual meeting, actually breathed, in some places, strains of eloquence and poetry. Young members, whose means do not permit the expence of an education, may here receive it gratis. A library, by no means inconsiderable, belongs to the institution, to which a collection of natural and mechanical curiosities has lately been added.

The Society for the Propagation of Useful Knowledge also originated in Boston. It has already published several works under the name of "American Miscellanies of Useful Knowledge," which answers the purpose remarkably well. The publications are sold at a very cheap rate, and contain information of great public utility. It would be a desideratum, indeed, if every city in the world could boast of a similar society. The march of intellect would then rapidly advance: slaves, now sunk into an abject state of ignorance and degradation, groaning under the yoke of tyranny and oppression, would then no longer bear the delusive quiet of their dungeons, but endeavour to shake off the fetters. Reflection is the natural offspring of an enlightened mind. It engenders a desire to recover rights inherent in man. Passiveness of thought gives way to a more active development of the faculties. The bonds of subserviency are gradually broken asunder; and the mind, once unshackled, breathes anew a pure and free atmosphere. Thus it is that an intellectual effort, sooner than violent and reprehensible measures, slowly, but with more certainty, prepares the attainment of an object of vital importance to the human heart—public and private liberty all over the world.

The Young Men's Association for the Propagation of Science and Literature; The Young Men's Benevolent Society; The Young Men's Society for Intellectual and Moral Exercises; The Young Men's (of the Baptist sect) Education Society:—these are the names of four of the principal societies created by the young men of Boston. The two first have already effected much good in their particular branches. The third was only formed a few months ago; it has an excellent collection of books, and several convenient saloons, where members, as well as strangers, have frequent opportunities of forming many interesting acquaintances, enjoying good company, and, at the same time, improving their minds by useful books and general conversation. The fourth is chiefly intended to form able clergymen, the great scarcity of whom is severely felt by the community. It would be no easy matter to imagine, at a distance, the indefatigable zeal displayed by this as well as by every other sect in the pursuit of its object. I know persons, particularly in Massachusetts (which may be called the school for the education system, now spreading all over the world), who sacrifice time, repose, and property, for the success of the good cause. Not content with labouring for their own country — offering, no doubt, a sufficient field for their exertions — they extend their liberal views to Asia, Africa, and Europe. At Burmah, at Siam, at the different African settlements, in many of the European States even, their missionaries are invariably found, whose education has been properly and carefully attended to before they were sent on their remote expeditions.

Societies of this description are annually increasing in the Northern States of the Union; and the friends of religion fondly anticipate the time when the true Gospel shall be promulgated in the North as well as the South, by such men only as possess intellectual capacity for preaching the commands of the Almighty.

Among the associations in Boston remarkable in their kind is that of the Peace Society; it has many adherents in the country. Its object is to inculcate a general aversion to war, as perfectly irreconcileable with the principles of the Christian faith. "War is an immoral pursuit," said one of the members of the Society to me; "for the doctrine of the Redeemer was mildness, and effusion of blood and murder were foreign to him. War is even unnecessary, and history proves it. Does victory always crown a just cause? or success compensate for the blood spilt — for the hatred excited in the vanquished — or for that vindictive feeling which lies dormant, and only ceases with life? Envy, misrepresentation, and, above all, personal considerations, too often engender hostilities. Ambition and revenge not unfrequently induce a chief to launch the firebrand among millions;

and these, to show their subserviency, cut down and murder each other. For these acts of wantonness, so revolting to humanity, they are rewarded, acquire renown, and an immortal name.

"Christianity and philanthropy show us, however, that one nation seldom thrives on the ruins of another; that the prosperity of our neighbour invariably operates beneficially on our own. Could not a better tribunal be found, for the settlement of differences between nations, than an appeal to arms? Is there not enough of misery, disease, and trouble in the world? Whichever way we turn, do we hear of anything but misfortunes and acts of violence? To remedy these ought to be the real field for the exercise of true and meritorious heroism. To improve mankind, and lighten the sum of misery, this is the only glory worthy of man. Patience, self-denial, courage, and reason, are qualities not less required on the field of benevolence than on that of battle. Divest poetical descriptions of heroic deeds, so enchanting to our youthful ears, of their exaggerated and lofty garb, and substitute the form of simple truth, and the brilliancy of warlike achievements will soon vanish before our too blinded imagination. But if, after all, the doctrine should still prevail that war is indispensable, then the formation of Peace Societies become the more important, to proclaim to the world the absolute necessity of a Christian love for peace.

"Oh! could I but live to see the day when my beloved country, ruled by principles of peace and justice, and relying entirely on the protection of the Almighty, shall relinquish the idea of threatening the world with her fleets!"

Besides the institutions just mentioned, there are the Massachusetts' Public Hospital, the Lunatic Asylum, the State Prison in Charlestown, Day and Sunday Schools, all deserving the attention of strangers.

According to the information I received on the spot, the number of young men wholly devoted to study in Massachusetts, and whose age varied from fifteen to twenty, amounted to twenty-four thousand eight hundred and fifty. In the city of Boston alone, there were, in the year 1833, no less than three thousand three hundred and fifty children educated at the public expence. The charges are defrayed by the State, and amounted, in the year 1832, to fifty-six thousand nine hundred and forty-seven dollars, forty-one cents. It often happens that, after all current expences are paid, a surplus arises out of the taxes raised. Whenever this occurs, this sum is applied to the building of new schools, or to improving the old. This surplus has, upon several occasions, exceeded forty thousand dollars a year.

Independently of the children just stated, the Sunday Schools also educate a large proportion, who are all instructed in the Christian faith. The latter establishments have of late been very successful in this State, as well as in various parts of the Union, and may be called the religious Lancasterian system. One of these Sunday Schools, the members of which belong to the sect of Baptists, whose head-quarters are in Boston, had, in the year 1832, one hundred and forty-four schools, in which thirteen thousand one hundred and twenty young children were instructed by one thousand seven hundred and nineteen teachers.

America, it is well known, has no established religion. Fugitive pilgrims, persecuted in England for their religious opinions, sought in the New World that liberty of conscience which was denied them in the Old. Every opinion of the Deity was here unshackled. Religion was considered the exclusive property of conscience and God, and exempt from all other constraint. The State was distinct from the Church : neither had a right to interfere with the other, except to protect individuals in the quiet exercise of the creed which they conceived to be the only true one. Even the clergy was in most of the constitutions of the States by particular clauses excluded from all participation in public affairs. Thus one of the most important and eventful experiments, ever attempted upon so extensive a scale, was made, namely, whether religion may be sustained in a country without the protection or support of the Government. The period elapsed since the creation of the Republic certainly speaks in favour of its practicability : how far the experience of future times will justify it I do not venture to anticipate.

This freedom of religion has, however, been the means of forming a great many sects, the names of which, as well as their varied professions, it is no easy matter to enumerate. The difference in many is but trifling, and only perceptible in exterior forms. A great number are solely distinguished by insignificant modifications of the same creed. When a young clergyman, for instance, commences his career, to gain importance and make proselytes, he generally pretends to deviate from the other followers in the observance of some unmeaning exterior form, without, however, rejecting the fundamental principles upon which the sect is founded. His friends then lose no time in building a church for him. The adherents now meet to listen to the new preacher, and in a short time his congregation becomes so considerable that he obtains a comfortable livelihood by it.

The distinction between all these sects may be classed as follows:

1st. Difference of opinion with regard to the Redeemer.
2nd. Difference of opinion of the clemency of God.
3rd. Difference of opinion as to the forms of worship.

To the first class belong the Unitarians, to the second the Calvinists and others, to the third the Catholics, and a great many more. But, though few men agree in opinion as to the creed, yet it is easily discovered that the basis is the same with every one. As the common name of these sects is Christians, in like manner their different opinions coincide that there exists a Supreme Being, through whose infinite goodness the world is ruled and supported, and whom we must worship — that Christ was the Messiah alluded to in the Old Testament — that resurrection will take place — and that virtue and vice will, in a future state, receive their respective rewards and punishments. This bond of union, equally powerful in America as in Europe, which keeps together the prosaic Unitarians and the superstitious Catholics — although otherwise so widely different in their belief — does it not, I ask, establish the expediency of a general and free doctrine all over the world? Why should not a Lutheran be allowed to worship his Creator in the manner he conceives the most proper, in a country where perhaps the number of Catholics is greater than that of Protestants, and *vice versa?* Are not both Christians ? Can there be any difference before the throne of the Almighty between a follower of the Pope, who offers his prayers in a kneeling posture, and a Protestant, who performs the same holy office standing? Is it not enough that he is a pious man? What more do we want to know ?

The Calvinists have the greatest number of adherents in the United States. Next to them come the Methodists, Presbyterians,

Orthodox Congregationalists, Catholics, and followers of the Episcopal Church. In the New England States, the Congregationalists and the Presbyterians are the most numerous: but in the State of New York, the Presbyterians, Congregationalists, and Methodists, take the lead. In New Jersey and Delaware, the Presbyterians are the most numerous : in Pennsylvania they are also first; and then follow the Calvinists, Lutherans, and Quakers. In Maryland, Florida, and Louisiana, there are mostly Catholics: in Virginia, North and South Carolina, Baptists, Presbyterians, Episcopalians, and Methodists: in Georgia, Baptists and Methodists: in the Western States, the Methodists stand foremost, and are estimated at eight hundred thousand ; next to them, follow the Baptists, seven hundred thousand ; Presbyterians, five hundred and fifty thousand; Catholics, four hundred and fifty thousand ; and so on.*

I was fortunate enough to procure an approximating statement of all the different sects in the United States, which I hereby annex for the information of the reader.

---

* Vide History and Geography of the Mississippi Valley, by Flint.

SECTS.	Preachers.	Congregations and Churches.	Followers.
Calvinist-Baptists	2914	4384	2,744,000
Free-will Baptists . . .	300	400	150,000
Free Communion Baptists . .	30		30,000
Seventh-day Baptists . .	30	40	20,000
Six-Principle Baptists . .	25	30	20,000
Emancipator Baptists . .	15		4,500
Methodists of the Episcopal Church	1777		2,600,000
Various Associations of Methodists	350		175,000
Presbyterians (General Assembly)	1801	2253	1,800,000
Cumberland's Presbyterians . .	50	75	100,000
Various Associations of Presbyterians	74	144	100,000
Congregationalists, Orthodox .	1000	1381	1,260,000
Unitarians	160	193	176,000
Catholics		784	800,000
Followers of the Episcopal Church	558	922	600,000
Universalists	150	300	500,000
Lutherans	205	1200	400,000
German Reformed Church .	84	400	200,000
Dutch Reformed Church . .	159	602	125,000
Christians	200	800	275,000
Quakers, or Friends . .		462	200,000
Mennonites	200		120,000
Tunkers, or Dunkers . . .	40	40	30,000
Moravians, or United Brethren .	23	23	7,000
Shakers	45	15	6,000
Swedenborgians	30	28	5,000
Jews, and other Nondescript Sects		150	50,000

To enter into an analysis, and distinguish the difference between each of these sects, would be a task which my limits do not permit; I will therefore only succinctly touch on the principal ones. The Baptists, more numerous than the others, deserve the first place. Their doctrine is founded on the belief that baptism ought not only to consist in the act of sprinkling holy water, but to dip also the whole body in it, and further, that baptism should only be performed on full grown persons, and exclusively on those who sincerely confess and repent their trespasses, and are worthy of being admitted brethren of the Union. The Calvinist-Baptists believe entirely in predestination, and affirm that, by his sufferings and death, the Redeemer washed out the sins of those only who were chosen. But though differing in some trifling points with each other, they agree upon one important principle, equally desirable to all, namely, the propagation of the beneficial light of the Gospel. Their missionaries are every where to be found. In the remotest parts of the United States — in those regions where no white man ever dared to penetrate among the buffalo-hunting Indians — in Liberia (the new founded settlement on the coast of Africa of emancipated Negroes from America,) in the midst of the heathens of Burmah and Siam — even in enlightened France — these missionaries are to be found, establishing schools. It redounds not a little to the honour of the Baptists that they do not lose sight of the offspring of the unhappy beings whose extermination has been nearly effected by too close a connexion with the Whites.

"It is with deep regret we find," observe the members of the committee appointed in the year 1832, in speaking of the Indian Missionaries, in the seventh triennial meeting of the general congregation of Baptists at New York, "that the mass of Indians are unceremoniously swept away by the tide of destruction. Deprived of the inheritance of their ancestors, driven from their last asylum, obstructed in the exercise of their craft, humbled by irksome dependence, despised by neighbours, and wounded to the quick by a series of unjust acts, all chances of relief are obscured before their eyes; and they sink into a state of despondency, the natural consequence of a distracted mind. Let us not forget that this Indian race are our neighbours, and that their population once amounted to millions, when left in peaceable possession of the country we now inhabit. Their number has sensibly diminished by emigrants settled among them, indifferent as to their temporal or spiritual welfare. Should we not incur the just wrath of Heaven, if we abandoned them at this critical moment? We rejoice to think that the efforts of the missionaries may hereafter be productive of some permanent relief to our Indian brethren.

Already a great number have removed behind the shores of the Missouri — there is a wide field indeed for the missionaries!"

The zeal with which these persevering men labour for the success of their good cause is almost incredible. No pains, no obstacles, no maladies, can possibly dissuade them from exposing their persons to the dangers incidental among savages, or to the almost certain sacrifice of life in the unhealthy climate of India, whence few missionaries ever return to their native soil. This premature dissolution does not, however, discourage a single individual from proceeding on his praiseworthy pursuit. They hardly perceive the destructive effect of an Indian sun till death has marked them for his own. Fearlessly they traverse the sandy deserts of Africa, and never quit the improving and flourishing Negro colony in Liberia, till they have inculcated Christianity among the inhabitants.

But no project on the part of the missionaries attracted more attention in America than that of sending agents to France. Nothing showed more clearly the religious enthusiasm which inspires the sect. A few extracts from a speech delivered by one of the most eloquent and active men among the Baptists will not, I think, be unacceptable to the reader, as showing an attempt to prove the necessity of a similar step. "France," it says, "is in great want of missionaries. Christianity is there nearly extinguished. The sacredness of the Sabbath is abolished. Neither religious instruction nor devotion is to be found. The king reviews his troops; apprentices and artisans attend to their everyday business; the theatres are crowded with people; Charlatans continue their harvest among the credulous; the sounds of music are heard from every hotel; and the whole country is nothing but a scene of vice and profanation. Now is the time for us to act; every thing is ready; the Holy Bible is there accessible. France, once restored to religious sentiments, will, by the propagation of holy books, set a fine example to surrounding nations in Europe, and richly and nobly not only provide for herself, but enlist faithful servants in her cause. We, more than any other Christian nation, are bound to remember France in this awful crisis. Need I advert to the assistance she tendered our ancestors in time of need? Let us repay this loan of fleets and armies by sending her the Holy Gospel! The example of our democrats has shaken every throne. We have shown to the world the errors of governments and the rights of nations. We have disturbed all Europe. The contest shall not cease in France, nor shall our matchless institutions obtain any stability there, till the moral character of the people has been entirely renovated. Great misfortunes and changes must inevitably continue, blood be shed, anarchy triumph, till principles of virtue and truth preponderate. The people must be *taught* to obey, and *taught* to command. All this can only be effected by the Christian faith."

The sect of Baptists gained, in the year 1832, an accession of about fifty thousand members. During the same period, four hundred and thirty-eight new congregations were formed, and two hundred and nineteen new clergymen ordained, being at the rate of one preacher to two congregations: from the whole number of both, all over the United States, an aggregate of three of the latter to four and a half of the former appears. In the States east of the Alleghany Mountains, the proportion is about two preachers to three congregations: in the western again one to two. This is, in truth, a lamentable circumstance; but, as the subject now seriously occupies the attention of all Baptist associations, it is to be hoped that, in the course of time, a sufficient number of clergymen will be supplied. Societies are also formed for the specific object of giving a suitable education to young persons intending to devote their time to the promotion of missionary pursuits, affording the needy every possible support and assistance. The nineteenth annual report of the Northern Baptists' Education Society states as follows:

"Hitherto, little attention has been paid to the education of our clergymen. It is a notorious and lamentable fact, that barely one in fifty of our preachers has received the first rudiments of an English education. Most of them have been taken from the class of farmers or agriculturists, and have always been distinguished for piety and good practical common sense. Considered as preachers, they have been honest and laborious, many even gifted with extraordinary natural endowments, which, if cultivated, might have paved the way to the highest distinctions. Agriculturists are always the first to advance in a new country, till they are dispersed over the whole surface: such was also the case with our priests. As culture and refinement progressively advanced, so they gradually quitted their pristine abodes, and the consequence was, that they accompanied the great mass of people which emigrated to regions as yet uninhabited. This explains why Baptists are so dispersed all over the country. The country having undergone a complete change, the illiterate clergy have lost all prospect of success. Knowledge and improvements have made great progress: the nation participates in the general prosperity. Regions in the country, which a few years ago were but deserts, have now sprung up into villages and towns, which are the seat of wealth, knowledge, and cultivated taste; to retrograde is therefore impossible. One alternative is now left—either to give our clergymen a better education, or to abandon the field to others. The utmost attention is paid to accomplish the first object, by the care displayed in forming able preachers. Theological institutions are maintained at their expense, and the qualifications required from each clergyman not inconsiderable. "We shall soon be able," said one of the followers of this sect to me, "to send a whole phalanx of preachers all over the world."

As Philadelphia may be called the Capital of the Quakers in America, and Baltimore that of the Catholics, so may also Boston be ranked as the seat of the Unitarians. The principles of this last mentioned sect deserve, in justice, the name of "Liberal Religion!" Reason and conscience are, according to the tenets of its adherents, the only true guide through life. They believe nothing which is not clearly seen and demonstrated; miracles are rejected as incomprehensible; there is no enthusiasm among them; their doctrine is always confined to plain prosaic expressions: lofty poetry—that strain of figurative language, which for centuries past has made so many millions of martyrs—is entirely excluded. No axiom is more applicable to the pensive, serious, and scrutinizing inhabitant of the New England States than this: "What I do not understand, I reject as worthless and false." So said one of the most learned men in Boston to me—"Why occupy the mind with what is incomprehensible? Have we not enough of that which appears clear and plain around us?"

The followers of Unitarianism contend that like every thing else in the world, religion is exposed to changes and vicissitudes. The Christian faith—such as preached by the apostles—was suited for that particular age. In the ages that followed, it was not preserved in its pristine purity. One addition after another, and one alteration worse than the other, soon converted it into a convenient engine for disguising crimes of every kind. The reformation in Germany undoubtedly unravelled the holy truth from its dark recesses; but the purification did not go so far as the real friends of the Christian faith had wished. Darkness still remained. It was then Unitarianism sprung up, and all was light.

Those who profess the tenets of this sect do not believe in the Trinity: they contend that Christ was a great prophet, but had no divine inspiration. Repentance and an unimpeachable life, they say, are sufficient to obtain God's forgiveness. The martyrdom of Christ did not make God better disposed towards us than he was before. He only requires a true repentance from the sinner, and he forgives the past.

The greater part of the Bostonians, including every one of wealth, talents, and learning, have adopted this doctrine. I had frequent opportunities of hearing their principal preachers. Generally speaking, they possessed much dignity, both in delivery and action, explaining the discourse in a simple, conversation-like manner. Metaphors or poetical allusions were never introduced. The sermon, from beginning to end, appeared to me as a conversation in a room between a father and his children. The service in other respects differed very little from that of the Episcopal Church, but it was considerably shorter.

CHAPTER IX.

Les Revenants et les Sorciers plaisent au peuple, comme aux hommes éclairés ; c'est une disposition qu' inspirent assez naturellement les longues nuits des climats septentrionaux.

DE STAEL HOLSTEIN.

HAVING spent a few weeks most agreeably in Boston, I proceeded on my journey to the other States situated still more to the northward.

Charlestown, the first place I visited, is contiguous to Boston, and connected with it by means of two long bridges. It is a small town of little note, distinguished only as being one of the naval stations of the United States. One of the officers belonging to this service, remarkable for his politeness, accompanied me on my visit to view the station. It is far from being completed : even the plan of the proposed basin was very little advanced ; but workmen were actively employed in constructing and widening the place. Among the finished parts may be mentioned the residence of the commodore, the barracks, stores, and forges. A spacious dock, without exception the finest and largest in the United States, was then being constructed when I visited Charlestown the first time. Before I left the States, this stupendous work was already completed. The dock, built of granite, is finished in a style that reflects the greatest credit on the builder ; it is two hundred and ten feet in length, and roomy enough for the largest battle ship. The water is pumped out by a steam-engine. Two gates, of which one is floating, arrest the influx of the sea. The stonework alone is stated to have consisted of no less than five hundred thousand cubic feet.

Several men-of-war, frigates, and sloops, were lying there dismantled, and partly covered by houses or sheds erected for that purpose. All the ships are built of live oak, or *quercus sempervirens*, which grows in the Southern States. This building material is well known as being particularly hard, compact, and durable, and, consequently well calculated for the construction of ships.

Among the vessels shown to me was one whose fame had already reached my ears, and with which every one in America, old and young, is acquainted. This was the Constitution, a frigate of forty-four guns. She is one of the oldest ships in the American navy, was built in Boston, in the year 1797, and has upon various occasions showed her prowess in combating the English and the Tripolitans. Fortune has every where favoured her: not only has she escaped from far superior enemies, but has been victorious in several rencontres, capturing frigates, corvettes, and sloops of war, and carrying home a number of prisoners. For these repeated deeds of valour, she was called by the honourable name, "Old Ironside," by which she is distinguished to this very day. She is the pride and boast of Americans, particularly of the Bostonians, with whom she is a darling object. Few men-of-war have done more than this ship. Whenever Old Ironside proceeds to sea, all eyes are fixed upon her, confident that she will give a good account of herself: on returning, she is enthusiastically greeted by the whole nation.

At one extremity of Charlestown, there are two hills, called Breed's Hill and Bunker's Hill, known in history as the spots where one of the battles was fought during the revolutionary war, in which the Americans were obliged to give way. This took place in the year 1775, and has, strange enough, been called the battle of Bunker's Hill, although, properly speaking, it ought to have gone by the name of Breed's Hill, where the fight actually took place. Fifty years subsequently to this event, or in the year 1825, in the presence of General Lafayette and a number of revolutionary officers and soldiers, the foundation-stone was laid for a granite monument in the shape of an obelisk. The work, however, went on but slowly, and even in 1833 it was far from being completed.

The distance from Charlestown to Lynn is only a few miles. This little town, one of the oldest in the Union, has a population exclusively devoted to the manufacturing of shoes. Of six thousand inhabitants, one fourth may be said to be shoemakers. Some of the masters employ fifty workmen, and it was reported that one of them could turn out twelve hundred pair a week, being, if we take twelve hours in the day, at the rate of one pair of shoes for every fourth minute. The annual quantity of boots and shoes manufactured at this place amounts to a million, the greater part of which are disposed of in the Southern States. Contracts are generally made beforehand with the manufacturers. In every house in the town, with a few exceptions, workshops are to be seen, and the eye meets nothing but shoemakers at their last. This is truly carrying on the shoemaking business to a great extent.

Salem, also one of the oldest towns in America, was founded in the year 1626, and bore formerly the Indian name of Naumkeag. It contended a long time for commercial supremacy with Boston, but was at length obliged to yield the palm to its too powerful neighbour. Trade and navigation have of late years visibly decreased, and many of the principal inhabitants have in consequence retired from business, while some have removed to Boston. Much wealth is still to be found in Salem, of which the exterior appearance gives at first sight a good idea. The houses are tastefully and ornamentally built. The streets are rather narrow, but a stranger is so pre-occupied with the justly celebrated female beauties of the place as to have no leisure for finding fault with the architectural part of the town.

Salem possesses a museum, the most interesting of its kind in the United States. It belongs to a society, of which no one can become a member till he has doubled Cape Horn or the Cape of Good Hope. From every part of the world curiosities, antiquities, and costumes, together with other remarkable things, are brought hither, interesting to the antiquarian as well as to the naturalist. No traveller ought to quit this part of the country without visiting the museum of Salem.

Close to the town is Beverley, a small insignificant place, remarkable only in the annals of history, as having formerly contained a superstitious population. Many lives have here been sacrificed; and the barren hill is still in existence, where persons accused of witchcraft were hung up on tall trees. Tradition, exaggerated and fabulous no doubt, points out the place where the witches of old resided. Cotton Mather recounts in a work,* truly original for that age, that the good people who lived near Massachusett's Bay were every night roused from their slumber by the sound of a trumpet, summoning all the witches and demons.

And there that night the trumpet rang,
  And rock and hill replied,
And down the glen strange shadows sprang,
Mortal and fiend—a wizard gang,
  Seen dimly side by side.

---

* Magnalia, by Cotton Mather.

> They gathered there from every land
> That sleepeth in the sun;
> They came with spell and charm in hand,
> Waiting their Master's high command,
> Slaves to the Evil One!*

Newbury Port is a town which has seen its best days: it is now sunk into insignificance. It is situated near the Merrimac, one of the many beautiful rivers which traverse the immense continent of North America. The port is good, but deserted and empty. Within ten years, the bustle and trade have considerably decreased: mackarel-fishing appears to give exclusive support to a declining population. The exterior of the town, the houses, and streets, bespeak its decline.

On leaving this place, and proceeding by the suspension-bridge, built on four arches, and one thousand feet in length, the traveller enters the territory of New Hampshire. In this State are the celebrated White Mountains, the highest in the United States, with the exception of the Rocky Mountains. Among them, Mount Washington rises highest: its summit is five thousand three hundred and fifty feet above the level of Connecticut river, or about six thousand four hundred feet above that of the sea. Besides these mountains,

* Legends of New England.

there are several others traversing the State in various directions, interspersed with rich pasturage. Along the coast, nothing but stones, sand, and sterility, is seen ; but in the interior the soil is more fertile, and in many places covered with extensive woods. The climate is healthy, though cold. Concord, the capital, is situate in the middle of the State, on the River Merrimac.

Portsmouth is the most considerable town in New Hampshire, and the only sea-port. It is watered by the river Piscataqua, forming one of the safest harbours in the Union. The environs are embellished by neat country-seats; but the town itself has nothing striking. It has suffered considerably by frequent fires, and, as its trade has been visibly on the decline, no pains have been taken to rebuild the houses. The old town, which has hitherto escaped the effects of conflagrations, has such a wretched appearance that the spectator fancies himself removed to some small European hamlet, just emerged from the horrors of war, pestilence, or persecution. In the midst of these ruins, however, I found a standard of liberty, on the top of which a gilt eagle spread its wide wings ; beneath it, was written, in large characters, that it was erected for the celebration of the 4th of July, the day on which America declared her independence.

On a small island opposite Portsmouth is another station for the United States Navy, enclosing several ships.

When the traveller leaves the river Piscataqua, he enters the State of Maine: before 1820, it formed part of Massachusetts. Every step indicates an approach to the North: cultivated fields become more rare, the soil appears less yielding, forests increase, the pine — this child of the North — assumes its empire, the neat cottages so conspicuous in the New England States disappear. The whole country has a Northern appearance; and the inhabitants, with their golden locks and rosy cheeks, forcibly reminded me of my own far remote but much-beloved country. During several months in the year, the rivers and lakes are covered with ice, as in Sweden: forests lie under the weight of snow-mountains: fields, rocks, valleys, all are dressed in the white winter mantle. I fancied I recognised the heavy clouds, the fresh air; that I heard the sound of the sleigh bells; and I pictured to myself all the pleasures of a winter's evening, with snow on the ground, and dancing, and singing, and toasting, within doors. Such were the illusions of my fancy, entirely bent on Sweden, when first I entered Maine.

In the course of this day's journey, I passed through the small towns of York, Welles, Kennebunk, and Saco. The road was very indifferent, and the country generally bore the appearance of sterility and uniformity. Several manufactories are established near Saco. Not far from Welles is a rock called Breakneck Hill, forming a cataract forty feet high. According to tradition, a great number of Indians met here a melancholy fate. They were returning from a fishing excursion to the upper part of the river. Surprised by darkness before they arrived at the falls, they despatched a small party to make up a fire on the very rock which divides the cataract, intending thereby to guard against danger. Some Whites residing in the neighbourhood having obtained information of their intention, killed the party thus sent. Combustibles of every description were hastily collected, and a fire lighted on one of the banks below the falls. The Indians, in full reliance on their comrades, did not perceive the stratagem till it was too late to arrest the progress of their boats. All were precipitated down the falls in an instant, and perished by the side of each other, in a common grave.

It is not surprising if these and similar barbarities inspired a deadly hatred and a thirst for vengeance. It was probably under this influence that five hundred Indians are stated to have attacked a small redoubt, situate a short distance from thence, and of which some traces are still left. No white men happened to be in the redoubt when assailed: five women formed the only garrison. These determined to defend themselves, and to sell their lives dearly. Disguised in the attire of men, they fired on the enemy with so much effect that the Indians at length raised the siege and fled.

Every stranger visiting the New England States is struck with a prominent feature, characteristic of the inhabitants — namely, that of curiosity. All must positively know their neighbours' business. To elude answering inquiries is nearly the same as holding the questioner over a slow fire. He suffers more than a snake in an ant-hill, if the following questions are not immediately answered: "Who are you? Where do you come from? Where are you going? What is your business?" &c. The great Franklin was well acquainted with this characteristic, and was therefore in the habit, whenever he proceeded to the eastward, and arrived at a place, to call together all the inmates of the house where he stopped, and tell them that his name was Benjamin Franklin, that he came from such and such a place, that he intended to go to another, that the object of his journey was so and so, and, finally, that he intended to return by such and such a route. This was an excellent way to prevent questions, and always insured him tranquillity. When travelling in a stage coach, nothing is more common than for one traveller to ask another the history of his life, and it is hardly possible to evade answering without incurring the displeasure of the whole company.

Our coach contained no less than nine inside passengers, travelling all the way from Portsmouth to Portland; before we had proceeded one-eighth part of the journey, we knew each other as well as if we had been educated in the same college. Inquiries were not limited to a mere personal biography: grandmothers, uncles, cousins, and aunts, were respectively brought into play, seasoned with appropriate anecdotes and comments.

Each narrative was always accompanied by the elegant expression, " says she," or " says he," generally exciting merriment with the auditory. To give a faint idea of the latitude to which curiosity is carried, I will report a short and humourous conversation which took place in the course of our journey between two gentlemen, immediately upon their stepping into the coach.

A. You come from Boston, I guess?

B. I left Boston yesterday.

A. You live there, I presume?

B. Not quite.

A. Perhaps from Cambridge, or Lowell?

B. (Did not answer immediately).

A. Well! from Lowell. Concerned in some manufactory there, I guess?

B. Just so.

A. How do the manufactories come on? Do they pay?

B. Tolerably well.

A. You have a large family, haven't you?

B. Not without.

A. Your father was probably also a manufacturer, I reckon?

B. Yes; you are right.

A. Pardon me, what was his name?

B. The same as mine.

A. Gilford, Dickens, or Gorum, perhaps?

B. No, Sir; neither of these names.

A. May I be allowed to ask who I am speaking to?

B. My name is . . . . . .

A. Really! Well, there was a gentleman of that name I knew ten years ago at Plymouth; he must surely have been your brother. Was he not?

B. No, but probably my cousin.

A. Cousin! then you have no brothers?

B. Yes, two.

A. They are also engaged in manufacturing, I calculate?

B. Only one of them.

A. And the other, what is he doing? Gone into business, I suspect.

B. He is a farmer.

A. Has he a large family?

B. A considerable one.

A. He must have a large farm, many sheep, cows, swine, geese, &c.

The questions and answers were thus interruptedly continued for more than half an hour, when A had at length exhausted his inquiries. B, who, to judge by his laconic answers, appeared little pleased with these fatiguing questions, now began to repay his antagonist in the same coin, and did not leave off till A had given him a circumstantial account of his whole family, father, grandfather, great grandfather, brothers, sisters, cousins, and their relations, with anecdotes relating to each, together with the particulars of their occupation, income, property, &c. When the colloquy was concluded, both appeared heartily tired. I could not refrain from indulging in a hearty laugh, and should probably have continued it for some time, had not my neighbour in the coach thought proper to break it off, by placing me under examination. At length the stage entered Portland.

This rising town is the seat of the Legislature for Maine, and lies on a peninsula, extending into Casco Bay. A few handsome private and public buildings may be seen; but the streets are neither paved nor Macadamized, so that, although the summer was not yet over, they were in such bad condition, that passengers ran the risk of being every minute engulphed in a mud-hole. The trade of this place is considerable: the active population has particularly directed its attention to ship-building, for which it is distinguished. The principal exports hence are deal, timber, and fish. An observatory has been erected on an eminence at one end of the town, from the top of which the prospect is very beautiful, and in clear weather the white mountains in New Hampshire may be seen.

One evening, during my short stay at Portland, I met a very well informed and experienced man, lately returned from a visit to the interior of Maine, where he had been examining the soil of some uncultivated and wild tracts of land, part of which he intended to purchase at an approaching sale, for the purpose of cultivation. "That portion of land," observed he, "which is situate between the rivers Penobscot and Kennebec, but particularly near Augusta and Hallowell, is so well cultivated and thickly peopled, that one can scarcely fancy himself in Maine. But, farther on in the State, neither the axe nor the plough has ever been used. Great treasures are still to be found in the immense forests and in the maiden soil. The climate is no doubt rather severe, and does not offer all the advantages of a Southern or Western one; but it is at least healthy, and does not weaken the body. In Maine, no emigrant can grow in a twelvemonth, but he is sure to do it in ten years. Why should it therefore be said, that because a man can earn an independence in the course of one year in the South or West, it would be folly to settle in the North, and wait ten? What is gained in one respect is lost in another; for those who, in the first mentioned States, accomplish their object in one tenth part of the time, generally die ten years before those in the North. The emigrant may therefore choose between a short and pleasant life, and a long and laborious one. For my part, I prefer the latter."

The expression of these sentiments, which at first appeared to me as rather emanating from a partial source, induced me, nevertheless, to make further inquiry into the subject. Europe sends yearly shoals of emigrants to the United States. In the year 1833, there arrived at New York forty-one thousand seven hundred and fifty-two passengers, of which two-thirds may be said to be emigrants: if, therefore, we admit the number twenty-seven thousand eight hundred and thirty-four, and add thereto the same number, which come to other ports and from Canada, the aggregate sum of emigrants that annually resort to the United States will be about fifty-five thousand six hundred. Generally speaking, they possess a very small sum of money, after paying for their passage across the Atlantic, and with it they proceed either to the West, South, or North, according to recommendations given by individuals they accidentally meet. Those who take their chance in the Northern States, such as New York, Vermont, New Hampshire, and Maine, are for the most part deterred by fear of epidemics, pictured to them in the most discouraging colours, from visiting the Western or Southern States, as they are accustomed to severe climates. They purchase uncultivated land, either from government or private companies, at prices varying from two and a half to four dollars per acre: for land already cultivated they pay from one hundred to one hundred and fifty dollars. Those again, who proceed across the Alleghany Mountains, buy lots at one and a quarter to two dollars per acre: it is land in a virgin state, intersected with hills, valleys, and swamps.

It is certainly an unquestionable fact, that land in the "far West," as it is emphatically called, is by far more yielding than that of any of the Northern States just mentioned. An acre gives there upon an average seventy bushels of wheat, or ninety of Indian corn; whereas, in the latter, it only produces half that quantity. Thus, the comparative production varies a good deal; the price of produce equally so. The facilities of transporting the latter down the large Western rivers to great markets materially improve the condition of the farmers, by insuring higher prices for their commodities: still, the distance and loss of time are of such great moment, that they are often obliged to submit to heavy deductions before the net proceeds reach their farms. Wood, cut on their premises preparatory to cultivation, yields nothing: to send it down one thousand, perhaps two thousand miles, before it becomes of any value, is an expense without any corresponding remuneration. But, in the Northern States, particularly in Maine, this is by no means the case. There, it is worth from three to three and a half dollars per cord. With the produce of the timber, always in demand in the neighbouring cold States, the prime cost of the property is paid. The soil, once cleared, generally yields, the first year, from twenty to thirty bushels of Indian corn, which, sold on the spot, fetches about fifty cents, and if sent to Boston, from sixty-five to seventy-five cents. This seems to establish the fact, that emigration to the Northern States is not so discouraging as has been represented. That it is a toilsome task cannot well be denied; but settlers are, at least, exempt from sickness. By industry and perseverance, an independence may certainly be acquired, but it can only be effected in process of time.

In the Western States, again, emigrants have, in the first instance, to defray heavy travelling expences, before they arrive at their place of destination. They then must pay an exorbitant price for agricultural implements, always high in a distant and thinly-peopled country. Unacquainted with the climate, they invariably commit acts of imprudence. Destitute of means, whole families are obliged, at first, to live in the open air, exposed to the miasmas and vapours continually arising from the swamps. Diseases, often of a malignant nature, follow as a natural consequence. Deprived of medical assistance, they have to contend with their effects, and are at the same time obliged, with the sweat on their brows, to work for food! How often does the first year's experiment leave the settler a widower, childless, and fatherless! However, this dreadful state of sickness will gradually disappear, like a shadow, before the influence of civilization. As soon as the country becomes inhabited, the swamps drained and cultivated, and the woods changed into fertile fields, the climate will become more healthy, and the emigrant be freed from this fearful scourge — sickness and debility.

The dread of fevers and agues, however, prevents many Europeans from settling in the woody parts of the Western Countries. In the Old World, nothing is more common than to hear objections raised against emigrations to the United States. The country is represented as being the abode of every species of disease. By degrees, this erroneous impression will be removed. Encouraging statements, I have no doubt, will be transmitted by Europeans, enjoying comforts and health in their new settlements; and the day will come when the children of emigrants, who have gone through the trying ordeal, will be exhibited as patterns of health and strength.

Among numerous objections I remember having heard in Europe against the tide of emigration, were certain difficulties mentioned as emanating from various States. The nature of these, taken in unison with the personal risk and trouble inseparable from emigration, were, according to the opinion of many enlightened men, sufficient grounds for the intended exiles rather to remain at home in a state of poverty and misery, even with slavery and wretchedness as companions, than to take the chance of liberty and independence, since neither could be acquired, but at the evident risk of life.

No State, that I am aware of, throws any impediment in the way of emigration or colonization, except Massachusetts. There the laws are opposed to an alien holding land until he becomes a naturalized citizen. But, notwithstanding this exception, many foreigners purchase soon after their arrival tracts of land in the State. It is done by leases, for a period of ninety-nine years, equivalent to an actual purchase, in a country where property seldom remains long in the hands of one family. Massachusetts is, however, a State to which few emigrants resort. The land being poor, the major part of the population direct their attention to manufacturing pursuits, or quit for the Western Country. In States less populous, such as Maine, New Hampshire, Vermont, Ohio, Illinois, Indiana, Kentucky, Missouri, Mississippi, &c., the Legislature gives every possible encouragement to emigration. The price of land is very moderate, and may be bought on credit by mortgaging it. It is, besides, an adopted rule in these regions, that, whenever an emigrant arrives, for the purpose of settling, the whole neighbourhood assembles and assists in raising a temporary dwelling for him, that he may at least have shelter over his head for himself and family. This assistance, indispensable in a country where no workmen can be hired, added to the trifling amount of taxes, materially contributes to remove the first and greatest difficulties an emigrant has to encounter in a wild district. If he possesses property to the extent of one hundred dollars, he may, by hard labour and industry, the first year earn barely enough to support himself and family; the second he will do it easily; and the subsequent ones much better than he has been used to in Europe.

I have been assured that if a man proceeds to the States just mentioned, with a capital of two thousand dollars, he may purchase more land and houses than he will be able to manage. This sum might therefore be considered the maximum in the purchase of land in the uncultivated districts. Whoever embarks this amount the first year is looked upon as a very wealthy man. This applies to the most remote and still thinly-peopled States.

The price of beasts of burden, necessary for agriculture, varies according to the distance of the place from the ocean. Upon an average, thirty to forty-five dollars are paid for a cow, seventy to eighty for a pair of oxen, and ninety-five dollars for a strong working horse. But these high prices are not common; they can scarcely be considered as a criterion.

The principal produce is tobacco, cotton, rice, sugar, Indian corn, wheat, and rye. Tobacco grows mostly in Virginia, Maryland, Kentucky, and Ohio; cotton in Louisiana, Mississippi, Arkansas, Alabama, Tennessee, Georgia, South and North Carolina, and Florida; rice, in Carolina and Louisiana; sugar, in Louisiana and Florida; Indian corn in Kentucky, Ohio, Missouri, Illinois, and some of the Northern States; wheat, in Illinois, Missouri, and some of the middling States; rye, in the districts north of the River Hudson. In the Southern States, cotton, tobacco, sugar, and rice, are considered staple articles. In the Northern, again, Indian corn and wheat take the first place. I will advert to the first-mentioned articles in a future chapter, when speaking of the South.

The prices of the Northern produce, namely, Indian corn, wheat, and rye, are subject to great fluctuation in the Eastern or Western States, depending more or less on the contiguity of markets to the plantations. In the principal towns, bordering on the Atlantic Ocean, they have upon an average been for some time as follows: rye from the North from seventy to seventy-five cents per bushel; rye from the South sixty to sixty-five cents; wheat, ninety cents to one dollar; Indian corn sixty-five to seventy-five cents. In the interior, and in the Western States, where transport to a market is long and difficult, Indian corn has only brought fifteen to twenty cents. A great quantity of flour is made from wheat in the Central States, from Virginia to New York; the average price has, of late years, been six dollars and a half per barrel.

From Portland I returned direct to Boston. At an inn on the road, where we changed horses, a dancing party had just assembled, in honour of the termination of harvest. The entertainment, which is called "husking," is given by every farmer to his neighbours, who have assisted in plucking the ears of the corn-stalks.

The practice of voluntarily helping each other during harvest time is common in this part of the country, and arises from the scarcity of labouring men all over the Union. They cannot be obtained for money in many places; I should say that they are scarce, when compared to the great population of the country. The reason lies in the very republican principle that every one aspires to the condition of master, for the purpose of enjoying an independent station, easily obtained. In the Northern States, exempt from slavery, the population has increased to so great an extent that salaried assistants must be found on any terms; but, the number proving insufficient, they often demand higher wages.

In the Slave States, on the contrary, it is considered degrading to a white man to do any work that might possibly be performed by a Negro. As soon as a European, and particularly an Irishman, arrives in America, he immediately tries to get employment either as a servant or an apprentice, driven to it by poverty; but it is almost without example that the same man, after having imbibed republican notions of equality, ever remains beyond a very short time as dependent on another, however well he may be treated by his master or mistress. His head filled with ideas of liberty, and a few dollars in his pocket, he starts for some remote part, buys a tract of land for a trifle and on credit, cultivates it, or follows some profession on his own account. In the course of a few years he grows wealthy, and becomes perhaps in time a candidate for one of the highest offices in the State. It is not surprising then, that, with such prospects before him, a man prefers being master to servant; but, at the same time, wages consequently become high. Masons, carpenters, and joiners, are as much wanted in the country as in towns, owing to the number of buildings continually being erected. An able workman of that class earns at least one dollar per diem, and in many places in the country even two dollars and a half. A common workman in the interior, or what would be called a labourer, receives from ten to twelve dollars a month, besides board and lodging, &c., this only during the summer months: in winter he gets less, except in the vicinity of woods, where he is employed in cutting and transporting timber. An assistant gardener, who is acquainted with some other profession, receives about fifteen dollars a month.

I was told that this "husking entertainment" was a real treat to young people in the country. As soon as the Indian corn is cut, and safely lodged in the barns, all the neighbours are invited to attend and pluck the ears. This operation is seldom performed without much mirth and hilarity, generally enlivened by the circulation of some excellent cider. When evening approaches, tables are spread with abundance of provisions of every description, and dancing only ceases when Phœbus greets the company. In this manner were these people engaged when I entered the ball-room. There was not a countenance that did not express artless joy; the motion of limbs, the clapping of hands, the bending of knees, the inclination of heads to follow time, all was in harmony with the smiles on the lips and in the eyes. Here was a perfect illustration of the pleasures of a country life, so happily portrayed by poets. Joy reigned without ostentation. There,

> Brown corn-fed nymphs, and strong hard-handed beaux,
> Alternate ranged, extend in circling rows.

But the horses were harnessed, the coachman cracked his whip. Each traveller hurried to the stage. Thus we left the dancing party, and entered Boston on the following day.

CHAPTER X.

He who hath loved not, here would learn that love,
And make his heart a spirit; he who knows
That tender mystery, will love the more,
For this is Love's recess. BYRON.

No city in North America has more beautiful environs than Boston. One fancies himself actually brought back to garden-like England. Nature has no doubt vastly contributed her share; but the inhabitants of the city have also taken an active part in embellishing these beautiful, and in many places romantic, situations. The surrounding country is every where hilly and covered with wood. Cottages are seen in every direction, giving them at once a rural appearance. Woods, formerly wild, are now converted into parks, and so contiguous that the visiter may walk from one to another without perceiving that they are divided. Many of these country-seats resemble a terrestrial paradise. Those in particular situate on the still, elysian lake, Jamaica Pond, are the finest I have seen in the New World. The lake itself is not very extensive; but its banks, its waters, possess something of so enchanting a character, that no stranger has yet been able to contemplate either without rapture. Surely, yes, surely, its former inhabitants, the Indians, must have fancied this the spot of some great Spirit: numberless times must they have kneeled down on the grassy banks and worshipped Him who lived near this abode. "He who hath loved not," says Childe Harold's immortal bard, "here would learn that love; he who knows that tender mystery will love the more, for this is Love's recess." This idea may very properly be applied to Jamaica Pond.

I one day visited the new cemetery, planned in imitation of that of Père la Chaise at Paris, distant about four miles from Boston. It is but lately commenced, but shows already what it is likely to be. Situated on Mount Auburn, an eminence of which it bears the name, this cemetery offers to the view a variety of objects seldom witnessed in similar places. Hence may be seen hills and dales, rivulets and fields, intersected with roads and pathways, named like the streets in a city. And, in fact, why should they not be so named? What is a cemetery but a town of the dead?

It neither wants buildings nor inhabitants: the latter are there—but silent. Each step we advance in this receptacle of the departed reminds us of our equals, slumbering in repose in their silent dwellings. Above their quarters we see names written in gold. Is there no intercourse between those who inhabit this mortal city? Silence itself!—is it not a painful language? Look at these weeping willows, these cypresses—what do they not announce? And this flower, but lately planted, spreading its fragrance through the air, this rattling and crystal-like stream, this plaintive tone of a solitary bird—is not all this a language that speaks to the heart? Death inspires here no dread: on the contrary, a glance at this beautiful cemetery almost excites a wish to die.

From the extremity of this eminence, Boston may be seen enveloped, as it were, in a dark fog. Neither bustle nor noise is perceptible. Here stands man alone in the presence of his Creator and his conscience. Above, nothing impedes the sight of the beautiful blue sky; beneath repose a world of equals. His eye is raised above the earth, and his thoughts are directed to regions where no looks have yet been able to penetrate. His breast, hitherto filled with worldly passions, now heaves with sublime and holy feelings. The inscription, in bronze characters, at the entrance of this burying-ground, further reminds him that he must himself return to dust. His own shadow indicates his insignificance in the great universe. The whitened bones scattered over the ground tell him to what he also must come. But he is not deterred : his reliance above is strenghtened. In the depth of his contemplations he fancies Religion whispering to his beating heart in the echo of the breeze, or in the thrilling note of the bird. He breathes, he fancies, a freer air; he forgets that he is still a wanderer on the earth. But, in the midst of these meditations, the sun is slowly returning; his lengthened shades melt in the mysterious twilight; the darkness of night covers with her mantle cities and fields; trees are motionless; flowers bend their sleepy heads; birds seek their nests; the serpentine pathways are illumined by millions of stars emblazoning the firmament; close to the Mausoleum of Genius* the evening star is seen in all her splendour.

* Miss Hannah Adams, authoress of several highly esteemed historical works. This lady was the first person buried at Mount Auburn. She died in December, 1831.

Approaching night soon forced me to leave this receptacle of the dead. Often did I renew my visit, and was each time more delighted with the spot. It would have been impossible for the inhabitants of Boston to select a more suitable situation for a cemetery.

It was on the 29th of August that lectures recommenced at the University of Cambridge, distant about three miles from Boston. This is the oldest and richest academy in the United States. The buildings are of brick, without any pretension to architectural beauty, bearing rather a resemblance to old barracks. The library, as far as number of books is concerned, has not its equal in the country: the volumes are computed at forty thousand. There is also a collection of minerals, but it is rather insignificant. The number of students annually resorting to this place is about three hundred; they are at liberty to reside either in the houses allotted by the University, or may take lodgings in town. They pay twenty-five cents a-day for board, furnished by the institution. The usual age at the time of entering is about sixteen; it is then expected they should have some knowledge of Latin, Greek, arithmetic, geography, and history. Every one has the privilege of conforming to the creed he thinks best, so that it may be said there is no prevailing religion at this University. At the expiration of four years the academical course is supposed to be completed; the student is then examined, and obtains the title of "Bachelor of Arts." He now enters active life at twenty; and may, three years after, without undergoing any further examination, take the degree of "Master of Arts," as it is called. I was told, that thirty years ago the number of students at this Academy was the same as it is now. This appears rather strange, considering the increase of population since that period; but it was explained to me in the following manner:—1st. In former times Cambridge was the only University in the country, whereas, now there are several others, among which is one in Newhaven, attended by five hundred students. 2nd. An opinion is prevalent, that a boy who has been several years at school has received a sufficient education, and does not require any more; that, instead of letting him proceed at the age of sixteen to the University to perfect his studies, it is preferable that he should learn a profession for his future support.

The ceremonies usual at the opening of the Academy commenced, at ten o'clock in the morning, by a procession to church, attended by the president of the University, the governor of Massachusetts, the professors, students, and strangers, invited upon the occasion. The church was already filled with spectators, and the upper seats occupied by ladies. The ceremony commenced by a prayer; after which the president invited the students, graduated as "Bachelors of Art," to deliver speeches. These orations were some in English, some in Greek, some in Latin, and all extempore. Each speaker had selected his own subject. One of them treated of radicalism, in a speech nearly interminable. Generally speaking, these orations were couched in such lofty language, and so many metaphors were introduced, that no one but the speaker himself could understand a word. When those who aspired to the higher degree of "Master of Arts" had also gratified the audience with endless speeches, the president, with much pomp, delivered their diplomas to about sixty graduates. A prayer concluded the ceremony; and the procession returned in the same order to partake of a sumptuous dinner, prepared in different saloons. The whole company consisted of five hundred persons. Prayers were read before and after the repast; and at the end a psalm was sung. In the evening, the president received visits from all the individuals who had attended the ceremony, on which occasion both host and hostess displayed the utmost courtesy and attention in welcoming strangers.

At Quincy, a few miles from Boston, John Quincy Adams, formerly President of the United States, has taken up his residence *en retraite*. This veteran statesman quitted his office, as First Magistrate of the Republic, in the year 1828, and was replaced by General Jackson. He only occupied the Presidential Chair for a period of four years, or from 1824, having lost his re-election, in consequence, as was reported, of a secret alliance between him and Clay. The community, jealous of its privileges, cried aloud against the machinations of the Heir Adams, * as he was nick-named, whom they suspected had acted contrary to the spirit of the Constitution; and this objection was sufficient to raise the whole country against him.

* His father, John Adams, was the only one of the Presidents who had a son. Hence he was called heir to the Presidential Chair.

All eyes were now directed to the hero of New Orleans, ever distinguished as a zealous member of the democratic party, and whose military achievements had already attracted the attention of the public. By this means, Adams lost all hope of being able to follow the example of his predecessors, in occupying the Presidential Chair, for a period of two terms, or eight years. From this exalted situation, to which Europe begins to look with admiration, he descended to the seat of a private individual in the House of Representatives. He, who by his veto could formerly frustrate the wishes of a whole nation, now only has a single vote in the Second Chamber, and passes summers alone with his wife, in the very same house where his father, John Adams, the former President, lived and died. *

This place of residence has altogether the appearance of a common farm-house, situated near the high road, shaded only by a few venerable trees, which add to the antiquity and gloom of the spot. The furniture is all

* It is a remarkable circumstance that two Presidents, John Adams and James Munro, died on the anniversary of the Independence: the former on the 4th July, 1829—the latter on the 4th July, 1832.

old fashioned — the drawing-room, for instance, being of red damask; and the walls ornamented with portraits of ancestors dressed in a kind of petticoat, and with powdered wigs. Mr. Adams was from home when I paid my visit, so that I had no opportunity of remaining long in a place with which so many agreeable recollections are associated. I met him, however, a short distance from his residence. The former President and Magistrate in the New World was seen walking with a knife in his hand, cutting willow-briars to make a stick! He is a man between sixty and seventy, but looks much younger. He is far from being tall; but has a fine open countenance, indicative of superior talents, which gains upon one by degrees. He recollected, with peculiar pleasure, Sweden, Stockholm, and many private individuals residing in that capital; and, on parting, left on my mind an impression of deep respect and veneration, which can never be effaced.

A few miles outside the Port of Boston is Nahant, a rock connected with the main land by a narrow promontory, where the inhabitants resort during the summer months, to avoid the oppressive heat. The waves of an agitated sea beat constantly against the foot of this rock, sending their white foam high in the air, rendering the rugged sides continually damp. The musical sounds of retiring waves are as pleasing to a townsman as the sight of the manifold sails which cover the surface of the sea. But it is more with the view of inhaling fresh air that this spot is frequented. The first time I visited it, I found all the houses occupied by people who said they required to breathe a freer air than the city could afford.

Nahant is, in my opinion, rather an unpleasant place. A calm day is a rare occurrence: the wind is so sharp and piercing, that one fancies himself under a European sky in November. A few miserable trees, scarcely deserving the name, are all that can grow on these rocks; and they are likely to remain in their present immature state for centuries to come. Among the natural curiosities shown to strangers, is a crevice in a rock called "the Swallows' Cave," represented in the "Northern Traveller" as a phenomenon. I am far from being of the same opinion as the author of this publication, though the cave may possess interest with some visiters. *Chacan a son goût.*

In the evening a ball was given in the hotel. Dancing consisted almost exclusively of quadrilles, here called "Cotillions." Waltzing had but lately been introduced in society, in spite of strenuous opposition on the part of elderly ladies. At intervals it was resorted to in the course of the evening, but subject to many restrictions and exceptions. A young lady, for instance, would by no means consent to waltz with a gentleman whom she did not previously know; and many a prudent mother gave strong injunctions to her daughter not to permit the cavalier to approach nearer than a certain distance. But a practice which surprised me more than any other was, that one of the musicians attached to the band constantly called out to the dancers the different figures they were to go through. The individual selected upon this occasion was a true original. His under-lip appeared perfectly unconnected with the upper one: his eyes seemed to suffer from the light, for he seldom or ever opened them. The instrument on which he performed was a broken violin; and he often beat time so loud with one foot, that the music was drowned by the noise. His features remained all the time unchanged, something like those of an Indian witnessing the representation of a tragedy for the first time. Without taking any notice of what passed around him, he called out as loud as he could, in a hoarse and shrill voice: "Advance!" "Retreat!" "Ladies' chain!" "Gentlemen's chain!" "Sideways!" and so on; until a double and long cadence announced to the company that the dance was at an end.

Report stated, that, not far from Nahant, a sea-monster had been seen. A number of persons positively asserted in the newspapers that they had, with their own eyes, seen the back of this stranger a considerable distance above the surface of the sea, enjoying the benefit of a sunny day. Guessings and calculations as to the nature of the monster were to be expected from a people ever anxious that every thing should be as clear as the sun at noonday. After much discussion, it was finally settled, that the animal could be nothing else but a sea-serpent. Incontrovertible proofs were adduced in support of this conclusion, and woe to him who ventured to question the existence of the animal! Some bold and incredulous individual hazarded, it is true, an assertion, that the pretended sea-serpent was nothing but a shoal of porpoises;

but this doctrine was soon overruled: and at present the fact of a sea-serpent having been seen in the neighbourhood of Boston is as well established in the minds of every one, as that mankind and animals in our days are only pigmies in comparison with the giants and mammoths of former times.

At Brighton, a small hamlet three miles from Boston, a cattle-fair is held every year in the month of October: it is renowned all over America. Cattle is sent to this place from the remotest parts of the country; I even remember having heard that a large drove of horned cattle, belonging to Mr. Clay, came to Brighton, all the way from Kentucky. In one single day, sales have been effected of no less than the enormous quantity of seven thousand hogs, eleven thousand sheep, and five thousand horned cattle. The fair had not commenced when I visited Brighton, but I found stalls and inclosures in every direction prepared to receive the animals on their arrival.

On returning from this excursion, I was overtaken by one of the most awful storms I ever witnessed. It came on so suddenly, that no person was prepared for it. A tolerably large proportion of hats took their departure in the first onset, and the owners ran foul of each other in quest of their property, carried away by the violence of the wind. But what particularly attracted my attention was, that within five minutes the streets were filled with fragments of paper, sailing whichever way the eye turned, together with a variety of vegetables, pieces of linen, and other materials, entirely interrupting the view. I happened to mention this circumstance to one of the citizens of the place, and received the following remarkable answer: "No nation on earth," said he, "uses a hat for so many purposes as a Yankee: it serves him at once for a head-covering, a writing-desk, a larder, and a portmanteau. In it the merchant deposits patterns of various descriptions: the doctor uses it as an apothecary's-shop: the married man, returning from market, converts it into a depository for potatoes and other vegetables: to the traveller it serves as a knapsack. Nothing has been more severely censured among enlightened people than the reform lately introduced in the shape of hats. By the present fashion, it is next to impossible to put more in its inside than a pocket-handkerchief and a dozen of cigars. Should, unfortunately, the present form be still more curtailed, then there will be no enduring the caprice of fashion, and who knows but a dreadful revolution may be the consequence!"

That this picture is somewhat exaggerated, cannot well be denied, but entirely without foundation it certainly is not. A hat has unquestionably more offices to perform in these States than in any other country. To stuff it with newspapers, letters, and cigars, is of common occurrence. Can it then be wondered at if, when a sudden gust of wind dislodges it from the head, a shoal of imprisoned objects should seek to take advantage of their liberty?

It was in the middle of September that with much regret I quitted hospitable Boston, on my return to New York. I directed my course through Pawtucket and Providence. The former place has considerable cotton-factories, worked by water-power from the river Pawtucket, which runs through the town, and forms the boundary between the States of Massachusetts and Rhode Island. Providence is the capital of the latter State, and about one mile distant from the mouth of the river. The town was founded as far back as the year 1636, by a puritan clergyman of the name of Roger Williams, who, on account of his religious principles, had been exiled from Massachusetts. It was then called by the Indians Mooshausick, but changed by him to Providence, in commemoration of his wonderful escape from persecution. The town is mostly built of wood, but has a gay and lively appearance. The cotton-factories established in its vicinity have greatly contributed to its rise as a trading place. Blackstone's Canal, uniting Worcester and Providence, commences in the latter. Among the improvements, from which great results are expected, may be mentioned two railroads now constructing between Boston and Providence and Providence and Stonington, which, when finished, will considerably facilitate the communication between New York and Boston.

One of the finest and most comfortable steamboats in America, the President, was then lying at the wharf, ready to start for New York. I hastened on board, and shortly afterwards the wheels were put in motion. It was not long before the capital of Rhode Island disappeared from our view, and, with the rapidity of lightning, the President passed ships, headlands, and villages. A few miles from Newport, Mount Hope appeared in the distance, the last stronghold of the vanquished, but magnanimous, King Philip. No Indian was ever more dreaded by civilized man. A century and a half has now elapsed since this hero of Pokanoket fell a victim to his own race, but even to this day his name is respected; and the least object supposed to have been touched by him during his life-time is considered by every American as a valuable relic of antiquity. This extraordinary man, whose real name was Metacom, succeeded his brother in the government of the Wampanoags. The wrongs and grievances suffered by this brother, added to those which he had himself experienced from the English colonists, induced him to engage in a war, with the design of driving all the intruders from a country of which they had obtained possession only by cunning and violence.

Had this contest terminated as he expected, America would, perhaps, at this time, be inhabited by the Red men of the wood. The issue might, perhaps, have been less doubtful had not one of his followers defeated his plan by a premature explosion, and before he had had sufficient time to summon and concentrate his warriors and allies. From this time no smiles were seen on his face. But, though he soon perceived that the great enterprise he had formed was likely to be frustrated, yet he never lost that elevation of soul which distinguished him to the last moments of his life. Ever indefatigable and undaunted, he flew, armed with a tomahawk, from race to race, encouraging those whose firmness began to waver. By his exertions and energy, all the Indian nations occupying the territory between Maine and the River Connecticut, a distance of nearly two hundred miles, took up arms. Every where the name of King Philip was hailed, accompanied as it was by murder and flames.

But fraud and treason soon accomplished what open warfare could not effect. His own followers gave way to numbers; his nearest relations and friends forsook him; almost alone, he still defied the power of his adversaries, and, when least expected, rushed in among them like a lion springing from his den. He—the last offspring of a mighty race of chiefs—driven from the abode of his ancestors, without subjects, abandoned by allies, hunted like a deer, exposed to hunger and thirst, hardly venturing to lay down his royal head on a solitary rock in the forest, when a ball at last struck his heart—was still the same fierce hero who once commanded a victorious army of thousands of warriors. Philip fell as a traitor, and his head was carried round the country in triumph; but posterity has done him justice. Patriotism was his only crime, and his death was that of a hero.

Without stopping at Newport, another fashionable watering-place, I continued my journey to New York. A short distance from Newport, our steamer was obliged to stand out to sea for several hours, in order to double a point called Point Judith, before arriving at smooth water, between the banks of Rhode Island and Connecticut, on one side, and those of Long Island on the other. Here is the entrance to East River, one of the inlets to New York. In fine weather, this trip is extremely agreeable. Numberless church-steeples, villages, and country-seats, embellish the scene in rapid succession. Here and there, lighthouses are seen, and, at short intervals, steamers, apparently in a blaze. By the aid of a beautiful moon, we perceived countless sails ploughing the deep, whilst her dazzling light played on its surface.

Towards morning we approached a place, which, owing to its shallowness and rocky stiuation, is considered very dangerous by navigators. The celebrated Knickerbocker, in his History of New York, affirms that the Devil himself had been seen in that neighbourhood, sitting on the back of a hog, playing the violin; and that he fried fish to announce the approach of a storm: in consequence of which, the Dutch Governor of New Amsterdam called this pass Hell Gate, which name it still bears.

The steamer, however, fearlessly pushed through the narrow passage, and successfully repulsed the waves that opposed her progress. High rose the sea, but she pursued her way, and steered not an inch from her course. It was then high tide, it is true; but, on several subsequent occasions, when passing the same way, I never perceived that the whirlpool at Hell Gate had any particular effect on the speed of the vessel. It is not near so dangerous as that at Bingen, on the Rhine.

The President arrived at New York before any house was yet open, so that the passengers had the pleasure of perambulating the streets a few hours, until half-sleeping porters thought proper to leave their comfortable beds and admit the weary travellers.

CHAPTER XI.

Promote, then, as an object of primary importance, institutions for the general diffusion of knowledge.

WASHINGTON.

NEW YORK was now what it had formerly been. The cholera had subsided, and with it the dulness and panic it had occasioned. Broadway, as usual, was crowded with pedestrians and equestrians. Wall Street exhibited its regular quota of anxious men of business; brokers were seen fagging and bustling about, as if emerging from a vapour-bath. Numbers were flocking to the Banks, either to make deposits or to withdraw them. Pearl Street was literally blockaded by goods and carts. Every corner presented an auction of some kind or other. Omnibuses were racing in all directions. Around fruit-stalls were grouped amateurs of pineapples and melons, anxious to gratify their appetite, long checked by the presence of the cholera.

Dinners, balls, and suppers, were the order of the day; and it seemed as if people were determined to indemnify themselves for past privation by present enjoyment. Niblo's Garden and the theatres proved insufficient to hold the numbers that thronged to them. Lottery contractors availed themselves of the medium of the press to congratulate the public on the disappearance of the epidemic, and invited their customers, while yet fresh from the country, to make a speedy investment in the lucky wheel. *

Doctors' gigs — the only vehicles lately parading the streets — were now intermingled with carriages of every description; and their emaciated horses began to show life again. Apothecaries'-shops were deserted, whilst the dealers in rice smilingly calculated the large profits they had realized.

At one o'clock, P.M., it was hardly possible to get along in the most frequented streets,

* In no place have I seen so many Lottery Offices as in the City of New York. They are numberless in Broadway. Their puffing exceeds all belief. Each collector called heaven and earth to witness that he was the luckiest among his worthy colleagues. One of them went so far as to affirm, that he had paid prizes to a larger amount than would liquidate all the debts of bankrupts in the United States. This is carrying things a great length. The Legislature of New York has at last enacted a law, prohibiting all lotteries after the 1st January, 1834.

owing to the number of belles and dandies occupying the pavement. When three drew near, it was advisable to remain in the house; for, at this time, all the gold-making, light-footed, mercantile fraternity were seen hastening home; and it is at all times a dangerous experiment to obstruct the course of voracious stomachs and thinking heads. Who could have supposed that a city, deserted but a few short weeks before by nearly its whole population, and its trade reduced to a state of complete stagnation, could so soon have been resuscitated?

Opposite to New York, on Long Island, is a small town called Brooklyn, which, though only divided from it by the river, may be said to be a faubourg. Cleanliness is certainly not one of its characteristics: the streets are covered with mud, and it may be called the focus of Irishmen.

Part of the United States' Navy is stationed at one end of Brooklyn: it is less considerable than at Charlestown, but this station appears the more important of the two. Several men-of-war and frigates were laid up under covered buildings, and a few new ships of the latter description were ready to be launched. The quantity of naval stores was also considerable. It was here that the steam-frigate Fulton unfortunately exploded in 1829, by which accident many persons were killed.

The Americans have seven stations for their navy, viz. Portsmouth, Charlestown, New York, Philadelphia, Washington, Norfolk, Pensacola. The whole number of ships amounts to forty, seven of which are men-of-war, ten frigates, fifteen corvettes, and eight schooners. Of these, only twenty-one were laid up in 1832: the remainder were in commission in the Mediterranean, West Indies, South Seas, and Coast of Brazil. Five new ships and seven frigates were, about this period, on the stocks.

The United States' Navy is under the immediate direction of the Secretary of the Navy at Washington. The highest rank in the service is that of captain or commodore: the question of appointing admirals has been long agitated, but was not finally settled when I left America. Of captains there are about forty belonging to the service, and their pay, when on duty, is from two to three thousand dollars a year.

The American naval officers are in general perfect gentlemen. By being a great deal in active service, they have seen much of the world, and, on board their ships, or wherever they are met on shore, show a degree of tact and good breeding, which redounds much to their credit. Like all seamen, they are frank, liberal, and stanch in their friendships. I had frequent opportunities of associating with some of these officers during my residence in America, and still retain the highest respect for their merits, and gratitude for attentions almost lavished upon me. A foreigner is never considered a stranger among them. Their artless and upright manner of acting inspires confidence at once. Rudeness and pride do not exist among them, from the youngest officer to the commodore of a squadron. With such seamen, it is not surprising that the Navy of the United States gains daily more and more respect among other nations.

About fifteen miles on the other side of New York, in the State of New Jersey, is a small manufacturing place called Patterson. A railroad had been commenced, but was not yet half finished, so that I had to pass over an extremely rough road on my visit to this place. The town, with a population of eight thousand inhabitants, has within twenty years risen from nothing. Cotton goods are here manufactured. The factories, seventeen in number, contain thirty thousand looms, working two million pounds of raw cotton annually. There are besides several sail-cloth and nail-factories.

Patterson is situated near the River Passaic, by whose aid all the works are carried on, and which afterwards precipitates itself down a perpendicular rock seventy feet high. This cataract is not particularly distinguished for its mass of water or elevation, but merely for the picturesque beauty of the surrounding scenery. It is Trenton in miniature. The stream meanders slowly and half dormant between two banks covered with verdure, and expands its smooth and crystal surface over a clear rocky bottom, till it approaches an opening in the same rock. Through this opening rolls the whole mass of water, as if from a narrow path down a dark, and from above invisible, precipice. So near are the walls to each other in some places, that the water fills the whole channel. Above, a noise is heard proceeding from below, not unlike thunder at a distance. The spray envelops in an incessant vapour this slippery, and to weak nerves really frightful, precipice.

Report states that this spot was, a few

years ago, the theatre of a horrible catastrophe. A clergyman, dissatisfied with his wife, I cannot recollect exactly for what reason, pushed her down the precipice. When the water reaches the bottom of the pit, it rolls foaming and agitated a few hundred yards between the close rocks, beneath a feeble bridge thrown across the precipice by the hand of man: it then takes a sudden turn in nearly an opposite direction to its former course, and insensibly disappears between bushes and shrubberies, below which are seen the factories, that are put in motion by its agency.

In the month of October every year the city of New York has an exhibition of American manufactures, patronized by a society called the American Institute. Its avowed object, as the prospectus states, is to promote and encourage within the State of New York, as well as in other States, native industry in agriculture, commerce, manufactures, and mechanical arts; and to further improvements in all branches, by the distribution of rewards to those who make any such improvements, or excel in any of the said branches. The exhibition first took place in the year 1828, and has since been continued annually. The number of members amounts to three hundred: out of these, four presidents are chosen (one for each of the four branches) who award the prizes. Every American citizen has the privilege of sending goods of home manufacture to this exhibition. But, when the exhibition is over, the goods must be taken away by their owners.

It is to be regretted that the funds of this useful and excellent society do not permit purchases of the exhibited goods, independent of the prizes awarded, so that a regular collection might be made, which at all times would prove interesting. Upon the present plan, it is next to impossible to ascertain what progress has been made in the manufacturing of an article in the course of a twelvemonth; it requires the aid of a good memory to pass a correct opinion in this respect. I saw a great number of works in wood and iron, glass, woollens, and cotton goods, models, and machinery, all finished in a style and with a correctness reflecting the highest credit on the artisans, and proving the wonderful progress that the country has made: not having, however, seen any other exhibition, I cannot hazard an opinion which department in particular had made the most improvement within a year.

In one of my rambles through New York, I happened one day to approach a house, from the interior of which I heard a kind of soft noise. Curious to ascertain the cause, I entered. On stepping in, I found myself in the midst of one hundred and fifty black children, all of whom turned their large white eyes towards the stranger as he entered. It was a free-school for Negroes. The teacher, an uncommonly active and clever woman, managed this whole Negro flock very decidedly. The little rebellious urchins looked up to her with a confidence, which proved at once that she filled her situation with dignity, and that she was rather a tender mother than a severe instructress. Her look was sufficient to bring any little naughty girl to reason, and a word from her lips struck with awe numbers of noisy boys quarrelling about the space of a quarter of an inch on their forms. Gentle reproof was the only correction adopted by her. The children, educated free of expence, are instructed in reading, writing, arithmetic, geography, religion, and sewing. At sixteen or seventeen they leave the school, when some are put to the trades of masons, chimney-sweeps, carpenters, or smiths ; others again become seamen, cooks, and servants. The girls all go to service. To aspire to something higher in society is quite out of the question, although they are free-born citizens; and the law makes no distinction between a black and a white man in the filling of the most important offices. The prejudice, however, against their colour is so strong, that a white man would rather starve than accept a menial office under a black. To become masters of sloops or other vessels, or to be master in any profession, is therefore an impossibility. They have the privilege, since the year 1829, of voting in the State of New York ; but, even in this respect, they are treated rather with a stepmother's hand. To be eligible to vote, a Negro must possess an unincumbered property of two hundred and fifty dollars; whilst a white man, in the same State, is only required to be twenty-one years of age, and to have resided one year within its limits. To be worth two hundred and fifty dollars is not a trifle for a man doomed to toil in the lowest stations ; few Negroes are in consequence competent to vote. They are in fact very little better than slaves, although called free.

I counted about one hundred and fifty children in the school; but the instructress informed me that their number often exceeded two hundred. Any one may go or stay away, as he thinks proper: it is therefore difficult to ascertain the number of daily attendants.

This school is conducted on a system of its own, not unlike that of the Lancasterian. The children are kept in the strictest subordination, and the more advanced in knowledge teach those who are less so. This useful institution, as well as another of the same kind, is under the patronage of the "New York Manumission Society," which educates in this manner more than seven hundred children of the African race. The members of this laudable and benevolent association belong chiefly to the Society of Quakers, those real friends of mankind.

In the year 1832, there were, in the State of New York alone, nine thousand six hundred organized school districts, educating four hundred and ninety-four thousand nine hundred and fifty-nine children. Besides these, the same State counted fifty-five gymnasiums, intended to form teachers, and four universities: the former were attended by three thousand seven hundred students, the latter by more than five hundred. Further, in every village and town, private schools for children of both sexes are established, all numerously attended; and, if a calculation were made of the total number of young people receiving instruction within the State of New York, the result would be, at least, five hundred and fifty thousand, or about one to three and a half of the whole population. Since the year 1816, when the present system of education was first adopted, the number of school districts has increased from two thousand seven hundred and fifty-five, to nine thousand six hundred; and of school children from one hundred and forty thousand one hundred and six, to four hundred and ninety-four thousand nine hundred and fifty-nine; consequently, there is an accession in the course of sixteen years of the former, six thousand eight hundred and forty five; of the latter, three hundred and fifty-four thousand eight hundred and fifty-three. In the higher classes of learning, the following changes have occurred:—

In 1790, when the whole population of the State did not exceed three hundred and forty thousand one hundred and twenty, there were only one university and two gymnasiums, with about forty students in the former, and about one hundred and fifty in the latter. In 1810, when the population of the State amounted to nine hundred and fifty-nine thousand and forty-nine, there were two universities, and one medical university, and twenty-five gymnasiums, with two hundred and twenty students in the universities, and one thousand four hundred and ninety-five in the gymnasiums.

In 1830, when the population had risen to one million eight hundred and sixty-eight thousand and sixty-one, there were four universities, besides two medical universities, and fifty-five gymasiums. The number of students in the former amounted to five hundred and six; in the medical, to two hundred and seventy-six; and in the gymnasiums, to three thousand eight hundred and thirty-five.

The expences of public schools are defrayed by a school fund, raised by taxes and local contributions. The school fund was first collected from the citizens as far back as the year 1809, but did not accumulate to any degree of importance till 1816, from which period the commencement of the system of education may be dated. This school fund now possesses a capital of two millions of dollars, the interest of which, and the voluntary contributions of parents and guardians, together with a tax levied on every citizen, amounted in the year 1832 to one million four thousand and eighty-two dollars and forty cents. Of this sum, three hundred and forty thousand one hundred and seventy-nine and a half dollars were expended in fuel for the different schools, and in the purchase of books; and six hundred and sixty-three thousand nine hundred and two dollars and ninety-five cents in salaries to teachers. The whole amount of annual expenditure for the schools in the State of New York is made up in this way, that when the State has contributed its share, or, what amounts to the same thing, when the school fund has paid the interest accrued, the citizens are taxed to furnish an equal sum, and to build schools and provide fuel; whatever money is afterwards required to cover other expences is raised from the parents and guardians of the children. The State has thus only to pay one-tenth part of the charges: about three-tenths are raised by taxes, and the remaining six-tenths are defrayed by the children themselves.

I annex an important and interesting document, extracted from a periodical, published at Boston, under the title of "Annals of Education," showing not only the number of young people educated at Schools and Universities, but presenting a point of comparison between the school education in the United States and that in Europe, and also between the higher degree of education at Universities in America and other countries on this side of the Atlantic.

The State of New York stands foremost on the list of school children. It counts in the proportion of one to three and a half of the number of its inhabitants; the New England States one to five; Pennsylvania and New Jersey one to eight; Illinois one to thirteen; Kentucky one to twenty-one, and so on. By way of comparison, I may just mention, that Würtemberg has one to six; Bavaria and Prussia one to seven; Scotland one to ten; France one to seventeen and a half; Russia one to three hundred and sixty-seven!

But, if the United States take the lead with regard to school education, they are far from occupying the first place in academical instruction. Scotland has there the advantage. The Eastern States of America belong to the first class in this respect, and emulate Baden and Saxony. The Middle States are upon a level with Würtemberg, Sweden, Portugal, and the Low Countries. The Southern, again, are upon a par with Switzerland. Finally, the Western may be classed with Denmark, Naples, and Austria. The States lately peopled in the West are about equal to France and Ireland, and Russia leaves the latter at an awful distance.

UNITED STATES.				EUROPEAN COUNTRIES.			
	Number of Students.	Proportion to the Population.			Number of Students.	Proportion to the Population.	
Massachusetts	770	1	792	Scotland	3249	1	683
Connecticut	327	1	960	Baden	1399	1	816
New Hampshire	241	1	1118	Saxony	1360	1	1040
Vermont	186	1	1509	England	10549	1	1132
Maine	238	1	1611	Hanover	1203	1	1303
New Jersey	193	1	1661	Bavaria	2593	1	1312
South Carolina	325	1	1789	Tuscany	909	1	1402
Pennsylvania	688	1	1928	Spain	9867	1	1414
New York	986	1	1940	Prussia	6236	1	1470
Rhode Island	50	1	1944	Würtemberg	887	1	1731
Maryland	175	1	2554	Sweden & Norway	2687	1	1732
Virginia	457	1	2650	Portugal	1604	1	1879
Kentucky	249	1	2766	Low Countries	2998	1	1979
Georgia	173	1	2985	Sardinia	1722	1	2420
Mississipi	45	1	3040	Switzerland	767	1	2655
North Carolina	233	1	3170	Denmark	578	1	3342
Tennessee	211	1	3245	Naples & Sicily	2065	1	3590
Ohio	285	1	3290	Austria	8584	1	3760
Louisiana	46	1	3335	France	6196	1	5140
Delaware	23	1	3336	Ireland	1254	1	5767
Alabama	84	1	3634	Russia	3626	1	15455
Missouri	28	1	5003				
Indiana	65	1	5101				
Illinois	28	1	5624				

A statement like the preceding can never be expected to be so accurate as might be wished, containing only the number of those who study at public institutions. It is well known that many young people in Europe receive a highly finished education, without ever visiting these public places: this is equally the case in the United States, particularly among those who study the law. Another circumstance, which renders these calculations questionable is, that nothing is more common than to have the names of double the number of students that are actually present at the University inserted in the rolls. But, setting all these difficulties aside, I still believe that the above table is as near the mark as can possibly be expected.

A liberal form of government depends, in a great measure, on the enlightened state of the people: hence education, in the United States, is nearest the heart of every American citizen impressed with a love of his country. He dreads no dissolution of the Union, so long as the facility of learning keeps pace with the increase of population. He looks upon education of so much importance, that, if any individual in the community should happen to disregard that object, he thinks he deserves to be visited by such a variety of reverses as to make it incumbent on him, if not for the sake of the public good, at least from motives of self-interest, to give his children or pupils the first rudiments of a common education, such as writing, reading, and arithmetic.

Although this opinion seems pretty general in America, and all voices are loud in favour of the system of education, yet there still exists not only a great reluctance on the part of parents to send their children to schools, but also a real want of schools and teachers. To remedy the former evil, a Society, under the name of "American School Agents' Society," has been formed for sending agents in various directions into the interior, for the purpose of persuading parents and guardians of the utility of education and improving schools.

In the city of New York there is a Society exclusively occupied with this object. The want of schools and teachers is supplied by the indefatigable exertions of several religious sects; and in the mean time the end is partly accomplished by the existence of Sunday schools, where every charitable person may give instruction, and by which disinterested assistance thousands of children have been taught to read, write, &c.

According to authentic accounts, however, the number of children in America, deprived of the means of education, is about equal to that of the more fortunate who obtain it. More than one million is stated to be the number of the former. Of these, two hundred and fifty thousand are to be found in Pennsylvania, eighty thousand in the State of New York, (thirteen thousand alone in the City of New York). In Indiana, it is contended, there are twenty-two thousand children, and in Illinois twenty thousand, who cannot read; and nearly the same number of full grown persons in the same situation. New Jersey has eleven thousand five hundred children without any kind of education, and in Kentucky, in 1833, about one third of all children were in the same lamentable condition.* Here is a wide field for Philanthropy to exercise her love for mankind.

Invited to attend a meeting of the American Bible Society, which assembles every month, I had an opportunity of seeing and forming acquaintance with some of the best informed and most benevolent characters in New York.

* Annals of Education, September, 1833.

This Society, considered the most extensive in America, has nearly nine hundred auxiliary Societies, and was instituted in the year 1816. Its income amounted in 1832 to the considerable sum of eighty-four thousand nine hundred and thirty-five dollars and forty-eight cents, of which one half was received for the sale of Bibles and Testaments. The Society prints all its books at its own expence, and has seventeen printing-machines, worked by steam. The secretary attached to this institution assured me that one thousand Bibles might be printed in a single day if necessary. All these Bibles and Testaments are very neatly printed, and published in different forms, to suit all ages and all classes. A Bible in the English language may be obtained at from forty-five cents to one dollar fifteen cents; and the expence of a Testament in the same language is from nine cents to sixty cents. Besides these, the Society publishes Bibles and Testaments in English and Gaelic, and in the French, German, Dutch, Spanish, Irish, and Indian languages. A resolution was passed by this Society, in the course of 1832, appropriating the sum of thirty thousand dollars to printing and circulating the Holy Scriptures, not only among native Americans, but also among foreign nations. One third of this amount alone was set aside for the purpose of translating the Bible into the different Indian tongues spoken in the United States. Several parts of the New Testament are already translated and distributed among the Indians in the West; and it may be mentioned as a remarkable circumstance, that auxiliary Bible Societies have lately been formed among the Chickasaws and the Cherokee nations, which are making incredible progress. A translation of the Gospel of St. Matthew was then preparing for the last mentioned nation; and, when completed, an edition of three thousand copies was to be printed in a small place called New Echota. This Bible Society printed in the year 1832 a smaller quantity of Bibles and Testaments than usual, in consequence of the large stock on hand. It amounted to only ninety-one thousand one hundred and sixty-eight, which, added to those previously issued from the press, formed an aggregate of one million five hundred and thirty-three thousand six hundred and sixty-eight Bibles and Testaments, printed since the organization of the Society in 1816.

CHAPTER XII.

For modes of faith let graceless zealots fight;
His can't be wrong whose life is in the right:
In faith and hope the world will disagree,
But all mankind's concern is Charity.

POPE.

IT was towards the end of October that I bade adieu to New York, and set out upon my long intended journey to the South. My first visit was of course to Philadelphia. A steamer hurried me from New York to New Brunswick, in the State of New Jersey, in about four hours. From the latter place, all the passengers were conveyed in a number of stage-coaches over a plain and uniform country, and on a very indifferent road to Trenton, a distance of twenty-seven miles, in the course of five hours. To enumerate how often the drivers indulged in a drop of the "inviting liquid" is a task I could not undertake with any degree of accuracy; but that it was an event of frequent occurrence I can assert without fear of contradiction ; so much so, that the patience of the travellers was often put to the test. Prayers, threats, oaths, and blustering, were all in vain: the "knights of the whip" were insensible to remonstrance, or pretended to suffer under the influence of deafness. Three times the coaches were changed, and three times ten, at least, if I mistake not, the horses were watered, till at length we obtained a sight of the small town of Trenton, on the River Delaware.

It was early in the afternoon when we arrived; but, the steamboat having already taken her departure for Philadelphia, and the landlord of the hotel finding it in perfect accordance with his interest to keep the passengers over night, spared no pains to convince us that it was literally impossible to proceed any further that evening. For my part, I did not much object to remain till the following morning, although, to speak with the veracity of an historian, the prospects within doors were not altogether of the most promising character; but a young dandy from New York, one of the exquisites of Broadway, who had travelled in the same carriage over the rough road, made out a long list of grievances and objections as to the comforts and conveniences of the bed-room; and concluded a very eloquent appeal, by insisting on an immediate retreat from quarters absolutely irreconcileable with the ideas of a "perfumed and accomplished gentleman." So great was his perseverance, and so impressive were his oratorical powers, that a charitable coachman who happened to be present was at length induced to listen to a proposal, the tendency of which was to take us the same evening to Philadelphia. We took leave, in consequence, of our landlord, who was highly dissatisfied with the effect produced by the eloquence of the dandy.

It was midnight before we reached our place of destination. To find accommodation at such an unseasonable hour is a thing I have been taught by woful experience never to expect in America. Upon this occasion, I had to enjoy the benefit of a nocturnal drive through the streets of Philadelphia, from house to house, without a chance of success — alone, and unacquainted with the place — till daylight at length began to dawn upon me. An honest watchman (to the credit of the profession be it mentioned) at last took compassion on me, and indicated a house where I could at least, as he observed, get shelter for the night. But rest was out of the question. A creaking bed, a broken pane of glass, with a pair of inexpressibles filling the gap, and a confined atmosphere, formed the sum total of my comforts. Add to this, the size of the room, more suited for a dwarf than a full-grown person; and it is, after all, but an imperfect picture of my lonely lodging. By way of a substitute for a candle, a dismal lamp was handed to me, from which issued a smell so obnoxious to the spiders and rats (co-occupants with me of this cage) that these little animals were actually taken ill with it, and kept in constant motion till the sun at length broke in upon them. To lie down in such a place, when exhausted with fatigue, is easily done; but the waking in the morning inspires reflexions of a serious stamp. A glance at the scattered objects around is enough to banish the inmate. I lost no time, as may be supposed, in taking leave of my comfortless quarters, and removed to Head's Hotel, the best, without exception, in the United States.

Philadelphia is, if I may be allowed the expression, a coquettish city. Like a young and agreeable lady, she takes peculiar care of her exterior appearance, endeavouring to please all. Every object appears as clean and bright as if a personage of note were expected. The exterior walls of the houses are washed and scoured; as to the streets, they are proverbially clean. Every thing announces wealth and comfort. There is certainly nothing extraordinarily grand; but on the other hand nothing mean. No palaces are observed; but, again, no wretched dwellings. Here the real and true republicanism is exemplified: it is as distant from democracy as from aristocracy. The inhabitant himself, the easy, though not purse-proud Quaker, bears the stamp of it. The only possible fault that might be advanced against the aspect of this city is its uniformity and sameness. This is perhaps fatiguing to eyes accustomed to the crooked streets of Amsterdam and Hamburg; but the latter are again as disagreeable to him who resides in the parallel streets of Berlin or Philadelphia.

The city is situated on a narrow stripe of land between the Rivers Delaware and Schuylkill, and built in squares. The streets are either in a line with the rivers, or at right angles with them: the former are numbered 1st, 2nd, 3rd street, and so on; the latter, again, bear the name of trees, such as chesnut, walnut, &c. The city is least inhabited on the Schuylkill side ; but, from the gradual increase of population, it may be inferred that this part will be also built upon in a few years.

It cannot, with propriety, be said that Philadelphia is a great commercial city. She has, it is true, both foreign and inland trade ; but the vicinity of New York is a great obstacle to her aggrandizement. A large proportion of her business with Europe is transacted through the medium of New York ; and, in spite of all efforts, she cannot possibly cope with her too powerful rival. The locality of Philadelphia is an insurmountable impediment in this emulation : both rivers are closed by ice during the winter months, rendering access impossible ; whereas, the entrance to New York is open the whole year round. The Delaware is particularly adapted for navigation ; it is navigable about thirty miles above Philadelphia. The Schuylkill is chiefly used for the transport of large quantities of coal, forming one of the principal branches of commerce in the State. This coal is extracted from extensive mines in the upper part of the country, which yield very abundantly, and it is obtained without much difficulty. It is very hard in its composition, and ignites very slowly. It is a common practice to mix it with Liverpool coal, and the heat is then great. The price is much lower than that of Liverpool coal.

But, if Philadelphia cannot boast of an extensive trade, she may justly be proud of the literary talents she possesses, and of her public and benevolent institutions. No city in the Union, not even excepting Boston, can venture upon a comparison. The American Philosophical Society, and the American Historical Society, are two learned academies, counting among their members men in all parts of the world, and ranking highest on the list of all literary institutions in the United States. The first owed its origin to the indefatigable exertions of Franklin, and has subsequently ranked among its presidents men of the highest standing in literature and knowledge. The actual president is the well-known and venerable patriarch, Mr. Duponceau, who, at the age of eighty, has not yet given up the occupation of writing, or of promoting the welfare of the Society. In the prosecution of this object he has a powerful assistant in Mr. Vaughan, another gentleman of eighty, whose urbanity and attention to every foreigner visiting Philadelphia has been the theme of universal panegyric.

It was by this respectable individual I was one evening introduced to the "Wistar Parties," as they are called, meetings which are held every week at the residence of one of its members. Here both scientific and literary men meet; every one, in fact, that Philadelphia contains, laying claim to genius or talent.

The intention of these *réunions* is to bring together individuals of different occupations, from which, no doubt, there results much good. It is only to be wished that, with a view to accomplish the object, the members would assemble a little earlier in the evening, and not convert useful meetings into fashionable *soirées*, commencing about midnight. The evening is spent in conversation on different topics, embracing both the productions of the literary world, the latest inventions, and the politics of the day.

Among public benevolent institutions, the Sunday School Association, the Pennsylvania Hospital, and the House of Refuge, may be particularly mentioned.

The usefulness of Sunday schools is no longer questionable with those whose thoughts have been seriously occupied with the plan of education in America. Philadelphia is their head-quarters. The Sunday School Association there established is not only connected with all the other associations of the same kind, but prints, on its own account, a number of useful books on religious subjects, adapted for children, in which particular care is taken to exclude every thing that might appear unpalatable to the different sects in the country. A Methodist may therefore make use of them, as well as a Baptist or a Unitarian. By the sale of these books the Association nearly defrays its own expences: each member pays, besides, a trifling sum, sufficient to make up any little difference that might arise. Any well-known respectable person disposed to sacrifice a few hours on a Sunday to the instruction of the school is at liberty to do so. It is a voluntary choice, without any kind of remuneration.

The Pennsylvania Hospital, instituted in the year 1751, by voluntary subscriptions among the citizens, was originally intended as a receptacle for unfortunate lunatics, and those afflicted with any disease not contagious. It was opened to the public in the year 1752; from that period to 1832, no fewer than twenty-nine thousand six hundred and sixteen patients have been received and taken care of, of whom fifteen thousand two hundred and ninety-three were so destitute that they had no means of paying; and fourteen thousand three hundred and twenty-three contributed towards the expence. Of this number eighteen thousand four hundred were completely restored to health, and three thousand one hundred and eighty-eight died in the hospital. The number of lunatics, during the same period of eighty years, amounted to three thousand seven hundred and eighteen, of whom five hundred and thirty died at an advanced age or from accidental disease, and one thousand two hundred and eighty-nine were cured. At the moment I write, there are about two hundred and forty patients, more than one half of whom are insane; these are treated with a tenderness and mildness, which cannot be too much commended.

The Quakers, who have always taken an active part in the direction of this institution, have invariably recommended a mild treatment towards the unfortunate beings suffering under mental aberration; and this humane system has now been pursued for the last thirty years. Here, as well as in the prisons, the superintending officers are strictly enjoined to treat the individuals under their care as parents would their children. Not only must they abstain from every thing bordering on cruelty, but they are expected to speak in a friendly manner, to reason with them on the real cause of their malady, to inspire confidence by salutary advice, and, finally, to try to prove to them that the present mode of treatment will lead to their perfect recovery. That this mild method actually exists in this lunatic asylum cannot be doubted; for in no madhouse—and I have visited a great many in the course of my travels in Europe—have I seen insane persons so quiet and calm as in this. I could no where discover the appearance of chains; and yet it was contended that no danger was to be apprehended from the raving of those labouring under what is called *mania a potu*, or *delirium tremens*, the highest stage of insanity. Experience has proved, that occupation or labour produces a salutary effect on those not arrived at this degree of mental alienation, and is, in addition to a mild treatment, unquestionably the safest and speediest remedy for this dreadful malady.

"Where recovery is possible," says the printed description of this Hospital, "it is effected by labour; and, where it is nearly hopeless, labour gives at least a sound sleep and general composure, seldom found in the indolent lunatic." The men are employed in weaving, wood-cutting, and so on: the women sew, spin, knit, &c. Books and newspapers are given to those disposed to read. Even music is encouraged among them; and the visiter is not unfrequently struck with surprise, on hearing the sound of flutes and pianos in these, of all on earth, least harmonious corridors. But the most incredible part of all is the introduction of the game of chess among the insane. It borders almost on madness to assert, that a person, suffering under an alienation of mind, can possibly sit down to a similar game, and, left to himself, form plans of attack and defence. More rational is it to suppose that a being so circumstanced would be the last for whom the game of chess could be a pastime. None requires more attention, more reflection, and yet numbers of lunatics are seen playing at chess!

The building, however, is rather too small and confined for the purpose; and many inconveniences, I was told, were incurred daily, in consequence of the insane being under the same roof with those afflicted by other diseases. The repeated fits of laughter and noise of the former continually disturbed the latter, who required unbroken rest. But, independently of this, the proximity had in reality a baneful effect on the physical recovery of the sick. The mirth or laughter of a maniac is at all times awful, and dejects the strongest mind; but, when it is within the hearing of an invalid, it makes a still deeper impression, for his mind is already dejected, and this additional pressure renders him still more miserable, and may eventually check a perfect recovery. It ought, therefore, to be a subject of serious attention with the benevolent inhabitants of Philadelphia to build a separate asylum for lunatics, and appropriate the Pennsylvania Hospital exclusively to bodily diseases.

In the middle of the square of this Hospital is a bronze statue in honour of the immortal Quaker, William Penn. The pedestal is of white marble. Penn is attired in the same costume that he used to wear in his life-time; the square-cut coat, long waistcoat, and cocked hat, have always a peculiar appearance, and particularly so when copied in bronze or marble. His features are in perfect harmony with the character which he displayed. Every time I took a view of this statue I fancied that I recognized more and more the friendly Quaker, landing on the shores of the Delaware, and bargaining with the Indians for that very piece of land now bearing his name. He holds the conventional document in his hand—a memorable epitaph of Penn.

In a separate building, not far from the Hospital, may be seen one of West's most admired paintings, representing the Redeemer healing the Sick in the Temple. The artist made a present of this picture to the Hospital, in consideration of his being a native of Pennsylvania. It was impossible to make a more appropriate and handsome donation: its exhibition insures an annual income of four hundred dollars, and has, since its first exposure to the public, yielded an aggregate sum of twenty thousand dollars; in truth, no trifling gift, still increasing in value every year! The picture is of great size, and all the figures are as large as life. Several groups are admirable, particularly those in the foreground. The principal characters, however, are here, as in every one of West's paintings, handsome, but without expression.

The House of Refuge, as it is called, is one of the most useful and benevolent institutions in later times. Prison-reports of various countries relate with horror the very lamentable consequences which have resulted from indiscriminate intercourse between young offenders and those whose whole career has been a series of crime. Levity may, in the first instance, have prompted the former to the commission of petty offences: by daily associating with the latter, and listening to their counsels, they become initiated, and crime insensibly loses its blackness. They now learn things of which they were before ignorant, and are led from step to step, till murder at last crowns the work, and the scaffold ends a wretched life.

To prevent the contamination of the young by old and experienced delinquents, Houses of Refuge have very properly been instituted. They are neither prisons nor schools, but partake a little of both. Children of either sex, who have committed and been convicted of offences, are not only received here, but even those who, through misfortune, the influence of demoralizing example, or the negligence of parents, are found strolling about town and country, ready to perpetrate any criminal act for which opportunity may present itself. The objects are, therefore, two-fold — to punish those who have already been guilty of crimes, and to guard against the commission of more. Punishment is, however, not the main intention. The infliction of stripes is only a temporary remedy, leaving hardly any impression on the unfortunate being to whom they are applied. Education and reform are the real object of the House of Refuge.

It was in the city of New York, as far back as the year 1825, that the first institution of this kind was attempted. Philadelphia followed the example three years subsequently. Citizens, whose feelings were alive to the sufferings of unfortunate children, united, and formed a society, which built at its own expence the present House of Refuge. The State sanctioned this charitable institution, and enacted a law, setting forth that all convicted delinquents, who were minors, should be sent, not to prison, but to the House of Refuge. But, although the State has given this private undertaking the form of a public institution, yet it possesses no control over its affairs. It is under the direction of the people; and that the management in such hands tends materially to its prosperity is proved by the flourishing situation of several institutions similarly circumstanced, and by their beneficial effect on young people.

When a child is sent hither by a Judge, no time is fixed for the duration of the detention: how, in fact, could this be done? It is not within the sphere of man to decide beforehand what period is required for the proper and suitable education of a child. It depends entirely on the difference of dispositions. The managers of the institution are the best judges when liberty ought to be restored: and they have, in consequence, authority, if a liberated child does not answer the anticipation entertained of its moral improvement, to take it back again. But this guardianship ceases altogether as soon as the individual becomes of age: if then detected in any criminal act, it is handed over to the prisons.

On entering this school of reform, the child is informed of the rules which must be observed, and the two following simple maxims are deeply impressed upon his mind: Never tell a falsehood—Do the best you can. The name is then entered in a book, and the child is introduced into the first class. In fifteen hours of the twenty four, he is instructed in various things, attends to work, &c. Four hours are allotted to school, and eight to the pursuit of some profession — for example, shoemaking, carpenters' work, tailoring, and so on. For each meal he is allowed half an hour, and the remaining hours are devoted to rest. A short time is granted for recreation and gymnastic exercises. The children have separate bedrooms, and are thus cut off from all communication, which might lead to demoralizing consequences.

The children are divided into classes, according to their behaviour and advancement in knowledge. Promotion or degradation is considered sufficient to maintain discipline. The rewards are suitable for children, and flatter their vanity, while they encourage a continuance of good conduct. A premium, to which great value appears to be attached, is the appointment of monitor, whose duty it is not only to superintend the other children, but to attend to their personal cleanliness and that of the rooms. Punishment consists in being degraded from the higher to the lower class, privation of recreation, solitary confinement in the day-time, curtailment of food, and, finally, in case of great extremity, whipping. Every evening, the children are summoned before the manager, to give an account of their conduct in the course of the day. The result of the investigation is entered in a book kept for that purpose, where each child has an account current. At the end of the week the balance is struck, and if the credit-side (speaking in the language of an experienced bookkeeper) be in favour of the child, he is rewarded with books, paper, pocket-handkerchiefs, &c.; if, on the other hand, he happens to be debtor, degradation follows, and loss of supper on Sunday evening, or something to that effect. Upon some occasions, the children are even allowed to sit in judgment on those who have committed an irregularity. Twelve jurymen are then appointed, and deliver their verdict with a solemnity proportionate to the gravity of the offence, and the sentence is immediately carried into effect.

When the child recovers his liberty, the manager always takes care to obtain for him some employment, either as servant, apprentice, or agriculturist. A residence in town is avoided as much as possible. On leaving the institution, he receives, as a present, a Bible, together with written advice how to behave in future.

That this system produces incalculable benefit cannot be denied. According to reports made of the behaviour of the children after regaining their liberty, I find that about two-thirds conduct themselves reputably. With such results before me, I cannot help admiring a plan, which not only corrects faults and dangerous propensities, but inculcates, at the same time, a taste for regularity, industry, and propriety; which gives useful knowledge, and enables the child subsequently to support himself in the path of virtue.

I was, however, informed that to reform children after the age of sixteen is a task of great difficulty. Theft is the prevailing offence among boys sent to the House of Refuge, and immorality that of the girls; these two crimes, it appears, leave the least hope of amelioration. Yet daily experience shows that it is not impossible.

The House of Refuge at Philadelphia cost originally about sixty-five thousand two hundred and thirty dollars; and the yearly expences amount to twelve thousand, including salaries to officers and superintendents. The amount of the children's labour is only two thousand dollars; the difference of ten thousand being made up by the institution. The yearly deficit is owing to the children not being kept continually at work, as practised in prisons ; but this is, after all, a minor consideration, if the great object is attained. The ten thousand dollars are richly repaid by the redemption of fifty children—reclaimed, and changed into useful members of society.

Besides the institution here alluded to, I ought not to lose sight of several others equally benevolent, all of which I was fortunate enough to visit during my residence in Philadelphia. To enter into a detail of them all would exceed my limits ; and being, moreover, nearly upon the same plan as similar institutions in Europe, with which the public is acquainted, it is unnecessary to refer to them further than by mentioning their names. At the head of the list I will place The Widows' Asylum. This excellent and well supported institution is followed by The Orphans' Institution, Deaf and Dumb Asylum, Magdalen Institution, Asylum for the Blind, Naval Asylum, &c.

No city in the Union has such beautiful Banks as Philadelphia. The United States' Bank, generally called the Mother Bank, is an edifice of fine effect, situated in one of the principal streets in the city. The architectural part is copied from the Parthenon at

Athens. The portico is of marble; and the pillars of the Doric order. The interior, however, is not in harmony with the exterior. There, every thing appears rather heavy, mean, and less pleasing to the eye, probably to serve as a contrast to the exterior, which partakes, at least, of the classic, if it is not altogether faultless. The Pennsylvania Bank is another building shown to every stranger. It is much smaller, does not strike the eye so much as the former, but has unquestionably a neater and more suitable appearance. The façade of this Bank, as well as that of the late Mr. Girard, is of white marble, without any pretension to Italian architecture.

The new Mint was not yet finished when I visited Philadelphia; but a fugitive glance convinced me that it will be upon a grand scale, combining taste and convenience. This is the only city in the Union where coin is struck.

In a long gallery, called The Arcade, is Peale's Museum. The contributors to this interesting collection count among their number many natives of the country, now no more. A great many objects of curiosity may be seen, particularly implements of the Indians settled on the western shores of the Mississippi. But what attracts the particular attention of every visiter is the almost perfect skeleton of the mammoth, not long ago dug up in a distant part of Pennsylvania, at the expense of Mr. Peal. The few bones wanting to complete the whole frame are hardly perceptible, except upon close inspection. An elephant placed beside this gigantic animal appears as diminutive as a calf beside an elephant. The shape or figure is, however, not unlike the latter, although the dimensions of the bones and joints are three times the size.

The Indians have a singular tradition with regard to this animal, which deserves to be quoted: "About ten thousand months ago," it states, "it pleased the Great Spirit to drown in one day all living animals, with the exception of the mammoth, who, closely pressed by the rising waters, took refuge on the top of an elevated mountain. But the flood reached this retreat at last, when the animal began to scream so hideously, that the Spirit himself was frightened, and saved it from perdition. This is the reason why, of all gigantic animals which inhabited the earth before the Deluge, the mammoth is the only one of which any traces are left."

A few steps only from this Museum is the Statehouse, justly celebrated in the annals of American history, as being the place from which emanated the declaration of independence. This old building is of brick, still of its pristine colour, with two wings, distinguished only by a peculiar simplicity in the architecture. Age has given it rather a dismal appearance; but even this proved gratifying to my eyes, particularly when travelling in a country where every thing is new and fresh, and where antiquities are as scarce as young cities in Italy, sprung up from nothing. Historical recollections, moreover, attach to this building so much interest, that it is next to impossible to approach it without reverence. It was within its precincts that America shook off her fetters. Here it was, also, that the first impulse was given to the extraordinary revolution which ended in the total emancipation of the Colonies. It was here, in short, that a handful of bold patriots, by a stroke of the pen, risked the chance of an ignominious death as rebels, or the immortal glory of heroes of liberty. It was here that the signatures were affixed to an Act which has already had, and will for ages to come, have an immense influence on the destinies of the world.

CHAPTER XIII.

Narrow is thy dwelling now! dark the place of thine abode! With three steps I compass thy grave, O thou who wast so great before!

OSSIAN.

THE environs of Philadelphia are really of the most enchanting character, particularly those in the vicinity of the Schuylkill, whose romantic borders cannot but be highly admired. The country is intersected with villas vying with each other in beauty. To point out any one in particular would be doing injustice to all the rest. Two I visited, belonging to Messrs. Pratt and Borie, from which I enjoyed a most extensive and beautiful view of the Quaker City. To my great astonishment, however, I was told that these mansions are hardly ever inhabited. Every thing on earth is subject to some objection: even in the midst of the finest wheat, thistles will sometimes grow — so with the elysian shores of the Schuylkill. An unwholesome and fatal miasma rises invariably from this seducing stream, and woe to him who ventures to settle in its neighbourhood! A cadaverous look soon replaces the wholesome complexion, and health flies away in the midst of enjoyments of an enchanting nature! This lamentable circumstance reduces property in these parts to little or no value; the villas are compared to the prohibited fruit, the tasting of which entailed death. They appear like places lately visited by the plague, or neglected by owners too fond of a town residence. Each bower bore the stamp of desertion, and the footpaths were covered with grass. The works of man had a dead appearance in the midst of lively nature.

But Philadelphia's boast, that of which the inhabitants may justly be proud, is the waterworks at Fair Mount, which supply all parts of the city with abundance of excellent water, for the consumption of private houses, as well as for the cleansing of the streets, and for extinguishing fires whenever they happen. The eminence, called Fair Mount, lies close to the city, and rises from the banks of the Schuylkill. A place more suitable for this purpose could not have been selected. The stream is conducted through a dam to a kind of basin, near the foot of the eminence, where several large wheels are worked by the mass of water. These wheels, in turn, put in motion a number of pumps, the aggregate power of which is so great that, when all the wheels are going, a quantity of water, equal to seven millions of gallons, is raised in the course of twenty-four hours. Upon the eminence, the water is collected in reservoirs, containing nearly twelve millions of gallons. It is conducted hence to the city by means of pipes, which, like the veins in the human body, serpentine in various directions; it is at last brought to the houses, and circulates under the streets. By this excellent arrangement, plugs, placed purposely at regular distances, need only be opened, and all quarters are supplied. This simple aqueduct cost the city no less than one million seven hundred and eighty-three thousand dollars: the annual expence, which is proportionably trifling, is borne by every housekeeper, who has on the other hand the great convenience of water in every part of the house, even in the garret. In fine, nothing in or about Philadelphia deserves more to be seen than these water-works.

The new prison is also worthy of the attention of every stranger. I shall pass over any detail of this institution for the present, intending in a future chapter to treat more at large on this subject, pointing out the difference between the penitentiary system adopted here and that which goes under the name of the Auburn system.

Very often it occurred to me, during my travels through the United States, as a singular circumstance, that I hardly ever discovered any public monument in commemoration of Franklin. Statues, busts, and portraits, are everywhere seen of Washington — even the names of Lafayette and Kosciusko are not forgotten by grateful Americans. But Franklin, the great Franklin, has not received that tribute to which his memory is unquestionably entitled. In a dark corner of a smoky tavern in the country, or as a sign-post, his head may sometimes be seen suspended ; but this honour is any thing but enviable, particularly when it is taken into account that the likeness to the original is in general so questionable, that both painters and landlords are obliged to write beneath the ugly countenance in large gold letters : "This is Benjamin Franklin." — I expected to find in Philadelphia a variety of memorials relating to him: but even here the memory of this extraordinary man has been treated with a niggardly hand. His remains are interred in a churchyard in the middle of the city. I hastened thither, in full expectation of finding a splendid monument raised by the American nation. I saw only a flat stone over his grave, with this inscription:

BENJAMIN }
& } FRANKLIN.
DEBORAH }
1790.

This simple and unostentatious epitaph, although unexpected, leaves nevertheless a deeper impression on the mind than the most costly mausoleum would produce. The life of Franklin, like his marble, was without pretension. The name alone, Benjamin Franklin, is it not a speaking monument? He who was content with a frame-house during life-time was too great a man to court, after death, a marble tomb. As a private citizen, he returned to the same mother earth that witnessed his birth, and for whose prosperity he had lived. Near his silent grave now stand the children of his revolutionary brethren, watching its sanctity, as if it were the property of the whole nation. And such it is in fact. The dust which covers America's first and greatest philosopher undoubtedly belongs to the people. The simplicity of the grave is its greatest ornament. Woe to the hand that would destroy its effect by an attempt at splendour!

A portion of the United States' Navy is stationed at the southern extremity of Philadelphia. The largest man-of-war probably in the world is building here, and is justly shown as a prodigy. It is enclosed in a wooden shed, on the roof of which is a reservoir of water in the event of fire. When launched, she is intended to carry one hundred and forty-four guns, and will be named the Pennsylvania.

The President and Vice-President of the United States are, as it is well known, elected to their respective offices for a period of four years. In Pennsylvania, the election takes place in the following manner: four months before the duties of the office are entered upon, electors are chosen by the people, who afterwards vote. A similar day of election took place on the 2d of November in Philadelphia. The friends of the respective candidates, Jackson, Clay, and Wirt, had, during the preceding week, used every exertion to influence voters to avail themselves of their privilege. No pains had been spared, and no inducement neglected. In England, where I have likewise attended popular elections, the zeal of the friends of the candidates is certainly very great; but in America it is carried to a still higher pitch. Both old and young, poor and rich, men and women, feel such an intense interest in the issue of the contest, that the least result which an impartial foreigner can possibly expect is, the dissolution of the Union, effusion of blood, and civil war. Whichever way I turned, I heard the severest censure directed by one party against the other. In one place, appeared a number of Clay-men attacking and tearing down the hickory trees.* In another, a numerous and savage mob was seen dancing round similar trees erected in the streets, calling out — "Jackson for ever!" Not far off, a procession of anti-masons, to whose party the last-mentioned candidate belonged, was seen moving and laughing at their antagonists. In another group, were observed a number of the most

* A kind of walnut tree, distinguished for its toughness and durability. President Jackson went always among the lower classes by the name of Old Hickory. The reason is variously stated. Some pretend that he obtained this nickname after a victory gained at a place called "Hickory Ground." Others assert that the quality of the wood is applicable to his character. I cannot say which of these versions is the correct one.

influential politicians in the city, haranguing the people on the brilliant prospects of their cause, the certain defeat of their opponents, the matchless qualifications of their candidate, and the duplicity, vacillation, and deception, of the other two. It was evident, that the prevailing policy was to keep up party-spirit by holding forth encouragement, and to acquire new adherents, either by the propagation of false statements or by attempting to frighten the opponents.

The State of Pennsylvania is divided into certain districts, where elections take place on the same day. Philadelphia constitutes a district of itself. The city, however, is so extensive, that it is necessary to subdivide it into wards, to facilitate the elections. Commissioners from each ward assemble in the Statehouse at eight o'clock in the morning of the day appointed. Each of them had his own particular box placed near the avenue of trees fronting the house. The voters approached these boxes whenever they wished to give a vote, and delivered a printed card, on which the name of the electors was inscribed, and signed by the voter. It being understood that none except those who belong to the ward of which the box bears the name are allowed to vote, it may be supposed that the person who receives the vote must know the respective voters. But, if any doubt arises as to the eligibility of the party, the commissioner has the privilege of insisting upon his oath, and the production of receipts for paid taxes. Before the boxes thronged a number of people belonging to the three aspiring candidates, distinguished only by the different names on voting cards, and which were pasted on boards and carried about in the shape of flags. Some of these cards had the portraits of the candidates for the presidency; on others were written or printed eulogies of them. The conflict near the boxes was often attended with bloodshed, and several of the combatants were carried away from the field of battle wounded and disfigured. These fights continued the whole day uninterruptedly; and about ten o'clock at night the boxes were shut up, when a retreat was effected by the straggling party to other parts of the city. The uproar spread in every direction; yells and discordant sounds were heard in all parts; the arrival of an enemy, or of the plague, could not have caused a greater disturbance. I took a walk late in the evening to look at the different transparencies which each party had exhibited before their committee-rooms. An attack, perfectly organized, took place on one of these rooms, and the assault was only repulsed by the besieged after a most obstinate resistance, when about fifty wounded were left on the field of battle. These scenes did not end till morning.

On the following day, the inhabitants of the city were officially informed that the anti-Jackson party had a majority in Philadelphia of about one thousand nine hundred votes. Returns were also transmitted from different parts of the State in the course of this and the following day, showing the issue of the election; but, when all these were summed up at last, Jackson's party appeared to have the ascendency, and his election in Pennsylvania was consequently secured. This result, quite contrary to the wishes of the majority in Philadelphia, did not, however, create any disturbance among the party who but a few evenings before had displayed an almost revolutionary zeal in the cause, and actually shed blood to secure victory over the Jackson men. On the contrary, they heard the announcement of their defeat with a composure worthy of imitation; I observed even some, who had commanded at the late attack on the committee-room, laugh at the issue of the election. This singular circumstance was often adduced to me as the perfection of the electioneering system. A strong feature in its favour it undoubtedly is; but to say that the system is altogether perfect is an assertion by no means admitted by all enlightened citizens in America.

Does a country in reality derive any benefit from elections which leave an equal power in the hands of the rich and the poor? Is it reasonable, that an individual, whose interest it is to maintain order and peace in a State, who has every thing to lose and nothing to gain by convulsions, should have no more to say than the less fortunate, who only knows by reputation the candidate he is going to vote for? To answer this question in the manner I often heard borders in a great measure on chimera. I was told, for instance, that every citizen in the United States has more or less reason to vote in an independent way; the facility of gaining a livelihood being so great, that free men must of necessity take some interest in the tranquillity and prosperity of the country—that education is a sufficient guarantee against the influence of bribery and corruption. I certainly am not of this opinion, and have only to adduce, in support of my dissent, the result of the elections of late years. The Constitution may perhaps be literally the same as in the time of Washington; but democracy has recently made such extraordinary strides, that former apprehensions of aristocratical ascendency have now been converted into a dread of mob-rule.

At the Presidential Election in 1828, numberless Irish emigrants had great influence on its issue; in 1832 also the poorer classes determined the result. This progressive power among the lower masses is the more to be apprehended, as a corresponding and equally rapid accession among wealthy and enlightened citizens cannot possibly take place. What will be the consequence? If ever the beautiful republican ship should strike on a shoal, it would be at the period of a Presidential election.

No State has so democratic a Constitution as Pennsylvania. To be qualified to vote, it is only necessary to reside within the limits of the State, and pay a few taxes. I was told, but I am not quite sure if the statement be correct, that with a view to strengthen a certain party in the State, a number of people were engaged to settle within its territory, whose taxes were paid for them. Thus, a great many voters were secured, who at the subsequent election proved of essential service. This, however, does not apply to every State. In some, a residence of two years is required before the privilege of voting is granted. In others, again, it is necessary to be a resident only six months to become an eligible citizen.

Pennsylvania ranking as the second State in the Union with respect to population, and sending no fewer than twenty-six members to Congress, great importance is naturally attached by each party to obtaining her suffrages. No exertions, as it may be supposed, are left untried to secure this object, which, once attained, is adroitly used to influence the elections in other States. In the State of New York, the elections took place three days later than in Pennsylvania. To encourage their friends in New York to greater exertions, and to determine those who were yet vacillating the victorious party in, Pennsylvania sent off extraordinary messengers, who travelled with the rapidity of lightning. This prudent and deep-laid scheme had the desired effect. Both these principal and influential States declared in favour of General Jackson. The force of example operated on the minor ones, and the election was conclusive.

As a native of Sweden, the city of Philadelphia could not fail to inspire me with intense interest. History records that, during the reign of Gustavus Adolphus the Second, deservedly surnamed the Great, a colony of Swedes was sent out from the mother country, and settled on both banks of the Delaware. This part of the New World appeared to them so inviting and delightful, that they gave it the name of the Land of Canaan; and to the spot where they landed that of Paradise. How much is it not to be regretted that posterity, regardless of the past, should allow these elysian fields to be so completely neglected, and wrapped in the mantle of oblivion, that not a trace can now be discovered! The only thing now known of this terrestrial paradise on the shores of the Delaware is, that its situation was near Cape Henlopen, a short distance from the sea. The colonists purchased tracts of land of the Indians, occupants of these parts, and threw up a few fortifications, namely, Fort Christina,* Fort Elfsborg,† and New Gothenburg.‡

The Dutch, whose principal city was then New Amsterdam, (afterwards called New York,) pretended that the country round the Delaware belonged to them, having paid it a visit before the arrival of the Swedes: this insinuation, however, did not prevent the latter from settling; nor could this pretension be supported afterwards, for the Indians had totally destroyed all the fortifications erected by the Dutch, and murdered the garrisons. The Swedes now kept peaceable possession of the country, and passed their time, according to traditions on record, with little or no care. William Penn speaks of them thus: "They are a plain, strong, industrious people, yet have made no great progress in the culture or propagation of fruit trees, as if they desired rather to have enough than plenty or traffic. As they are people proper and strong of body, so they have fine children, and almost every house full; rare to find one of them without three or four boys, and as

* Of this fortification there is no trace. It was situated near Wilmington, twenty-seven miles south of Philadelphia.

† Fort Elfsborg was near Salem Creek, east of the Delaware.

‡ New Gothenburg, or Tinnicum, between Fort Christina and the present city of Philadelphia.

many girls; some six, seven, or eight sons. And I must do them the justice to say, I see few young men more sober and laborious."

It was in the year 1655 that this happy and contented little colony was attacked by the Dutch, conducted by Stuyvesant, who, in a sanguinary battle, eulogized by the immortal Knickerbocker,* vanquished his enemy, and obliged the colonists to submit to the Dutch authority. But this victory was of short duration; for, in the year 1664, both banks of the Delaware fell into the hands of the English, who became rulers of the Swedish emigrants. But the latter preserved, to the latest times, the customs and manners brought from Sweden, and continued to have, up to the year 1831,† Swedish clergymen residing among them. Their number amounted, in the year 1700, to about one thousand two hundred, all speaking the Swedish language: in another century this number had so sensibly diminished, that divine service was no more performed in the ancient mother tongue. Even the Lutheran religion ceased at length to be preached to the offspring of Swedish emi-

* Knickerbocker's History of New York, by Washington Irving.

† This year died in Philadelphia the last Swedish clergyman, the Rev. Doctor Nicholas Collin, loved and respected by both countrymen and strangers.

grants, being replaced by the doctrines of the English Protestant Church.

In the account transmitted to England in 1683, William Penn thus expresses himself: "The Dutch have a meeting-place for religious worship at Newcastle; and the Swedes three, one at Christina, one at Tinnicum, and one at Wicacoa, within half a mile of this town." The last mentioned church at Wicacoa,* which in Penn's time was only half a mile from Philadelphia, is now within the limits of the city. It is a simple brick building, not painted, something like a country church in Sweden, and erected in the beginning of the sixteenth century on the same spot where the former church stood. The inside is painted white, without ornaments. Above the altar is the pulpit, which, as well as the organ-loft, was covered with black when I visited it, as a token of respect to the memory of the Swedish pastor, who died in the preceding year. Some of the remains of former clergymen are interred beneath the altar, among which are those of Anders Rudman and John Dyllander, whose memories have been honoured by tablets. On the right side, near the wall, is a simple monument of marble, to the memory of

* An Indian name, signifying pleasant place.

Doctor Collin's wife: the husband also reposes beneath. In the pulpit and near the altar, I discovered several Bibles and psalters, printed in the Swedish language, during the reigns of Charles XII and Frederick I. None can vote in this church unless he can trace his origin to Sweden.

Behind the church is the cemetery, on examining which I found a great number of names unquestionably Swedish, such as Gestenberg, Swänson, Lungren, Robertson, Jonson, and so on; others again, evidently of Swedish extraction, although corrupted in America, as, for instance, Williamson, Meddermark, &c. Several families are still extant in Philadelphia, but they are so intermixed with others that no accurate statement as to their number can be obtained. They have completely adopted the customs of the country, and cannot even in their appearance be distinguished from native Americans. They delight, however, in conversing about Sweden —as if the love of country still ran in their veins—and never deny hospitality to any one who intimates that he comes from the land of which the Swedish bard * thus speaks:

The rock yields steel, and heroes know to handle it.

* Esaias Tegner.

My stay at Philadelphia this time was very short: winter approached with rapid strides, and the journey I had in view was pretty long, and required a considerable portion of time. A steamboat transported me from the friendly city: passing many tracts formerly belonging to the Swedish Colony, I also left behind, in the course of a few hours, Chester, (formerly called Upland); further on, Christiana; and arrived at Newcastle, (Fort Kasimir of old) from which a railroad has recently been made, running to Frenchtown, on the River Susquehanna. The banks of the Delaware, south of Philadelphia, are low and marshy; the soil is, however, productive, and yields rich crops. The railroad from Newcastle, though only sixteen miles in length, passes through two States, Delaware and Maryland, the former being, after Rhode Island, the smallest State in the Union: the population in 1830 was only seventy-six thousand seven hundred and thirty-nine. Delaware belongs to the number of States chiefly occupied with all kinds of manufactures; the communication has lately been greatly facilitated by the opening of canals, uniting the River Delaware with the Chesapeak.

The journey over the railroad did not take

more than seventy minutes. At Frenchtown I went again aboard an excellent steamboat, which brought me in five hours to Baltimore. The Susquehanna is the largest river in the Union: it takes its rise in the State of New York, and meanders in various directions partly through that State, partly through Pennsylvania, and partly through Maryland, till at length it empties itself into the Chesapeak, after travelling more than five hundred miles.

CHAPTER XIV.

> Such is the patriot's boast, where'er we roam,
> His first, best country ever is at home.
>
> GOLDSMITH.

BALTIMORE, in point of size, is the third city in the Union. It is situated on the River Patapsco, which discharges its waters into Chesapeak Bay. The inlet to the port is narrow, fortified by two projecting points of land opposite to each other, one of which, called Fort McHenry, is mounted with heavy cannon, to protect the city in case of necessity.

When our steamboat, with the rapidity of lightning, entered the harbour, amidst boats, steamers, and ships, and I saw the multitude of steeples, domes, and monuments, rising above the houses, in the form of an amphitheatre, I could not help expressing my admiration to a young American, close to me on deck.

"Every stranger is delighted with this place," answered he, "and I don't wonder at it. There is something so pleasing in the exterior of Baltimore at first sight, that it is impossible not to like it: the splendid public buildings, the beautiful churches, the interesting monuments, so gratifying to every American, the convenient and handsome private houses, have given to this city a name it richly deserves, and which none in this hemisphere, not even excepting Philadelphia, can dispute. It is known by the name of Monument Town. But, after all, these are not the principal attractions in Baltimore, those of which every citizen justly boasts. Hospitality, politeness, and unsophisticated manners, are the distinction to which the city lays claim."

This picture was, in truth, very correct. It is not the exterior beauty of the ornamental part of the buildings, or the regularity of the streets, that I now admire in Baltimore, after having visited and become better acquainted with it; it is the sociability, the free and easy manners, of the citizens, their extreme politeness to strangers, and the unostentatious information so generally diffused among them, which have left an indelible impression on my mind. I have never yet met a foreigner who, after visiting Baltimore, does not speak of it with rapture. But why repeat a fact so universally admitted? Who can feign ignorance of its attractions — of its amiable and beautiful women? Both have passed into a proverb in America, as well as in Europe, and are therefore nothing strange to those who may feel disposed to follow me in my proposed peregrinations.

Among buildings, justly deserving to be noticed, are the Cathedral, the Unitarian Church, and the Exchange. The first, in particular, the Roman Catholic Church, is the largest in the United States; the exterior is, unquestionably, the handsomest of all, the American Protestant churches being generally remarkable for their simplicity and bare white walls. A dome, with a skylight, gives to this church a most agreeable light; and Guerin's celebrated picture of Christ's Descent from the Cross, presented by Charles X., ex-King of France, and the many little chapels, always found in Catholic churches, together with the marble altar at the choir, and the ornaments, tapers, and flowers on the altar — all, in short, forms a singular contrast with the neighbouring Unitarian church, where the utmost simplicity prevails, and which is nevertheless as imposing to a true Christian as a temple decorated with paintings and images, lighted by a multitude of tapers, and filled with incense.

The monument of Washington, the only one of its kind worthy this great man, consists of a large marble column, with his statue on the summit. The pillar is one hundred and seventy-five feet high, twenty in diameter at the base, and fourteen at the top; the statue alone is fifteen feet high. The sides of this column are perfectly smooth, though the original intention was, I believe, to decorate it, in imitation of Trajan's column at Rome, with a bas-relief, representing scenes from the life of the American Cincinnatus. That this project was not carried into effect is universally regretted, and, I fear, it is no longer thought of. The monument, however, is on the most elevated and conspicuous part of the city, in Howard's Park, at the end of Charles Street, and offers the finest view of Baltimore, the river, and the country for several miles round.

Another monument also adorns this city. It is erected to the memory of those Americans who fell in the battle with the English before Baltimore in 1814. There is always something so interesting in the public expression of gratitude and respect for services rendered to the country, that even the most trifling monument seldom fails to excite a lively impression in all Americans. They retain, with feelings of gratitude and pride, the names of men who have, in a moment of peril, saved country, contemporaries, and an unknown posterity. Far be it, therefore, from me, like many other preceding travellers, to censure this monument as heavy and tasteless! Let it not be forgotten, that it was raised by surviving parents, children, relatives, and friends; it was not the united efforts of a nation. Whatever defects it may possess, they must vanish before the eyes of all spectators disposed to view it in this manner; and, if this piece of sculpture cannot be compared to many masterpieces with which Italy abounds, it answers at least its purpose perfectly well, and this, I believe, is the limit of its pretensions.

During my short stay in this city, a death occurred, which caused as much sensation and regret all over the United States, from Maine to Louisiana, as when a beloved and esteemed Monarch in Europe dies. Charles Carroll, of

Carrollton, the last surviving signer of the Act of Independence, on the 4th July, 1776, expired in the month of November, 1832.

The event was certainly not unexpected, as his age was nearly a century; but whoever had seen the aged man in later years, surrounded by a numerous family circle, in which he shone with so much lustre, and heard him speak of the State fabric, to the erection of which he had lent his aid, could not help venerating the aged patriot. He might be compared to a link between former times and the present. Although he did not fill any public station subsequently to the year 1801, yet he was not forgotten by his grateful countrymen, for whose liberty, independence, and prosperity, he staked life, property, and glory.

This circumstance alone, that he was the last of the bold revolutionists who separated the Colonies from the Mother Country, would have been sufficient to illustrate his name for ever. His star continued bright after all the others had set; and the rising generation looked up to it with an almost religious veneration.

Carroll's career was fertile in events: with delight, yes, I may add, with the fire of youth, he recalled to memory, but a few days preceding his demise, the many important epochs he had witnessed, and how, regardless of consequences, and only acting for the public good, he had hazarded his own immense estates, for the honour of being foremost in the ranks of those on whom the world then bestowed the epithet of rebels. His long career gave him, moreover, an opportunity of seeing his young country twice engaged in a sanguinary contest with the modern rulers of the ocean, and yet able, a few short years afterwards, to pay off the greater part of a considerable national debt.

Destiny, however, did not permit him to descend to the tomb before the dreadful voice of rebellion in South Carolina reached his ears. The flame of discord, always destructive to a republic, kindled before him when on his death-bed. Carroll trembled at the idea of witnessing the annihilation of Washington's magnificent work; from his pale lips parted a sincere prayer to Him, to whose bosom his affrighted spirit soon fled.

Thus died Carroll, he who, like a true virtuous Roman, answered a man, who rather sarcastically observed that, of all the signers of the Act of Independence, Carroll hazarded the least by the insurrectionary step against the lawful government, inasmuch as many persons in America bore the same name, and the English rulers, if victorious, would have had some difficulty in finding which Carroll it was: "Is it so?" said he: "then I will add another name to the one I already possess." And the sentence was hardly finished, before he wrote, in the important document, immediately after his name, the words: "of Carrollton," which addition has since been censured by people unacquainted with its origin, who have accused him of harbouring aristocratical notions under a republican exterior.

At his death, however, all private rancour ceased: friends and foes hastened round his grave to pay the last tribute of respect to departed greatness. The newspapers in Baltimore, as well as in other cities, were bordered with black in token of mourning, and all united in the expression of grief for the death of the deceased.

One of the journals inserted the following poetical lines to his honour, which I cannot refrain from copying: they may be called his epitaph, and certainly are not destitute of merit:

THE LAST OF THE ROMANS,
THE LAST OF THAT
SACRED BAND,
WHO, IN THE DARKEST HOUR OF THEIR COUNTRY'S STRUGGLES,
PERILLED THEIR LIVES, THEIR FORTUNES, AND THEIR
HONOUR,
FOR HER FREEDOM:—

CHARLES CARROLL, OF CARROLLTON,
The venerated and beloved,
The virtuous and the wise,
The patriot and the christian—
IS NO MORE!
He has gone down to the grave,
Full of days, riches, and honour.
Of no distemper, of no blast, he died,
But fell like autumn fruit, that mellow'd long;
E'en wonder'd at, because he dropp'd no sooner.
Fate seem'd to wind him up for fourscore years,
Yet freshly ran he fifteen winters more,
Till, like a clock worn out by eating Time,
The wheels of weary life at last stood still.

I fully anticipated witnessing a funeral different from the ordinary ones in America. We Europeans take it as a thing of course that the obsequies of a great man should be in proportion to his character. My residence in the United States had then been too short for me to imbibe other notions. When, therefore, informed that the body of the deceased was to lie in state, that the public authorities were to attend it to the last place of rest, and that even the President and the Secretary of State were expected from Washington, to follow in the procession, I naturally concluded that the whole ceremony would be conducted upon a scale of magnificence similar to what is observed with us. Under this impression, I proceeded to the residence of the deceased. Two staves covered with black crape were placed at the entrance of the house, and in front of it, half a dozen black women were playing as if nothing had happened. Their mirth and wild gestures actually excited my anger before I entered the gate; but this was a mere prelude to the indecorous, I may almost add, scandalous scene I subsequently witnessed in the room containing the remains of the great patriot.

The body was wrapped in a blue morning gown, and laid on a simple bed, in the middle of an apartment, which had probably been a parlour in the life-time of the owner. The bed was covered with a white sheet, overhanging the sides. Round it, were four tapers burning, and at the head a crucifix, to show that the deceased was of the Roman Catholic faith. The room bore not the slightest indications of mourning: all moveable furniture had been taken away; but curtains of the gayest colours were left, and produced a strange contrast to the silent victim of death, but a few paces distant. I found the room filled with spectators, the greater part of whom appeared to be Americans. They crowded round the body, and pushed each other, at the same time uttering reproaches, and laughing. For a long while I could not get near; but I felt indignant at witnessing a scene of merriment, and on hearing unbecoming observations close to the bier of a departed fellow-creature. They went even so far as to examine the morning-gown, to touch the lifeless body, and to place their hands on the forehead. I shuddered at this levity, and turned round in hopes of seeing some person belonging to the house, who could put a stop to these improprieties. I soon found an individual, appointed to superintend on the occasion — and, as long as he remained near the deceased, none dared touch him; but his presence did not silence the indecorous language and laughter, which continued all the time that I was in the room. When I surveyed the high forehead of the deceased and his noble features, I could not help fancying that he assumed a look of displeasure. Low, indeed, must he be sunk, who can joke and smile at the sight of a corpse. On the contrary, what an instructive and improving lesson is it not to him, who, by the side of, a lifeless fellow-creature, pauses in his ardent career, and reflects seriously for a moment, before he himself sets out on the long journey whence no traveller has yet returned!

But, if this preliminary ceremony displeased me, I was not the less disappointed on the following day, when the funeral took place. There was certainly a procession, but without order, without the least magnificence. The President, in signifying his regret at not being able to attend, despatched a few soldiers, with a view perhaps of giving greater *éclat* to the ceremony by the exhibition of elegant uniforms. I need only mention, that of the number of persons who accompanied the hearse a very small proportion were dressed in black. The majority were attired in grey, brown, or blue small-clothes and coats; some had white hats, a few even caps, and all carried umbrellas, to shelter themselves from the heavy rain falling at the time. At the cathedral the procession was received by the archbishop and a number of assisting functionaries, who went through the usual ceremonies practised by Catholics. No funeral oration was delivered; but, in its stead, pieces of solemn music and a kind of requiem were sung by a numerous band of amateurs, which produced a very impressive effect. When the service was concluded, a hearse conveyed the body to one of Carroll's estates, where it was deposited in the family vault.

Baltimore, although the largest city in Maryland, is not the capital of the State. Annapolis, a few miles to the south, and situated on Chesapeak Bay, has the honour of being the seat of the Legislature, without deserving it. It is a very insignificant place, with barely three thousand inhabitants; whereas, Baltimore, according to the last census in 1830, contained eighty thousand five hundred and nineteen souls. In the year 1820, the number amounted to only sixty-two thousand seven hundred and thirty-eight, consequently, there had been an accession in the course of ten years of no fewer than seventeen thousand seven hundred and eighty-one.

The prevailing religion is the Roman Catholic, which has been unremittingly maintained since the period of the first colony under Lord Baltimore. There are several other sects, such as Unitarians, of whom there is a great proportion; but, upon the whole, it may be said that the population of the State is almost exclusively Catholic, which is easily perceptible to any sharp-sighted stranger, this religion, it will be admitted, having certain characteristic features, more or less affecting the mass.

Traffic in slaves is permitted in Maryland, and carried on to great profit, particularly among the tobacco-planters in the interior. No baneful effect on the manners is, however, observable, until one approaches the southern parts of the State. In Baltimore, for instance, you perceive not in the streets that slavish ignorance and indifference, painted, as it were, on the features of the lower orders in the South: here are still numbers of free servants, who exercise a powerful influence over the less fortunate, who are slaves. In the more enlightened and respectable circles, prevail a frankness, liberality, and hospitality extremely pleasing to every stranger; and, at the same time, this good nature and kindness among masters entirely remove the humiliating part in the situation of a slave, and so reconcile him to his fate that he forgets his debased condition Any person, ignorant that slaves exist, would never be able to discover it, nothing in the houses or streets giving the slightest indications of it. A European, proceeding no farther south than this city, will certainly return under the impression that the situation of a slave is far from degrading. This discovery, to the shame of mankind be it said, is not made till you enter the State of Virginia. The principal exports from Maryland are wheat and tobacco, both of which are sent in great quantities to almost every part of the world. Baltimore is distinguished as a particular market for these goods; they are brought thither with extraordinary facility, through the agency of rivers, railroads, and canals. A company has lately been formed, whose object is to carry into effect one of the most gigantic projects in modern times, namely, a railroad, not less than three hundred English miles in length, to facilitate the communication between the eastern and western parts of America. This undertaking once accomplished, Baltimore will gain an incalculable accession of articles for export, and also an additional source of wealth and population. I will resume the subject of this railroad in a subsequent chapter.

At length, I quitted Baltimore, on my way to Washington, the capital of this immense Republic. The road leading to it passes over a hilly and sandy, though in many places picturesque, country. No tobacco-fields were observable, the soil in this part not permitting the cultivation of the plant; it is only in the interior of Maryland that it can be brought to perfection.

It was on a rainy, disagreeable, and uncomfortable November day, that I arrived at Washington. The first object which struck me at a distance was the Capitol, the wonder of America, where the members of Congress assemble. The situation of this edifice is on an eminence at one end of the city, facing the President's house at the other extremity: both are connected by a long and wide avenue, a mile in length, the only regular and close-built street in the city. The stage moved slowly and cautiously over an infinity of rubbish, stones, and deep holes, as the avenue was then undergoing repair. Few people were to be seen, and those consisted chiefly of slaves. Not a living being could I observe: there was none of the noise, confusion, and bustle, characteristic of a capital. Hardly a coach could be perceived: if one did appear, it was empty, or the driver was indulging in a comfortable nap on the box. In the streets, or rather roads, traversing the avenue which I entered, solitary houses were here and there observed, distant several hundred yards from each other. I could scarcely believe my eyes: I fancied myself in a village. Is this Washington, said I to myself, the capital of another hemisphere? My features must have expressed what passed inwardly, for an American, who happened to be in the same coach, asked me, half-smiling, whether, with my European notions of a metropolis, I was not rather disappointed in my expectations? He concluded these inquiries by adding in a serious tone: "Simplicity is the motto of a Republic. What you see is a true illustration of it. What can be more grand than that a country so extensive as the continent of North America should not require a larger spot than this for a capital?" I made no answer to this remark, just recollecting one of Washington Irving's expressions—"Washington, this immense metropolis, which makes so glorious an appearance on paper."

Congress had not yet met, nor had any of the persons to whom I had brought letters of introduction arrived from the four-and-twenty different States, to pass as usual the winter here: I had therefore no reason to remain longer than over-night. On the following morning I embarked, in company with a few friends, on board an excellent steamboat, and proceeded down the Potomac to a place called the Creek, distant only nine miles from Fredericksburg, a small but flourishing town in Virginia. The trip down this beautiful river was delightful beyond description. As soon as we left the district of Columbia, which contains only three cities, Washington, Georgetown, and Alexandria, (belonging to no State in the Union, but under the immediate rule of Congress at Washington,) the banks took the form of hills rising one after another as they followed the course of the stream, and appeared in many places, particularly at a distance, not unlike the waves of the ocean. Few rivers in America have left a stronger impression upon me than the enchanting Potomac. It was at once a grand and interesting sight: although the chill of autumn had already stripped the forests of their foliage, it was easy to discern what a variety of trees adorned the shores.

Potomac river divides the North from the South, and forms the boundary line. Maryland and the district of Columbia on the north side still preserve the aspect of a northern climate: Virginia, again, sighs under the burning heat of a southern sun, but, nevertheless, boasts of natural grandeur. The Potomac, taking its source among the majestic Alleghany Mountains, proudly rolls its mass of water a distance of three or four hundred miles, conscious that it may one day perhaps form the boundary between a Northern and a Southern Republic. But its greatest ornament, its greatest glory, is the unostentatious and hardly perceptible tomb of him — the last Roman on earth — him whom republican America idolizes, and whose memory even monarchical Europe venerates. The spirit of Washington still hovers over the beautiful regions, by himself selected and so beloved in life: and the Potomac, to embellish the scene, washes with her waters the foot of Mount Vernon.

I did not stop to undertake a pilgrimage to the tomb of the great man: the time was too short, and my intention was to return to Washington in the following spring. Mount Vernon, surrounded by small woods and parks, and still occupied by a namesake of Washington's, soon vanished from my sight, as well as Fort Washington, formerly called United States' Fort, situated on a rock on the opposite side. From the initials of the words United States' Fort, the English used to call it, in derision, Uncle Sam's Fort. This explanation of the words U. S. is now generally known all over America; in the western parts, in particular, it is so common to say Uncle Sam, instead of United States, or the government at Washington, that scarcely any other denomination is ever heard.

On arriving at Fredericksburg, I lost no time in taking advantage of the stage on the point of starting for Richmond. Here I was soon reminded of another circumstance, namely, my entrance into the Southern States, by the execrable condition of the public roads. The traveller has to choose between two alternatives—to be shaken to pieces, or be ingulphed in deep mud-holes. The roads are made of trees laid crosswise, emphatically called corduroy roads. It would, in many places, be quite impossible to effect a passage, if this precaution were not adopted, the soil being so soft, that the least rain is sufficient to make them impassable: the clay is often three feet deep, the wheels stick fast in it, and the carriage is consequently upset.

If the timber, thus laid across the roads, had been cut, and so placed as to fit, it would answer the purpose of a well constructed bridge; but, in so young a country as America, this cannot be expected. The trees are laid on the ground in their rough state, with the branches only cut off: in a thousand places the inhabitants had not even given themselves time, or perhaps voluntarily neglected, to take off the small boughs, so that it not unfrequently happened that, owing to these leafy branches becoming entangled with the wheels, the trees on the road were displaced. The question then naturally arose, which was the stronger — the wheel or the branches: but never did the driver attempt to check the speed of the horses, from apprehension that the coach would go to pieces. This idea seldom enters the mind of an American coachman; nevertheless, there is no country on earth where this precaution would be more advisable than in the southern parts of the United States, still so thinly peopled, that you may travel miles and miles through forests, without discovering a human habitation where assistance could be procured in case of necessity.

The cause of this indifference to horses and coaches is, that all stages carry mail-bags, which, according to contract with the post-office department, must arrive at their destination at a given time, otherwise the contractor is liable to a considerable fine. To evade this result, he gives the drivers strong injunctions to make all possible haste, let the consequence be what it may: they therefore proceed with the utmost celerity, regardless of the danger of breaking down coaches or killing horses. The consequence is, that accidents too often occur; and, on such occasions, if a carriage or team cannot be found in the neighbourhood, the driver takes the mail-bags, throws them upon a cart, and thus continues his journey, leaving the unfortunate passengers in the middle of the road, in a bog, or in a forest, many miles from any habitation.

To similar and numberless other inconveniences is a traveller exposed in the South; and, if he is lucky enough to arrive at the place of his destination alive, or with unbroken limbs, he may indeed think that he has had a narrow escape. I must, however, confess that accidents occur less seldom than might be expected on such roads, and which are hardly ever repaired; and the materials of which the coaches are built are so strong and tough, that holes, timber, stumps, roots, or trees, have seldom the power to break them. To the eye they appear very heavy and substantial, and to my taste far from handsome:

the iron alone, which is used for one, would be sufficient for two in England. No doubt they are perfectly suited to the roads: the springs, for instance, are almost always of leather, able to resist any shocks. It would be as impossible for an English carriage to be used here without being broken to pieces, as for English horses to trot on such roads, or for English coachmen to drive.

If railroads be desirable, they are certainly so in a superlative degree from the beginning of Virginia to Louisiana. Probably, many years will not elapse before such may be constructed in this tract of country by enterprizing Americans; and whoever then travels from Richmond to New Orleans, by way of Charleston, and will take the trouble of reading this brief description, (the remembrance of which almost makes me shudder) will in all probability not refuse a sympathizing thought to those, who, in former times, to the imminent danger of life, and under numberless inconveniences, performed this journey once, but certainly would not willingly undertake it a second time.

CHAPTER XV.

That feeling which tells him that man was never made to be the property of man.

SHERIDAN.

RICHMOND is the capital of Virginia. Few cities in the Union can be said to have a more beautiful and picturesque situation. It is built on a chain of hills, between which James River, navigable to this place, rolls its silvery waters. The public buildings, such as the Capitol, the Court House, and others, are erected on elevated points, and visible in every direction; their exterior, which would produce effect any where, contributes to embellish the whole. The bustle in the lower part of the town proves the flourishing state of the city; manufactories and institutions of various kinds add to the general activity, and give life to the picture.

I visited one day the Capitol, as it is called, or Statehouse, occupied by the Legislature of the State, not then sitting, but which generally meets on the 1st day of December, and is, as in all the other States, divided between a Senate and a House of Delegates. The first is composed of thirty-two members, elected for four years, one fourth of whom are changed annually, and the latter, of one hundred and thirty-four members, elected every year.

This edifice is situate on an eminence in the upper part of the city, and modelled after the well-known *maison carrée* at Nismes in France. Eight Ionian pillars adorn that part of the building fronting the lower end of the city. Two entrances, in opposite directions, lead to a kind of vestibule, in the centre of which is a marble statue of Washington. It is made the size of life, and represents him in the same simple garb which he was accustomed to wear. There is something so unpoetical in a coat in reality, that it is hardly possible for a sculptor to give to a statue of marble, dressed in the *costume de Marquis* of the seventeenth century, that life and spirit, which can alone impart a natural air to a cold and inanimate piece of marble; but, notwithstanding this drawback, the spectator is gratified in beholding this piece of sculpture. I do not question the merits of the execution; it has been conducted with talent, and a due observance of the ancient and modern rules of the art; I am, however, of opinion, and I hope the artist will kindly excuse what I advance in a spirit of candour, that it is the noble, well-known features, which, rather than the general treatment, must at first glance strike every one who attentively examines the statue. Washington had a peculiar, open, noble, distinguished, and ever-composed countenance: both sculptors and painters have succeeded in copying it without difficulty. So also with this statue: all those who have seen it, and known Washington during his life-time, are of one opinion that the sculptor has admirably executed the head: all portraits, busts, and statues of him that I have seen are perfect likenesses. The attitude, besides, is very natural: he rests his right hand on a stick, and the left on fasces. A plough is placed close by, and a sword hangs upon it, as symbols of the warrior and the agriculturist.

Immediately behind the palace of the Legislative Body is the Courthouse. The exterior is the most imposing part of the building: the façade has four rather handsome pillars of the Doric order, and the whole is crowned with a dome. The interior contains nothing remarkable, except a few portraits of Washington and Lafayette.

During one of my rambles in the city, I met with one of the most affecting mausoleums I had seen since my arrival in America. In an open colonnade, near the front of the Episcopal Church, and directly opposite to the entrance, is a sarcophagus, on which a great number of names are inscribed. It is a monument commemorative of a dreadful event which occurred here on the never-to-be forgotten evening of the 26th of December, 1811.

On the same place where the church and the monument now stand was formerly a theatre, where the first and most enlightened society in Virginia once found an agreeable recreation. A play was performed on that very evening, the name of which I cannot recollect, but which was extremely popular at the time. Many of the first families in town attended the performance: the house was filled with all the talent, beauty, virtue, and knowledge, that Richmond could boast of. In the midst of the performance, at the moment perhaps when the feelings of the audience were excited to the highest pitch — for thus Fate often sports with men — a loud cry of "Fire!" was heard. Panic-stricken, the whole assembly rushed towards the doors; but — great God! shall I continue to describe the last act of this tragic scene? Enough — they met the flames at the entrance — few ventured to brave them — some flocked together — their piercing cries and lamentations reaching even the ears of friends and relatives who had remained at home — smoke and flames enveloped the house sooner than could have been expected — a low murmur was heard from the interior of the building — relatives and friends rushed franticly to the spot — a thunder-crash suddenly drowned the roaring of the fire and the crackling of the beams — the smoke took another direction, as if in fear — a single immeasurable flame rose towards the dark heavens, and its light was more than sufficient to show to the horror-stricken multitude that walls and roof had irretrievably buried the unfortunate victims in their ruins.

A church was afterwards erected on the ruins of the former theatre; and, to remind those who enter the temple to worship God that about one hundred and twenty fellow-creatures here met a premature death, this monument was placed so conspicuously before the gate to the church that no one can go in without passing it. What an awful memento to sinners of the suddenness of death, often occurring when least expected, and in the midst of earthly enjoyments! With what excited feelings must not the citizens of Richmond visit this simple temple, and hear the consoling doctrine proclaimed; they cannot fail to recollect that all that now reminds them of those whom they bewailed is a common mausoleum, with a few black names cut in the stone! Yes, this monument speaks a powerful language to all hearts approaching this place consecrated to death. Let no one visit Richmond without performing a pilgrimage to this simple, silent, but yet eloquent mausoleum.

Another sight of a different character presented itself shortly afterwards, during my stay in the capital of Virginia: for the first time in my life I witnessed a scene, alike degrading to mankind and abhorrent and disgusting to the friends of humanity. Who can doubt that I allude to the slave-trade? The newspapers had several days previously inserted an advertisement to nearly the following effect:

On Saturday next, at nine o'clock A.M., will be sold by public auction the following excellent and good-looking Negro Slaves, &c.

Betsy, a Negro woman, twenty-three years of age, with her child Cæsar, three years old. She is a good cook; understands washing and ironing, and is warranted sound.

Julia, a Mulatress, thirteen years old; an excellent hand in the fields; strong and hearty; has a trifling blemish in one eye, otherwise warranted.

Augustus, a Negro boy, six years old; a good subject for a servant. Faultless.

The above slaves will be sold, without reserve, to the highest bidder; and the buyer may have one, two, and four months' credit, on offering unexceptionable paper, &c.

I was not behindhand, as it may be supposed, in attending the auction: among a variety of other saleable articles, such as pots, pans, beds, chairs, books, &c., the unfortunate slaves were sitting close to each other, all as decently dressed as might be expected from persons who are considered by their equals as mere animals. The mother, with the child in her lap, was the first who drew my attention. She had seated herself, or rather the vender had placed her, in such a situation that any one entering the store could, without difficulty, see both her and the child. Speculators went round and surveyed the unfortunate group with looks of curiosity and scrutiny, as if it had been some masterpiece from the chisel of a Canova, a Thorwaldsen, or a Byström. These cold-blooded and unfeeling beings treated the slaves with an indifference, a roughness, which made me shudder. Not only did they put questions which would have made any female blush in whatever situation, but which, on the present occasion, were still more offensive — not only did they divert themselves at the expence of the slaves, and indulge in *bons mots*, as piercing to the heart of every feeling man as the point of a dagger — they even examined them with the same scrutinizing eye as they would horses brought to market, inspected their teeth, eyes, feet, and shoulders; felt their sides, and finally pronounced their opinion "that they were tolerably good slaves, capable of doing much work."

The only one of these Blacks who appeared to feel her degraded situation was poor Betsy. Her eyes were constantly fixed on her infant; and if at times she lifted them up, it was at the commanding request of some buyer, desirous of ascertaining if they were strong enough to support work night and day; but the moment she had complied with the injunction, she looked down again on her babe, and answered every question without again raising them, or even casting a glance on the inquirer. This, however, was not the case with the other slaves: they laughed good-naturedly at every jest, looked upon the inspection as extremely foolish, and their large white eyes sparkled like brilliants in their heads with delight at the lively and witty talk of the "Gentlemen" who had come all the way from the country for the purpose of purchasing human creatures! Julia indulged in innocent playfulness, ignorant of the real character of the scene: the more harshly she was commanded the better she was pleased.

But the time for sale approached. Several buyers had assembled in the store, anxious to overbid each other for the possession of the Negroes. The auctioneer invited them to come out; and on a table before the door, in the middle of the street, one of the slaves at a time was exposed for sale. Betsy and her child had the honour of occupying the first place in the catalogue. Close to her side stood the auctioneer on a chair, and round them a number of people who, partly from motives of curiosity, partly from a desire to speculate, attended on the occasion. In the crowd I discovered at least a dozen Negroes and Negro women, who stopped in passing to gratify their curiosity. They appeared to listen with an extraordinary degree of attention to the progress of the sale. I could not avoid sympathizing with them, in witnessing the expression of feeling they showed towards their fellow-creatures.

"This proves sufficiently," said I to myself, delighted at the discovery, "how erroneous and incorrect the opinion is, that the Negro race is only a link between man and brute animals; and that these unfortunate natives of Africa are only half men, not much better than a certain species of apes!"

At that moment, I heard, to my horror, a burst of laughter from the crowd. I looked round, and observed all the surrounding Blacks indulging in so hearty a laugh, that I was nigh being smitten with the same fit, so ridiculous was the scene, and so many contortions did the various faces exhibit. Full of surprise, I inquired the cause, and was informed that one of them had happened to make a most striking and ludicrous remark, respecting the mother then about to be sold. Can there be anything more unfeeling, more unbecoming, than that persons, themselves slaves, who have often gone through the same ordeal of being sold like beasts, and who are consequently thoroughly acquainted with its iniquity, that these persons should jest and laugh at the natural horror and timidity felt by a mother at the time of sale?

"A woman to be disposed of!" commenced the auctioneer, with a loud voice; "who will start a price? She is an excellent woman, without blemishes! And a boy into the bargain! What shall I say for mother and son? Two hundred and fifty dollars. I thank you, Sir. Two hundred and fifty dollars once. Will any person give more than two hundred and fifty? Why, gentlemen, this is as cheap as cattle; look at her eyes, limbs, &c. Shall I say two hundred and sixty? Much obliged to you. Two hundred and sixty are offered, once. Two hundred and seventy-five dollars did I hear? Gentlemen, it is the cheapest lot I ever sold. Only two hundred and eighty dollars for the very best cook, laundress, and seamstress? Is she to be knocked down for a paltry two hundred and eighty dollars? Going for two hundred and eighty dollars. Three hundred dollars, two voices: I am glad to see you get into the spirit, gentlemen. Three hundred and ten is offered, once. Three hundred and thirty—three hundred and thirty-five—three hundred and forty: going for three hundred and forty. Really, gentlemen, I am astonished; allow an experienced cook to be sacrificed for only three hundred and forty dollars! By Jupiter, and all the gods in Olympus! such a woman as this for the trifling sum of three hundred and forty dollars! I beg you for a moment to reflect, gentlemen! and a boy into the bargain!"

Here the auctioneer was stopped by one of the buyers, a man whose features from the beginning had inspired me with horror, and who now, with the indifference and *sang-froid* of a real assassin, made the following observation: "The boy is good for nothing; he is not worth a day's feed. If I buy the mother, I will sell the brat immediately, at a cheap rate, to the first comer."

I cast a glance at the unfortunate mother, to observe what effect this barbarous expression might produce. She uttered not a word; but her countenance denoted profound grief and resignation. The little innocent child in her arms fixed his large dark eyes upon her, as if to ask, "Why do you weep, mother?" and then turned astonished towards those who witnessed this touching scene, with an expression which seemed to say, "What is the matter? What have ye done to my mother, since she is crying so bitterly?" I shall never forget this moment; it confirmed me for life in my former abhorrence of the traffic in human flesh.

The auction continued :—" Three hundred and forty dollars — three hundred and fifty, three hundred and fifty dollars — a better woman has never come under the hammer, I feel well satisfied — three hundred and fifty dollars for a woman worth at least six hundred dollars — three hundred and sixty dollars — going for three hundred and sixty dollars — three hundred and sixty dollars, once, twice, thrice — going for three hundred and sixty — for three hundred and sixty — going—going—going—for three hundred and sixty dollars — three hundred and sixty dollars, I say — make up your minds, gentlemen—you will lose her — going — going — gone. She is yours for three hundred and sixty dollars." A blow with the hammer concluded the bargain; the victim descended from the table, and the buyer carried her off.

None of the speculators had uttered a single word during the progress of the sale. When they overbade each other, it was not done in the customary way by means of words. They nodded to the auctioneer, who rolled his eyes round the assembly, sometimes in one direction, sometimes in another. Each movement with the head had probably a peculiar signification, for the intention of the speculator was never mistaken, and he added, accordingly, five, ten, fifteen, or twenty dollars to the bidding.

The other slaves were disposed of in the same manner as poor Betsy. Julia fetched only three hundred and twenty-six dollars; and Augustus one hundred and five dollars. Both were bought by the same individual who purchased the first lot. He appeared to be a young farmer, and I was assured that such was his occupation. I rejoiced at least to think that these unfortunate beings had not fallen into the hands of a regular slave-trader. True enough, his looks denoted the delight he felt at having made an advantageous bargain; but he treated his acquired property with mildness, and never addressed the slaves in a harsh and humiliating tone.

It may, perhaps, not be irrelevant to the subject to say a few words here of the condition of the slaves in North America, their intellectual capabilities, the danger and impossibility of a sudden emancipation, and the advantages likely to result from the system of colonization.

The first rule which every owner of slaves

has prescribed to himself, with a view to treat the Negroes properly, has been: "Let the light of education never dawn upon them. Keep them always in a state of complete ignorance. Let them never know aught of a happier existence than the slave life they now lead."

This maxim, so unworthy of enlightened minds, and so irreconcileable with the liberal principles of a free country, is, nevertheless, still prevalent in all the Slave States. It invariably guides the conduct of the planters, whose conviction seems to be irrevocable that a spark of light disseminated among slaves would be equivalent to a supply of arms, which they would immediately turn against the white population. This belief has entailed the most disastrous consequences, and been highly detrimental to the moral condition of the unfortunate Negroes. Born of parents, as raw and ignorant as savages, from whom they learn nothing but vice, they live days and years, without being able to understand any of those manifold natural wonders with which they are surrounded—without knowing for what purpose they are brought into the world—often without suspecting the existence of God. Their religion hardly deserves that name. Many a savage Indian in the wilds west of the Mississippi has better ideas of a Supreme Being, and greater veneration for the Creator, than a Christian slave, as he is called, in the Christian land of the United States.

The greater part of the Negroes profess the creed of the Baptists, at least such is the case in the States situated on the eastern coast of the country; but many are found who have no religion whatever, who do not know what it signifies, who are perfectly callous on the subject. Do the owners of slaves, similarly situated, it may be asked, know this state of things? I started this question to a well-informed man in Virginia, and received the following answer. "They are perfectly well aware of it, but care not a straw about it; for they think it better not to stir the ashes; the least spark may cause the greatest conflagration."

It is very seldom that a slave has learned to read: his knowledge of the Bible is confined to what others, more fortunate than himself, teach him —persons who, from being white, assume the exclusive privileges of thinking for and instructing the Blacks. Missionaries have certainly endeavoured to circulate among the slave-population religious tracts composed solely for this purpose, and written in a style suitable to individuals of so little information as the Negroes; but, as I stated before, few are able to avail themselves of the gift, and the object in view is far from being accomplished. In many places through which I passed, and where numbers congregated on Sunday evenings, I sometimes found one that could read. On him devolved the duty of reading aloud some religious tract, or a passage from the Bible; but I must in candour confess that this desirable thing was of rare occurrence. Upon nearly every occasion, I found the slave more disposed to indulge in some noisy amusement, which generally ended in drunkenness and riot, and destroyed all consciousness, at least for the moment. "Their moral condition," said a slave-proprietor to me, "is better or worse in proportion to their vicinity to high roads, where they come in contact with white men who, one way or other, spoil their morals."

To judge from what I have seen in America, I am inclined to think that slaves, generally speaking, are well treated by their owners. Exceptions there are, no doubt, from this rule: what else can be expected from persons who, like the speculator at the sale just mentioned, unfeelingly observed: "If I buy the mother, I will sell the boy immediately at a cheap rate to the first comer?" These examples of cruelty on the part of slave-owners are, strange enough, almost exclusively traced to persons brought up in the Northern States under early impressions of horror for slavery, who, from infancy, have shuddered at the very name of slave, and have been in the habit of hearing nothing but curses and execrations launched against heartless slave-proprietors. When these once settle in the South, they are obliged to procure slaves for the cultivation of their land, &c. for Whites look upon it as a dishonour to work wherever slaves can be found; but, unaccustomed to treat them in a proper manner, and never forgetting how much labour a man is able to go through in the North, they require of the slave as much willingness and activity as of the free servant. When this disposition is wanting, natural to a being obliged to work, and who, on that very account, does no more than he is actually compelled to do after all—but an inconsiderable portion when compared with the labour of a free man in the North—they then believe it to be the effect of indolence, and have recourse to the mistaken system of compulsion, in order to force him, by the infliction of corporal punishments and the severest treatment, to work more assiduously.

In States where the servants are free, very few are seen in families: this want of domestics is owing to the facility which every free man possesses of supporting himself in most parts in an independent way, as master instead of servant. One is therefore obliged to be satisfied with few attendants; but these few must do every thing that is wanted. In the Slave States again, where hands are abundant, the same work which is performed in the North by one man is divided among several: this is not taken into consideration by the planters from the North, who require that every slave shall contribute as much as the free servant. From this misconception, barbarous acts, which would otherwise never be thought of, are perpetrated. These, however, I am happy to add, seldom occur. Of the disgusting and humiliating scenes, and the unnatural cruelties practised by slave-owners in former times, there are now very few instances. Complaints of ill-usage towards servants are by far more common in certain despotic countries of Europe.

One of America's most humorous authors,*

* J. K. Paulding, author of The Dutchman's Fireside.

in a work lately published, intitled "Westward Ho," has given a lively and true picture of the difference between the life of a slave and that of a free man, and proves, in a masterly manner, that the situation of the former is by far not so deplorable as it is generally imagined to be. An old slave, he says, accompanied his master to Philadelphia, where a man in good circumstances tried to persuade him to desert, and by that means obtain his freedom. Pompey — this was the name of the slave — felt a strong inclination to have a taste of liberty; but observing, shortly afterwards, a few poor begging, wretched, and swearing Negroes, enjoying the sweets of liberty, he declined the offer, and hastened home to his master, to beg that he would buy the unfortunate free servants, and take them along with him to Kentucky.

If this anecdote is not exactly founded on fact, it has at least the colour of probability, for I once heard a slave in Alabama utter the same sentiments respecting free servants.

That, consequently, good and tender masters are to be met with, and that they are more numerous than is generally believed in the Northern and Eastern States, admits of no doubt. It is, moreover, their interest to treat slaves well. In many places, no inspectors or Negro drivers, as they are called, are to be found. Planters prefer looking after them themselves; but when this is not practicable, either from absence or other circumstances, they invariably choose persons of mild and humane dispositions. Slaves have, however, always the privilege of making their complaints or addressing petitions direct to the masters. Corporal punishments are still in use; but I have been positively assured that they are annually on the decrease, and only resorted to on occasions when slaves show symptoms of obstinacy or insubordination, and cannot possibly be brought to a sense of obedience by mildness and friendly advice; but, even then, the correction is far from severe. Upon the whole, they are well dressed and fed, and in many plantations treated as if they formed part of the family. The children play undisturbedly with their young masters: they are never put to work until arrived at an age when labour cannot prove injurious to their constitutions.

At break of day, slaves generally rise as soon as the sound of a bell announces the time of leaving their resting places. The day's work might easily be performed by a white man in half the time, for with them rapidity of motion is out of the question. The setting sun is a signal for retreat to their huts, which are built of logs, and close to each other. The slaves are always so divided that married couples with their children live separately from the others, and the single in distinct houses, each sex apart. When age renders them unserviceable, they are taken care of with paternal tenderness. Then every one is allowed a hut and a small piece of ground, with which he must support himself; but, although this is a more independent life than the former, they almost invariably prefer continuing slaves to the end of their existence, to avoid the necessity of thinking and providing for themselves—without which, as free persons, they would certainly starve.

A slave, well treated, seldom runs away; if ever he takes this step, he is either impelled by seducing promises, which he is too weak to resist, or acts under an erroneous impression of his duties as servant. In the first case, he soon finds his mistake; and then it is not unusual for him to return to his former master, and beg as a favour to resume the place he left from thoughtlessness. In the latter case again, he deserts, encouraged by religious fanatics, whose blind zeal induces them to propagate doctrines, inculcating that a slave is as much entitled to freedom as his master, and therefore there is no harm in taking that which by right belongs to him. That these men, instead of doing good, actually cause a great deal of evil among the slaves, is a fact fully demonstrated, of which I will by and by adduce proofs.

The idea that a free man must support himself without the aid of others is a powerful effect on beings unaccustomed, perhaps, their whole life-time, to think about their own maintenance. Many of them will not, at any price, accept liberty as a gift, and would, if emancipated, give themselves up to the first bidder. How many instances are there not on record, of slaves, who, after recovering their freedom, return to their former masters! The following anecdote, known all over America, the truth of which is unquestionable, illustrates the correctness of the preceding remarks:—

In one of the southern States died, a few years ago, a rich planter, who, happening to be without heirs, ordered in his will that all his slaves, to the number of several hundred, should be set at liberty, and his whole property divided among them. The executors appointed by the will bought large tracts of land in Ohio, divided them in equal shares among the slaves, built houses on each lot, and arranged every thing so comfortably, that the cultivation of the soil was the only thing that remained to be attended to. The slaves were sent thither, and obtained their liberty. The charm of novelty at first pleased them; but, by degrees, even this grew wearisome. They were obliged to think of the wants of the morrow, and to become initiated in an art perfectly new to them—that of economy. Fatigued with the blessings of liberty, which they did not know how to appreciate, and which varied so much from their notions of happiness on earth—which, be it said, *en passant*, only consist in idleness and a life without care—they lost no time in emigrating from their new colony, and returning to the State whence they came, where they voluntarily offered themselves at a sale to the highest bidder. Only a few had sense enough to remain in Ohio, and to devote themselves to agricultural pursuits.

I have before observed, that missionaries from the northern States display a mistaken zeal in the cause of humanity, by endeavouring to induce slaves to desert their owners, and that this zeal, so far from promoting the desired end, entails the most pernicious consequences. A disposition to disobedience and irritability among the slave-population towards the planters is too often manifested; and this feeling is so strong, that it may one day burst out in an open and sanguinary contest, in ferocity and barbarity, perhaps, not dissimilar to the Sicilian Vespers. The planters again, with a view to prevent desertions, which make considerable inroads on their property, adopt the greatest precaution to prevent slaves from having the least communication with itinerant missionaries, and thus defeat the hopes of the friends of humanity of seeing a due sense and love of religion inculcated in the minds of slaves. Some are even obliged, by way of example, to inflict corporal punishments, thus again disappointing the sanguine expectations of philanthropists to see this mode of correction abolished.

Another evil results from this irrational zeal: the slave recovers his liberty—but with it no property. In what manner is he all at once to support himself? I admit that he can work, and thus earn a livelihood; but is it to be expected that a being, unused to think or work for himself, shall of a sudden become sensible of the necessity of it? And, even if he does, is it to be supposed that he can immediately find an occupation, the produce of which will be sufficient to satiate craving hunger? Persecuted, moreover, by his former master, he is obliged for several days to continue his flight under the greatest privations to avoid a re-capture; in this emergency he can earn nothing. Is it then to be wondered at if these unfortunate victims of mistaken ideas are induced to commit thefts for the support of nature? Would to God they were never tempted to commit greater offences! Daily experience proves, however, that crimes of the blackest dye are perpetrated by runaway slaves; there is hardly a newspaper published in a State bordering on one in which slavery exists, that does not record atrocities of which these desperate and deluded beings are guilty. I could bring forward many more facts to establish the uselessness and danger of this interference of missionaries; but my preceding observations will, I hope, have represented the matter in a clear and intelligible light.

A man, therefore, brought up as a slave, and without any other notion of education than passive obedience, cannot be expected to govern himself, and does not understand the value of liberty. If all his passions, repressed by the yoke of thraldom, are at once let loose, his want of judgment encourages him to rush into momentary excesses, by way of indemnity for past sufferings. Passions are the only Supreme Being he worships, and, with a view to the gratification of them, no sacrifice is too great for him. He is ignorant of the Bible — it is only through the medium of others that he has heard of its Divine doctrines — he cannot read; and if he could, his mind is too uncultivated to allow him to surrender all the temptations and enjoyments of liberty to what he considers as the severe dictates of the Christian faith. He thinks that he has already suffered sufficiently under the lash of obedience. "Now is my time to do what I please," he contends; and his unbridled and irrational acts are in harmony with such dangerous axioms. In short, the emancipation of a slave, destitute of instruction, who cannot read, and who never learnt to think for himself, has seldom any other result than to incumber the community with a free man, who, from want of discrimination, commits lawless offences, for which he is amenable to justice, and punished. In this manner, from being an unfortunate creature, pitied by all, he becomes a culprit, held in general abhorrence.

It is not my intention—God forbid it should be so! to advocate a non-emancipation of slaves; I only mean to say that giving a man liberty does not conduce to the object in view, if other means are not adopted previously, to enable him to become, in the course of time, a useful member of society. This can only be effected by a suitable education.

Many Americans are of opinion that Negroes are differently organized from white men. Such a supposition is evidently false and ungenerous. The Negroes are not deficient in any of the properties which distinguish the Whites: they are sunk in a state of apathy, attributable to their slavery as well as to our prejudices. I often heard instances adduced, clearly showing that the Blacks had a good fund of feeling, and that they might be placed on a level with the Whites. The unhappy contempt invariably entertained for them by the white population in Slave States produces the effect that no action, no expression, however noble and great in its tendency, is taken notice of by the free. This prejudice is carried so far, that even the indigent Whites, who, in the sweat of their brow, must toil for food, and often perhaps beg for it, treat them as mere animals. In the playhouses, and in all places where public entertainments are given, they are separated from all other living beings by boxes exclusively allotted to them, in which a White would abhor to be seen. In New Orleans, this aversion is even extended to those descendants of the Negroes, who, by a mixture of several generations with Whites, have become almost white. Is it, then, surprising, if these debased and oppressed creatures, who never hear any thing but commands, who only behold cold and repulsive countenances, who are aware that all the world knows their degraded situation, and who are themselves shut out, as it were, from society — that these go, if I may use the expression, half sleeping through life; and that, totally indifferent as to the present and the future, they become perfect fatalists? "When my hour is come, I die," said one of them to me, when I asked his opinion of life and death; "it is, therefore, immaterial what I do."

But, it may be asked, cannot a general

emancipation be effected by an indiscriminate liberation of the slaves on the part of the owners? Assuredly, the object would then be attained; but another evil would at the same time occur, of too much consequence to be overlooked — the total ruin of the Slave States. As long as wages for free people remain so exorbitantly high as they now are in America, and as long as the difficulty exists of obtaining a free workman — the one a consequence of the other — the planters cannot possibly do without their slaves; for, deprived of their services, they can neither cultivate cotton, sugar, rice, and Indian corn, nor deliver these articles of necessity at so cheap a rate as at present. As the riches of these States consist in the produce of their soil, there would not only be a general ruin and distress in these parts, but the measure would also have a material and baneful effect on other States consuming the above-mentioned products.

But if, under these circumstances, an immediate emancipation of slaves is not advisable, what measures can be adopted to accomplish the so-much desired object, cessation of slavery? As dangerous and impracticable as emancipation now would be, as easy and unhurtful I believe would it prove at a future day, if the event be prepared beforehand with wisdom and due consideration. And this might be effected, if the Legislatures of the Slave States were to decree that only a certain number of slaves should be permitted to remain in each State, and that the yearly surplus, over and above that number, should be purchased and exported to a free colony. By the adoption of this expedient, the black population would be effectually kept in check — (in the two States of Louisiana and South Carolina, it is now more numerous than the White) — and remain stationary, whilst the Whites are gradually on the increase. I will here quote, by way of example, Virginia, which, according to the last census, contained little less than one fifteenth part of the whole white population of the United States, more than one-seventh part of free Negroes, but again between one-fourth and one-fifth part of all the slaves in the Union. In this State, the annual increase of slaves is between ten and eleven thousand. Of these about six thousand are sent for sale to other States; the remaining five thousand would therefore be the number for Government to dispose of. If purchases were made, particularly of children, the sum would be inconsiderable; and, making an average calculation of about one hundred and fifty dollars for each, the whole amount would only be seven hundred and fifty thousand dollars. These slaves should afterwards be conveyed, either to Liberia, or some other place in Africa: the expences for sending them out, and for their support in the colony for a few months, may be calculated at one hundred and twenty-five thousand dollars, or about twenty-five dollars a-head.

One of the principal objections to this project, is the difficulty in which Virginia is placed of laying out so large a sum as that first mentioned; the latter, again, can easily be set aside by Government for this purpose. Several proposals have been made to obtain the considerable appropriation of seven hundred and fifty thousand dollars, and among others, that of making those funds available which the Federal Government receives annually from the public tracts of land situated in the Western States.* The revenue amounts

* The old venerable Ex-President Madison, still living in retirement in Virginia, is of this opinion, and has, in a letter written not long ago, expressed himself in the following manner: "In contemplating the pecuniary resources needed for the removal of such a number to a great distance, my thoughts and hopes have been long turned to the rich fund presented in the Western lands of the nation, which will soon entirely cease to be under a pledge for another object. The great one in question is truly of a national character;

to three millions of dollars. If Virginia, which now possesses a larger proportion of slaves than any other State, more than Mississippi, Tennessee, Alabama, and Louisiana, put together, and more than four times the number of any of them, receives seven hundred and fifty thousand dollars; and the other Slave States in the same proportion, the whole sum will not amount to three millions. No appropriation, however, of this kind had been made when I quitted America.

If the slaves are prevented, by this or any other expedient, from increasing in number, and if, in the mean time, Missionaries or other Christian teachers are allowed unmolested to disseminate among the remaining slave-population the seeds of a true and intelligible religion, at the same time that, quoting passages from the Epistles of St. Paul, they promulgate maxims, having for their tendency that the servant must obey his master — if this simple plan were followed, the slave-owners would not be every moment in peril

---

and it is known that distinguished patriots, not dwelling in slave-holding States, have viewed the object in that light, and would be willing to let the national domain be a resource in effecting it. Should it be remarked that the States, though all may be interested in relieving our country from the coloured population, are not equally so, it is but fair to recollect that the sections most to be benefited are those whose cessions created the fund to be disposed of."

of their lives, nor would those States where no slaves are found be engaged in continual disputes with those in which they are permitted, on the subject of cruel and unnatural treatment; the slave himself would have a clearer idea of many things to which, as a man, he is entitled, without losing that affection for his master, or attempting to acquire liberty by violent means, which he would not fail to do when once acquainted with his rights.

In the South, I heard continual complaints respecting the unnecessary interference of the Northern States, in regard to the condition of the slave-population in the former — and their injurious and blind zeal in wishing immediately to redress this unfortunate state of things. A great deal of bad feeling has in effect been excited between the North and the South on this subject; and upon various occasions, of the most trifling nature, the slave question has been submitted for consideration, and this, too, with a warmth that often gave rise to altercations. All this will, I hope, soon disappear, in proportion as the communication between all parts of the Union is facilitated, so that the Southerns may intermix with the men of the North, and the latter have more frequent opportunities of visiting the plantations of the former, and of ascertaining, by ocular demonstration, whether the slaves are really so miserable as they are represented to be. The zeal of the Northern States has, meanwhile, had this effect, that the Southern have been roused from their lethargy. The slave-trade is now become more than formerly a subject of discussion; and the owner of several hundred is at all times as ready to discuss the question relative to emancipation, as the individual to whose mind the word slave only conveys something degrading and sacrilegious. It is therefore to be hoped that the day is not far distant when slaves shall cease to exist in the United States, when freedom shall be given to them, and not kept by violence from them.

CHAPTER XVI.

As some lone bird, without a mate,
My weary heart is desolate:
I look around, and cannot trace
One friendly smile or welcome face.
BYRON.

VIRGINIA tobacco is an article so well known all over the world, that I was not a little anxious to become acquainted with the method of cultivating it, and to examine some of the manufactories where it is prepared for the use of man. The soil in this State appears to be peculiarly adapted to the growth of this plant, which thrives here better than in any other part of the Union. Yet, with all its fertility, it is considered a bad plan to grow crops of this plant on the same ground for several successive years. Wheat and Indian corn are generally planted the year after a tobacco crop; in many places it is cultivated only once in three, four, or five years. I was surprised to find the dwellings belonging to the greater part of these tobacco-plantations in a dilapidated state, more resembling the ruins of some old mansion than the residence of rich Virginia planters. The reason assigned was, that the cultivation of tobacco absorbs so much time that none is left for the repairs of the house, or for attending to other branches of agriculture.

During my stay in Richmond, I visited one of the most eminent tobacco manufactories in the city. Three hundred slaves of both sexes, with their children, were working in it; they were hired by the proprietor at so much a year. The wages varied according to the strength and capacity of the slaves; for a young and strong man, for instance, eighty or one hundred dollars were paid, and for a child about half that sum.

America consumes a vast quantity of tobacco in chewing; the manufactory which I visited appeared exclusively occupied in preparing it for this purpose. The first process devolves on the oldest Negroes, who assort the different kinds of leaves. The stalks are then taken out, and the tobacco rolled on a table till it has acquired the necessary form. I shudder, when I think of those excessively dirty hands which handled the very tobacco that was soon after to be chewed by elegant amateurs. The most disgusting part, however, of the whole preparation was the manufacture of the tobacco of inferior quality, consisting of the refuse which had been thrown aside, on which the workmen were trampling and spitting the whole day, until it had formed a uniform and disgusting mass: it was then swept into another still dirtier room, and there rolled till it became of the required shape. The process ends in the usual way by sweating, after which the article is packed in cases and barrels. It is only necessary to witness these preparations once, to take a dislike to tobacco for life.

From Richmond I proceeded to Norfolk, and visited, in the course of my journey, several places which even to this day, although in ruins, revive recollections of the noble Pocahontas. The banks of James River are hilly, and covered with bushes and trees almost to the water's edge. Here and there may be seen a few Negro-plantations: their miserable huts, at small distances from each other, continue along the shore. Of James Town, the first English settlement in the United States, no trace is discernible, and of the many hospitable mansions of which Virginia formerly boasted, very few are left. A traveller, bearing in mind what this State once was, cannot help viewing every object with interest. From remotest times, history represents its inhabitants as distinguished by a chivalrous spirit; and this feature, more and more developed in the course of events, is now perceptible in a tendency to aristocracy. I mean only with regard to manners — for in other respects the Virginians are perfectly republican. During the revolutionary war, this State was not backward in sending her sons to fight the battles of the country: since then, it has furnished no fewer than four Presidents. In our times, Virginia still retains an important rank in the political relations of the Union, and Americans attach great hopes to her energy, in case of need.

The city of Norfolk is situated on the east bank of the river Elizabeth, opposite to two small towns called Portsmouth and Gosport, the latter remarkable only as being a station for part of the United States' Navy. Norfolk is a seaport, carrying on some trade, but to no considerable extent. The chief branch of business consists in timber, from the interior of the country, suitable for naval purposes, and contracts for this article to no small amount are made with Government for the use of the fleet. About a mile from the city, on a point of land, a marine hospital has lately been established, which deserves to be visited by every traveller.

The stage was at the door. Nine strangers, crowded together in the uncomfortable and heavy carriage, soon began to complain of the narrow space allotted to each for the convenience of their legs. My travelling companions and myself had, unfortunately, too much luggage, a circumstance that gave rise to a very animated debate between us and the owner of the stage ; but, on putting the question to the vote, we carried it *nem. con.* by paying a few dollars extra. At length we started.

Norfolk might still be seen at a short distance behind us, when one of the travellers called out that all the trunks and portmanteaus were unfastened, and that the least jolt of the coach would infallibly send them into the middle of the road. As the sky announced an instantaneous storm, threatening to soak all our carpet-bags, knapsacks, parcels, &c. our voices united in one common request, that the driver should immediately stop and look after them. He obeyed the mandate only in part, by pulling up his horses, adding an observation still foreign to my ears, but with which I became more familiarized in my subsequent travels through the United States, particularly in the South and West, namely, "that, as to looking after the baggage, it was no business of his." This explanation informed each of us that he must henceforth be on the *qui vive*, and attend to his own property. In the midst of a drenching shower, we were obliged to alight, and fasten the trunks ourselves, standing ankle-deep in mud ; but to shelter them against the rain was entirely out of the question. They were left to their fate ; and I need not assure the reader that they were filled with water before we arrived at our journey's end.

Not far from Norfolk, is a very large marsh called The Dismal Swamp. The road led through only a corner of it, so that I cannot assert that I have seen the whole of this swamp: but, were I to judge from what I did see, I should pronounce the Dismal Swamp to be one of the most desolate places in the world. Nature appeared really in mourning. The marshy soil was every where covered with bushes; and here and there cypresses, symbols of death, raised their gloomy heads. The ground was so saturated with moisture, that each footstep of the horses made a deep impression, which was immediately filled with water. Trees, half-decayed, lay about in all directions, and millions of frogs were leaping sportively across them, at the same time rending the air with their discordant notes. In some places I discovered a kind of grass or weeds growing, but weak and unhealthy. Branches of trees formed a haunt for hawks, falcons, and eagles, which diverted themselves by flying from tree to tree, whilst uttering shrill and deafening screams. The air itself was damp and cold. In the interior of this swamp, there are said to be several dry spots, where runaway Negroes have taken up their residence, and where they spend the remainder of a miserable life. Many are born there, but more leave their bones behind in this marshy and pestilential soil. Some time ago, a regular hunt took place after the deserters; but the inaccessibility of the spot to persons unaccustomed to this labyrinth proved an insurmountable obstacle, and prevented the pursuers from penetrating into its innermost recesses. Many of the unfortunate fugitives were, however, killed, or made prisoners: others hardly ever venture out of their hiding-places, and, rather than lose life and liberty, pass their time in the greatest misery, with but a scanty subsistence. It is thought that but few now remain in this swamp.

A canal has lately been cut in this neighbourhood, which unites Chesapeak Bay and Albemarle Sound, in North Carolina. Norfolk expects to derive great advantages from this communication, and time will show whether these anticipations are well founded or not.

Not far from a small place called Somerton, we entered the territory of North Carolina. The road was execrable, and consisted of deep sand, and bottomless holes, and here and there artificial corduroy roads, generally in so indifferent a condition, that they drew down the severest animadversions of the travellers. By way of change, streams and rivulets were sometimes crossed by swimming, and the numberless rivers in ferry-boats, or rather canoes, which invariably filled with water before we reached the opposite shore. Bridges were, no doubt, seen, and even frequently; but their dilapidated state made it more hazardous to traverse them than to take the chance of fording the stream.

The country presents a very monotonous appearance, consisting only of plains and woods. No mountains are visible; even hills are scarce. The wild forests seem to be endless, and sometimes reminded me of those in the North of Sweden, with the exception that American woods are composed of a variety of trees, such as oak of different kinds, cypresses, cedars, pines, &c., which is not the case with us. The soil is very poor, being chiefly sand, with a small proportion of good earth. The scattered plantations in these ill-favoured parts bore evident marks of the poverty of their owners; and, on more than one occasion, I felt persuaded that the poor condition of the people of North Carolina had not been overrated. All the houses near the roads deserve no other name than that of huts. Built of the trunks of trees, the branches of which are not even cut off, laid loosely on the top of each other, so that the ends only join, they afford but a wretched shelter against the inclemency of the weather. On the outside of these huts is a chimney made of brick, which gives a still more miserable appearance to the building. Fences are seen in abundance ; and every cultivated field has its inclosure. The planks or stakes are laid horizontally on each other, without being bound or nailed, and form angles with other planks also laid horizontally, thus making a solid support for the whole. Before many of the dirty houses, numberless peacocks strutted in full parade, displaying their plumes of all colours. They are raised in unusual numbers in this State, and the people carry on a kind of traffic, though not a very profitable one, with them, the price of such a bird being only one dollar.

The interior of the houses was destitute of every kind of comfort. In many places no furniture was to be seen. Instead of candles, splinters of lighted wood, carried in the hand, were used, and, to my great surprise, negligently thrown by the Negroes into a corner of the room, close to the wooden walls. Drinking-glasses did not belong to the catalogue of necessaries in these habitations ; goat-horns served as a substitute. But even these may prove acceptable, if the traveller has but a sufficient supply to fill them, which was not the case in the parts of the country which I visited.

Fields and meadows were scarce and far from rich, so that cattle looked poor and lean, and milk could not be obtained for several days. These circumstances may account for the continual emigration from North Carolina to Georgia and Alabama. On the following day, I met numbers of poor people on their way to these States, after having converted their little all into tangible property. They travelled mostly on foot, sometimes on horseback or on mules, accompanied by a waggon, covered with canvass, and containing, besides women and children, some miserable articles of household furniture. At night they bivouacked in the woods around a large fire, which formed a singular contrast with the sombre appearance of the forest.

Many of these emigrants return to their former homes poorer than they left them. Their scanty resources are generally insufficient for the purchase of good land in Georgia and Alabama. Obliged to be satisfied with inferior lots, mostly in the hands of speculators, they soon perceive that the soil is not better than what they have left behind. Disappointed in their expectations, they return to their place of nativity, after having spent their little property in travelling and other expences, and gained nothing but woful experience. This is a sad picture, but it will be easily recognized by any one who has visited North Carolina.

I saw very few living creatures on the road, as the number of travellers is very inconsiderable; both men and women journey on horseback. But, independently of these, I met scarcely any one except a Negro now and then, who, half naked and sleepy, was wandering in the woods. A white pedestrian I never observed during my whole journey through the Southern States. Near a church, situated in the midst of a wood, not far distant from the road, where divine service was performing when I happened to pass, I counted not fewer than a thousand saddle-horses, besides a few sulkies, a species of vehicle used all over the United States. All the horses were tied to trees, but not a creature was in attendance to look after them.

Indian corn was chiefly cultivated in these parts. Cotton-fields are not seen till you approach Fayetteville. Stumps and dead trunks of trees are invariably left standing in the fields, and give a wild appearance even to cultivated Nature. One night, our road led directly through a field of Indian corn, covered with the withered and dry stalks of a former crop, the whole looking as if it had been the prey of a great conflagration. The objects appeared so dark and gloomy, that it influenced, in some measure, the spirit of the travellers, and for a while we suspended our contemplations. Forests of lifeless trunks and half burned stumps met the eye in every direction ; and in the moonlight these might be taken for a phalanx of ghosts. We pulled up the windows of the coach, and continued silent.

The heat and confined air obliged me at length to let down a window, and, to my great surprise, I suddenly perceived an extensive field, perfectly white, as if covered with snow. The first impulse was that snow had actually fallen, and the lateness of the season rendered this supposition probable ; but the day had been remarkably warm, and the atmosphere was still rather oppressive, two circumstances little in harmony with a fall of snow. The whole seemed like a dream. Rubbing my eyes, I attempted to awake one of my neighbours, with a view to point out the singularity of the scene. He did not answer my appeal, and his oppressed respiration removed all doubt as to his being under the uncontrollable power of Morpheus, alike unable to enjoy the beauty of a fine landscape, and to answer questions. My curiosity was therefore highly excited, without being able to satisfy it; and it was only after the lapse of a few hours that I was informed that the snow-covered ground, as I fancied it, was nothing but a cotton-field, the first I had ever seen.

Cotton grows on short stalks, in pods or balls, which burst, like the buds of flowers, when the cotton is ripe. In the spring it is planted as thickly as possible; but, as soon as the plants grow up a little, the field is cleared of weeds, and they are left at a certain distance from each other. The flower is yellow, red, or white, according to the quality of the cotton; the best is snow-white, and in appearance like the lily. Like the sunflower, it follows the direction of the sun: in two days it generally withers. Negroes are employed in gathering and collecting the cotton in baskets, after which it is put into an iron machine in the form of a wheel, worked by horses, which separates the cotton from the seed. In this wheel there are several parallel spouts, set with small teeth, before which the cotton is laid, and by the motion of the wheel it is drawn between them, and then passes through the spouts till the seed is completely separated from it.

The cotton is now received into another wheel, also worked by horses, which cleanses it from every species of impurity by means of fine brushes placed within it. A press is afterwards employed to pack it into bales, and in this state it is sent to market. In many places it is usual to manure the fields with the seed not used for sowing; but of late years experience has taught the planters to set a higher value on it, as it contains a considerable quantity of oil, which is extracted by pressure, and is suitable both for burning and painting. This oil may, in the course of years, become an additional source of wealth to the planters.

At length, late in the evening of the third day, I arrived at Fayetteville, a small town in North Carolina, which may be said to have seen its best days. It owes its origin to a certain period of the last war, when the English were stationed in every direction off the coast, and all commerce with the interior was carried on through this place. Considerable capital was soon brought into play; and from an insignificant spot it gradually rose into a town of some consequence. But a conflagration of unusual violence unfortunately checked this prosperous career, and, on the 29th of May, 1831, reduced to a heap of ruins a town which it had taken a number of years to erect. By this sad calamity more than seven hundred houses were consumed, and the loss was estimated at nearly a million and a half of dollars. Strenuous efforts are making by the sufferers to rebuild the town; but the dwellings are scattered, and means are wanting to restore Fayetteville — at least for years to come — to its former splendour.

On the following day, about noon, I departed in another stage, determined not to stop until I reached Charleston. I found the country of the same character as to the north of Fayetteville: plain, woody, and sandy, it possessed the same features as the former, with the sole difference that swamps occurred very frequently, and rendered the journey any thing but pleasant, if not dangerous. This was particularly the case on the frontiers of North and South Carolina, between two small places called Lumberton and Marion, where the coach was continually in water, which rose in many places above the axletrees, threatening more than once to invade the coach itself. Nothing is more common, after heavy rains, than for the water to penetrate into the carriage; and passengers, to avoid drowning, are then obliged to have recourse to the roof. We luckily escaped this inconvenience, although continually on the alert to effect a retreat through the windows; but our trunks and portmanteaus were completely soaked. What particularly contributed to render this journey hazardous was, the constant crossing of rivers, intersecting the country in every direction. Many of these streams are very extensive, especially the Great Pedee and Santee, both of which in Europe would be considered large. The banks of these rivers, as well as those of the minor streams, Black River, Lynch River, &c., are of a very pleasing aspect, and afford a great relief to the eye, previously fatigued with the sight of swamps and plains of sand. Covered with wood to the water's edge, they rise and fall in a thousand different undulations, thereby intercepting the prospect in many places.

In passing Great Pedee, we embarked in a real Indian canoe, made of a single tree, which contained five passengers, the driver, a boatman, and a quantity of luggage and mail-bags. The current was so strong, and the boat so heavily laden, that the least motion by any member of the company would infallibly have precipitated the whole into the stream. But the boatman, who never ceased recommending us to preserve the equilibrium, steered us safely to the opposite shore, although guiding the bark with only one oar, which he used so dexterously, as to avoid several shoals and rocks in the middle of the river.

The following night I effected another passage, not less perilous than the preceding: between Georgetown and Charleston there are two rivers, the Great and Little Santee, united by a canal. The country between them is nothing but a swamp, so excessively low as to be inundated by the water of the streams. When this is the case, no traveller can possibly pass, unless he chooses to proceed by the canal. In the day-time this is attended with no inconvenience; but the necessity of effecting the passage in the darkest part of the night, still more obscured by a dense fog, and this too in a ferry-boat, the bottom of which was so decayed that the water rushed in every minute, deprived me,

I candidly confess, of all the gratification I should otherwise have derived from the sight of so characteristic a landscape. Two Negroes, the one lame, the other with but one arm, formed the complement of rowers.

On the arrival of the stage, they were roused from a sound slumber, and appeared to be half asleep during the whole passage; indeed I fancied at times that I perceived symptoms of snoring: but, whether this was founded in reality or the effect of imagination, I will not pretend to determine, for they never discontinued rowing until the steersman, also of the African race, in a loud voice informed them that we had arrived at the place of destination. To be able, however, to steer the course in the dark, across large rivers, and through a narrow canal, required no ordinary acuteness on the part of the steersman, however experienced and well acquainted with the localities. The dense fog prevented him from distinguishing any object at a greater distance than a boat's length from us, and the unsteady reflection of the evening star in the water was the only mark which guided and enabled him to calculate the direction he ought to follow. This calculation proved correct in every respect, and we at length reached the opposite shore without the slightest accident.

The country south of Fayetteville to the vicinity of Georgetown is poor, and regarded by agriculturists as unfit for cultivation. The rich soil generally found in the Western States induces numbers of farmers from parts less fertile to resort thither, and to leave all land neglected which requires many hands and more labour, on account of its poverty. The price of land in this part has, in consequence, considerably decreased, no more than forty or fifty cents being paid for an acre covered with wood. If I may credit what was said, I should be inclined to think that the rich soil is not so indifferent but that it might, by industry and perseverance, be rendered productive. I believe, moreover, that, with very little exertion, the swamps might be drained, and converted into fruitful fields. In this conclusion I am the more confirmed, when I take into account the statements of experienced and respectable persons in the neighbourhood, who admitted that the sand is merely on the surface, and that, if the furrows in ploughing the fields were made deep enough, a large proportion of good earth would be thrown up, capable of producing

Indian corn, potatoes, &c. The population in these parts consists chiefly of the offspring of emigrant Highlanders.

The forests are of great extent; to the traveller they appear endless. Of the different kinds of wood with which they abound, oak appeared to me to prevail; of this species, the varieties were very numerous and such as I had never seen, being distinguished by a trifling difference in the shape of the leaves. Near Georgetown, the well-known live oak, so suitable for naval purposes, grows in great abundance. It is only found near the sea-shore; the leaves are slender and pointed. There is, also, in the Southern States, a species of fir, which is peculiar to this part of the country. To the age of three years it is one of the most splendid plants that can be seen, and would be a real ornament to any park. The trunk is perfectly straight, with a thick crown at the top; the whole resembling a young palm-tree. It is usual in the spring to set fire to the brushwood, which has sprung up in the preceding year, with a view to make room for grass and to give it additional vigour; this operation, however, destroys great quantities of young firs, and oak-trees take their place. The same thing occurs if a number of the latter are cut down: firs in turn rise on their ruins, precisely on the same spot. Besides these principal species of trees, I saw considerable quantities of evergreen hollies, with their red berries, cypresses, laurels, junipers, &c. all intermingled in the woods.

In the course of this journey, I had frequent opportunities of seeing rattlesnakes, which are found in great abundance in the Northern woods. Their bright eyes sparkled among the bushes, which concealed every other part of them from view; but they were generally discovered, when stretched out on the ground, taking the benefit of a sunny day. In this attitude, they are absolutely harmless, as they cannot bite till they have formed a ring or circle, thus affording ample time for escape. The most dangerous enemies of this venomous animal are deer and hogs: the former never come near unless it is stretched out, when, with the rapidity of lightning, they jump on its head, and trample it with their fore-feet till life is extinct. The hogs again give the snake a regular chase; it does not possess sufficient strength to penetrate their hard hides, and vainly diffuses its poison over the bristles: the chase is never given up till the snake is dead, when they devour it in the most voracious manner. Another species of snakes, called moccasins, is often found in the woods: they are larger than the rattlesnake, equally venomous, but more dangerous to man on account of their giving no warning before they bite. Many remedies for the bites of these animals have been tried, but none have yet effected a cure, or saved the life of the patient. The Indians pretend to be acquainted with a method of healing the bites of poisonous serpents; and experience has shown that, if any thing can effect a recovery, it is their simple application. The following is one of their remedies. Take an herb called gold of the earth, or golden rod, lay part of it fresh on the wounded part, make a kind of tea of the remainder, and let the patient frequently drink of it. Administer afterwards a copious dose of salts, and then a few drops of turpentine. The slough will, by degrees, assume the colour of the snake, and drop off of itself. This remedy is said to have been very successful: recovery, however, is hopeless, if the snake in biting has punctured a vein. No human power can then rescue the victim from death; to assuage the excruciating pain is the only thing that can be accomplished.

Many experiments have been made to discover the best means of defence against venomous serpents. I heard a farmer in North Carolina assert that if the hands are rubbed with an herb called the rattlesnake masterpiece, or the root of it is kept in the pocket, any snake will drop down as if dead, and writhe in excessive pain, like a worm in an anthill. I could not ascertain what herb it was, nor do I know if he meant the leaves of white ash, which are said to have a wonderful effect on the rattlesnake. The following experiment was lately made; and, as I entertain no doubt of the authenticity of the statement, I here report it. A few sportsmen were chasing a deer, and happened to fall in with a rattlesnake. Having heard of the effect of the ash leaf on this animal, they hastened to cut off a couple of branches from trees within their reach, one of ash, the other of sugar-maple. Armed with these, they approached the snake, which immediately prepared for battle, hissing with rage. I will finish the story in the words of the narrator himself:

"I first stretched forth the branch of the ash, and rubbed the body of the animal gently with the leaves. It immediately lowered its head to the ground, stretched itself out, instead of coiling itself up, fell backward, twisted, and threw itself into every possible attitude except that of a circle, and appeared to be in the greatest agony. Satisfied with the trial, I laid the ash aside: as soon as the snake perceived this, it again rose, and resumed the same threatening posture as before. I now held out the other branch. In an instant it threw itself upon it, concealed its head among the leaves, and drew back, and re-commenced the attack, advancing its whole body with the celerity of an arrow. After repeating this several times, I suddenly changed the branch, and again rubbed it gently across the back with the ash leaves. No sooner had I done this than it fell backward a second time, and no more ventured to look at its enemy. Curious to see what effect blows from this weapon might have upon it, I struck several times at its slippery body, expecting to see the animal foaming with rage: but the blows did not produce the effect I anticipated; they only served to increase its uneasiness and pain. At each blow, the snake buried its head as deep as it could in the sand, as if to find a passage under the earth, and thus escape its enemy."

But I must resume my narrative of the journey to Charleston. Towards evening, the day following our departure from Fayetteville, we arrived at a small place called Georgetown, on the river Great Pedee, not far from the sea. It was here I first discovered a rice-field, which appeared to me to look like one of oats; the plant itself is not unlike the latter. All rice-fields are in low situations, and require to be often under water, which circumstance occasioning great dampness, the neighbourhood of the plantations is extremely unhealthy, and often fatal to the miserable slaves, who are frequently obliged to stand up to the middle in water.

The stage stopped at a distance of about two miles from Charleston, where the passengers embarked in a boat, rowed by six Negroes, the merriest slaves, without exception, I ever saw. The numberless anecdotes with which they amused us proved sufficiently that these beings, at least, were not unhappy under the yoke of thraldom. Their songs continued till the boat landed us at the port, after having passed the bay between Charleston and the sea, which forms the entrance to the city. The sun had just risen, when I found myself in the streets of Charleston.

CHAPTER XVII.

Le meilleur de tous les plans de finances est de dépenser peu, et le meilleur de tous les impots est le plus petit.

SAY.

CHARLESTON is the second city in size in the Southern States; it counted in 1830 a population of thirty thousand two hundred and eighty-nine souls. Its advantageous situation on an isthmus between two rivers, the Ashley and Cooper, at a small distance from their outlet into the sea, places it in the rank of the most considerable city for commerce, with the exception of New Orleans, south of the Potomac, a rank which I firmly believe it will continue to occupy for a long period. Viewed on the map, the city bears a strong resemblance to New York, but in reality there is no comparison. Charleston, closely examined, has an old and dilapidated appearance, whereas New York is quite the reverse: there, every thing bears the stamp of freshness. What contributes to give Charleston a different feature is the piazzas and balconies attached to every house; and these, in addition to the trees planted in the streets, called Pride of India, soon inform the visiter that he is arrived in a southern latitude.

The houses are chiefly of brick, and plastered: heat, heavy showers, and dust, have, however, taken off the plastering in many places, so that the buildings have a very shabby appearance. This was particularly observable in the churches, the exterior of which indicated only misery and destruction. Almost every house has a garden adjoining, filled with flowers, shrubs, and trees, peculiar to these warm regions; many flowers were in full bloom, although the month of December was at hand. Few streets are paved; they are consequently in a very bad state after the least shower; but, generally speaking, they are regularly planned and tolerably wide.

The climate of Charleston, in winter, is as pleasant and healthy as it is oppressive and dangerous in summer. During my residence there in the last month in the year, the most delightful summer heat continued uninterruptedly, so that great-coats were absolutely useless: many of the principal inhabitants have never used these superfluous articles. At certain periods, however, the city is considered extremely unhealthy: those who can afford it then remove to the plantations, or visit the Northern States. Even a residence at the former places is, during the great summer heat, attended with attacks of dangerous fevers, attributable to vapours rising from the rice-fields and swamps: the rich planters then lose no time in returning to the city. Thus, removals take place from the beginning to the end of the year, to avoid infection.

The principal exports from this city are cotton and rice, immense quantities of which are shipped for Europe. The well known Sea Island cotton is chiefly exported from this place; it brings considerable sums into the State. Nothing but bales of the latter article and barrels of rice are seen in the lower part of the city; the streets and quays are sometimes so filled with them, that the agility of a sailor is required to effect a passage. The ear is continually annoyed with sounds proclaiming the price of these articles, and merchants and dealers are incessantly engaged in drawing samples from the bales, for the purpose of trying the goodness of the article, by pulling out long threads between their fingers, or dipping their hands into the barrels of rice, to examine its whiteness and purity. This branch of commerce has been for a long time, and still continues to be, a source of great wealth to the merchants of Charleston: but its prosperity is not proportionate to that of other cities. Many reasons have been assigned for this stationary condition, and among others, the vicinity of the rival city of Savannah, which possesses the advantage of a water-communication with the interior of the country, and has consequently a locality preferable to that of Charleston. To remedy this disadvantage, a railroad has lately been commenced between the latter city and Augusta, from which beneficial results are expected. This railroad was expected to be finished the following year, and I have yet to learn whether the anticipations so fondly entertained have been realised or not.

St. Andrew's Society is a benevolent institution, having for its object the education of poor children. It has branches in all parts of the Union, and is reported, much to the credit of its members, to do a great deal of good. It has a large building in Charleston, where public assemblies and meetings are held.

I attended one of the latter, convoked to pay a tribute of respect to the memory of Sir Walter Scott, the account of whose death had but recently reached the city. Several orators, natives of South Carolina, had here an opportunity of giving specimens of innate eloquence. The extraordinary talents of the deceased as a poet and novelist were represented in colours which soon drew the most enthusiastic applause from all parts of the hall, and clearly evinced a disposition on the part of the audience warmly to contribute to the proposed subscription for raising, in some conspicuous place in the city, a marble bust in commemoration of the Scottish bard.

Among the speakers, none produced so powerful an effect on the audience as General Hayne. This remarkable personage, the boast of his native city, has lately played an important part during the eventful period of the Nullification project, and is now Governor of South Carolina; he is in the prime of life, with the vigour of youth and a seductive eloquence, and will always prove a dangerous antagonist to any enemy who may attack him. His language is pleasing, but vehement.

Frequently, when the subject is interesting, he raises his voice to an astonishing pitch, and thunders in the hall till all the members tremble.

As a public speaker, General Hayne is exactly the reverse of what he is in small and familiar circles; there, he is hardly to be recognized. The violent declaimer, whose looks, like the thunders of Jove, breathed only fire and flame, is the mildest and most modest of men in society. His voice there might be taken for that of a diffident youth; and his eyes, which at other times seem to threaten a whole community, are fixed on the ground. It appears as if the oratorical chair produced a magic effect on a man naturally mild, and had the power of converting, at certain periods, the peaceable citizen into an ambitious military chieftain. Generally adored by the State over which he rules, and admired for his talents even by those opposed to him in politics, Hayne is one of the greatest men now living in America, and will one day, no doubt, shine in the page of history.

At this period, the attention of the whole Union was directed to the State of South Carolina. A voice was there heard, whose threatening language, like a black cloud, the precursor of thunder, spread over the horizon, and chilled the blood of many an aged man. Numbers of deep-thinking statesmen had, undoubtedly, predicted a similar explosion of discontent in the Southern States, particularly in South Carolina, excited by what was called " The American System," which consisted in affording protection to home manufactures, and encouraging internal improvements, at the expence of trade; but, by skilful management, this explosion had for a while been checked, and it was hoped that the first impulse in the South had somewhat abated, when, all of a sudden, accounts arrived that a Convention had been convoked at Columbia, the capital of South Carolina, the members of which assumed the name of Nullifiers.

This party, in a mass, showed at once a hostile attitude to the Federal Government. Its first step was to issue a proclamation, dated in November, 1832, in which the members declare, "that, as Congress, by its unjust and unconstitutional tariffs of the 19th May, 1828, and the 14th July, 1832, has overstepped the power conferred on it by the people, we, the inhabitants of the State of South Carolina, in Convention represented, declare and ordain that these acts, tariffs, or laws, are null and void: that, from the 1st of February next, the people are absolved from paying any duties, and that all those who hold any civil or military office in the said State must, within a certain period, swear that they will obey, execute, and defend, these regulations. And we declare, moreover, that we are firmly determined to abide by, and carry into effect, the tenor of this proclamation—that we will not suffer any act of violence to be exercised against us by the Government of Washington: that we will consider any violent aggressions as attempts to force South Carolina to secede from the Union; and that the people of this State, in the event of secession, will consider itself free from all political connection with the other sister States of the Union, and organize a government of its own, and act in the character of a free and independent State."

Proclamations were, moreover, issued by the same Convention to the people of South Carolina, as well as to those of other States. In the first, it was attempted to be proved that the new tariff, adopted by the Congress of 1832 as law, to take effect in March 1833, was altogether unjust and contrary to the principles of a free government: that, if carried into execution, it would seal the fate of South Carolina, by reducing it to poverty and misery. The following are briefly the arguments adduced:

"The Government of the United States is altogether what is called a Federal Government—an alliance between different Sovereigns. The Federal Constitution, again, is a compact, a confederation, a union, by which so many independent States have mutually agreed to exercise their sovereign power at certain periods, when they are all equally interested in the subject under discussion; as, for instance, when war, peace, commerce, foreign negotiations, and Indian treaties, are in question: on all other occasions they may may act separately. Such is the true meaning of the Union. For the sake of convenience, a common agent has been appointed: this agent is the Federal Government, which represents the confederated States, and executes their will. Its power is perfectly derivative: it is a political corporation, which, like other political corporations, derives its authority from another source—namely, the States. But, if the States have invested this Government with power, they may also withdraw it. All hereditary sovereignty rests, therefore, with the States; it is only a moral obligation, which they voluntarily imposed on themselves, and certainly not a want of independence, which prevents them from exercising this authority.

"By the Declaration of Independence, South Carolina became a free and independent State, and, as such, she has a right to exercise the same acts as any Sovereign. As, in all alliances between independent princes, each party has a right to decide on the best means of obtaining indemnity for injuries received, so it belongs, in the present contest between South Carolina and the Federal Government, exclusively to the former, by delegates duly appointed by the people, and in Convention assembled, to determine whether the federal compact is infringed, and what measures the State ought to resort to for its re-union. South Carolina, therefore, neither can nor will yield to the Federal Government, still less to the Supreme Court of the United States—a mere tool of the Government, itself only a tool of the States—a right which belongs to her as a free State, and without which the whole sovereignty would only be a bubble—an empty name.

"Can that Government be called free, which levies taxes with impunity, in order to encourage one branch of industry to the detriment of others, if such a tax is not actually prompted by some great and inevitable public call? Other nations appear disposed to remove restraints on commerce; our Congress, on the contrary, is determined to lay every impediment on the importation of the very goods which we barter for the produce of the South, and thus throw the whole weight of taxation on this part of the Union. A people which has fought for liberty can suffer such wrongs no longer. With the last session of Congress, all hopes vanished of seeing justice guide the proceedings of the assembled representatives of the Confederation. One alternative only remains for this State: it is, citizens, RESISTANCE, not physical, but moral. It is a matter of indifference by what name it may be distinguished in the world — whether Nullification, State interference, State Veto, or something similar; if it be only resistance against oppressive measures, it is the path which duty, patriotism, and self-defence, point out. And this resistance is even constitutional, for the act itself which prompts it is unconstitutional, and nullification was already considered constitutional by a particular committee, appointed in 1798.

"Yes, Government is aware of it, and will not venture by military interference to force this State into obedience. Such a step would only lead to disunion between the members of the Confederation: it is, besides, in opposition to the spirit of the age. Look at England, which has lately accomplished one of the greatest reforms ever recorded in her annals—a reform which her wisest statesmen would, ten years ago, have considered impracticable without a civil war and great effusion of blood. The people are now every where enlightened, and this intellectual experience obliges Governments to exercise reflexion, moderation. Citizens, our dispute will be amicably adjusted, we are well persuaded, and nullification will consolidate instead of tearing asunder the Union.

"But the die is cast; we have solemnly declared our determination not to pay any taxes till abuses and grievances are redressed. Prepare yourselves, citizens, for the ensuing contest, and be ready to meet it as becomes free men. We call upon you by every thing that is sacred not to abandon the cause till we have obtained justice. Do your duty to your country, and leave the rest to God."

In the last address again, namely to the people of the twenty-three other States, the Convention says—"No government has ever exercised greater violence than that now attempted by the Federal Government against South Carolina, by compelling it to purchase at an exorbitant price articles manufactured at home, instead of foreign ones at a cheap rate. This Government, originally formed to protect, improve, and extend commerce, has done more to destroy it than all land and sea-pirates ever could.

"South Carolina, an agricultural State, whose commerce consists in bartering the produce of her soil for foreign manufactures, would, if trade were free, at least receive one-third more for her own commodities; for the duties of about fifty per cent. now laid upon them amount annually to the sum of three millions of dollars, whilst the whole produce of cotton in the same State—and cotton is the chief article of exportation—does not exceed six millions. Let us suppose, for a moment, that another State, New Jersey, for instance, manufactured the raw material to nearly the same amount, ought not both States to enjoy the same advantages? And yet is it so? The fifty per cent. duties fall only on South Carolina: this is not enough; they are paid to protect the manufacturers of New Jersey, who are at last benefited by it. What right have the manufacturing States—for the Federal Government is in our eyes only their tool—to prevent South Carolina from exchanging, directly or indirectly, the rich produce of her soil against such foreign goods as contribute principally to the wealth and prosperity of the inhabitants? It cannot be assumed—for truth opposes this objection—that, by bartering our produce against cheap European manufactures, we injure any of the privileges of the home-manufacturers, although it would undoubtedly be more in accordance with their wishes if we bought their inferior goods at higher prices.

"South Carolina is now upon the same footing with these States as the Anglo-American Colonies were formerly with the mother-country, with this difference only, that we suffer infinitely more than our ancestors. Must we remain indifferent spectators to this violence, and patiently give up an inheritance sealed with the blood of our forefathers? A people who voluntarily submit to oppression, and know that they are oppressed, deserve to be slaves: history proves that such a people invariably find a tyrant. A tyrant has never yet made slaves; but a slavish disposition in the people produces tyrants. The smallest community animated with a free spirit never has a master. May, therefore, none of the other States in the Union be induced to take precipitate and violent steps, in the vain expectation that South Carolina shall be found to waver in defending her rights and her liberties, merely because she has a population of only half a million instead of twenty!

"This dispute can be settled only by a modification of the tariff, or by a general Convention of all the States. Should South Carolina be separated from the Union, other agricultural States, as well as some in the West, will follow her example, compelled by necessity. How is it possible, that Georgia, Mississippi, Tennessee, even Kentucky, can feel inclined to pay to the Northern States a tax of fifty per cent. on articles of consumption, merely for the privilege of being united to them, when they are able to obtain all their supplies from the ports of South Carolina, without paying one cent. in duties? The secession of South Carolina will therefore entail a dissolution of the whole Union.

"Under these circumstances, we earnestly recommend that the other States may duly consider the step which they are taking. We do not believe that the Federal Government will venture by military force to maintain the tariff system; but if, in spite of our warnings, such an act of madness should be resolved upon, we hereby most solemnly declare that this system of oppression shall never succeed in South Carolina until slaves only remain to submit to it.

"Rather would we see the territory of the State converted into cemeteries of the free than inhabited by a population of slaves. These are the principles which animate us: true to them, we are determined to embrace the pillars of the temple of Liberty, and, if it must fall, let us be buried in the ruins!"

Besides these two important documents, another was also issued by James Hamilton, governor of the State of South Carolina, who, n a message, dated Colombia, 27th November, 1832, informs the Legislature that it is its duty to sanction the interposition of the revolutionary Convention; recommends the placing the whole State upon a war footing, in order not to be unprepared in case of aggression; but hopes at the same time to see an amicable adjustment of the dispute in question by the interference of the other States.

Thus far had the Nullifiers advanced, when

I arrived at Charleston. Every thing seemed to indicate that a revolution was on the eve of breaking out. The excitement among the hot-headed inhabitants was very great: a spark would have sufficed to set the whole in a flame. Of Union men there was also a considerable number, men who disapproved the principles of nullification, and who, partly from apprehension of a civil war, partly from attachment to the former state of things, endeavoured to extinguish the wide-spreading conflagration; but their efforts only served to irritate the minds of the others still more, and the flames of revolution continued to burn uninterruptedly in every corner of the State. Enthusiasm prevailed among women as well as among men; the zeal of the former was so great, that many a maiden in South Carolina enjoined her lover to display his prowess before he should be permitted to press her hand to his lips, and receive a return to his ardent declaration of love. Societies were formed by these modern Amazons, the object of which was to keep up the enthusiasm of the men. At a public meeting held at Charleston, during my residence in the city, General Hayne delivered a very violent speech, in which the word disunion was used, when the ladies immediately testified their feelings by tokens of unbounded approbation. White handkerchiefs waved continually at every sentence pronounced by the orator, and their bright eyes flashed fire and flames. It would indeed have required but very little exertion to induce these patriotic heroines to take up arms and march for Washington, to besiege and take the Capitol and the White House* by assault, and make the President himself prisoner.

All these threatening measures at length reached the ears of the Government at Washington. But General Jackson, far from allowing himself to be intimidated, determined immediately, by prompt and energetic measures, to destroy the weeds which began to grow up on the American soil. Congress had just commenced its sittings; and, in a message from the President, dated 4th of December, he informs the members of the circumstance, in a manner which led to the belief that the threats had had some effect, or that the Federal Government was still undecided how to act. But this illusion was soon dispelled; for, on the 10th of December following,

* The White House in which the President resides at Washington.

a proclamation was issued, the language of which sounded like an alarm-bell, accompanied by the unexpected annunciation, that Government had ordered several detachments of troops, both of the land and sea service, to enter the rebellious State.

"A number of the most enlightened and disinterested Statesmen," says the President, among other things, in his proclamation, "have invested Congress with power to regulate the revenues of the State, and yet every State wishes to arrogate to herself the right of opposing it. These two prerogatives appear in direct opposition to each other; yet it is contended that such an absurdity exists in the Constitution. I consider the attempt assumed by a State to annul any law duly enacted by the United States as irreconcileable with the existence of the Union, expressly contradicted by the Constitution, and contrary to the spirit and principles on which it is framed, and finally, destroying the great object for which it was intended. Complaints have been made that the laws do not operate equally. This may be said of all laws that have ever been, or ever will be, made. Man, in his wisdom, has never yet discovered any system of taxation, operating in an equal degree. If the unequal operation of a law constitutes its unconstitutionality, and if all such laws can, for such reasons, be annulled by any State at pleasure, then indeed is the Federal Constitution unfit to make the least effort for its conservation. We have hitherto relied on it as the safest link of our Union. We have hailed it as a work framed by the soundest and wisest men in the nation. We have contemplated it with holy veneration, as the palladium of our liberties. Are we in error, fellow citizens, to attach this importance to the Constitution of our country? It forms a Commonwealth, but not a Confederation: its character is the same, whether effected by a convention among the States, or in any other way. Each State has, in union with other States, delegated so much power as is necessary to constitute a single nation; and has, therefore, from that moment, relinquished the right of seceding from the Union; for such a defection not only dissolves the ties of an alliance but destroys the concord of a nation. To advocate that any State may at pleasure secede from the Union is the same as to contend that the United States is not a nation. It would be a solecism to pretend that any part of the nation may break off all connexion with the other parts, to their detriment and ruin, without committing a crime. Secession, like every other revolutionary act, may be excusable, if oppression gives rise to it; but to call it a constitutional right is to confound the meaning of the expressions. The laws of the United States must be obeyed. I have no unlimited control over them — my duties are clearly defined by the Constitution. Those who told you, fellow citizens, that you may, unmolested, obstruct the march of the laws, have deceived you — they could not be deceived themselves. They know that such a resistance must be repelled. Their object is secession from the Union; but be not misguided — secession from the Union by violence and with arms is treason. I conjure you, fellow citizens of the State in which I was born,* if you value the cause of liberty, to which you have devoted your lives, if you value the tranquillity of your country, the lives of your principal citizens, pause; withdraw from the archives of your State the dangerous edicts promulgated by the Convention — announce to its Members that all misfortunes are light compared to those which will follow a secession from the Union — de-

* General Andrew Jackson is a native of South Carolina.

clare that you will never fight under any other than the star-spangled banner — and that you wish to see your names go down untarnished to the latest posterity. You cannot destroy the Constitution of your country — you can only disturb its tranquillity, check its prosperity, eclipse its future fame for durability; but tranquillity shall be restored: once more shall happiness and prosperity thrive in your native soil, and the dark stain which now disgraces the character of your State be expunged, and remain a perpetual stigma on the authors of these troubles."

This Proclamation gained universal applause: one voice alone was heard from the confines of Canada to the extremity of the Floridas. Even in South Carolina the people began to waver, and the chiefs of the new party paused for a while to recover themselves, and to consider whether they had not gone too far in their inferences as to State-rights to withdraw from the contest. The situation of the Nullifiers became still more alarming, when, shortly afterwards, a Bill passed Congress, authorising the President to enforce the payment of duties, if not voluntarily liquidated: this Bill was afterwards called "The Bloody Bill," a name by which it is now generally known. In addition, came the unexpected circumstance, that the neighbouring States, Virginia, North Carolina, and Georgia, having nearly the same interests at stake as South Carolina, and on whose co-operation it had confidently calculated, had disappointed its expectations, induced partly by jealousy, partly by other causes. In this posture of affairs, it was not strange that Messrs. Calhoun and McDuffie, representatives of the Nullifiers at Washington, acceded to the compromise which Mr. Clay, father of the manufacturing system, proposed, although they easily perceived that the reduction of duties suggested had rather the appearance of being advantageous to the Southern Slave-States than was so in reality. The voice of Nullification became in the mean time weaker and weaker, till it died away altogether — at least it was never heard openly threatening a dissolution of the States. The party is, however, far from being dispersed: like the snail, it has only retired within its shell. The day may yet come, when the progress of the doctrine of State-rights in the Southern parts may attract the serious attention of the Northern.

CHAPTER XVIII.

Who could guess
If ever more should meet those mutual eyes?
BYRON.

READY to continue my journey, I embraced the opportunity of a steamboat going to Savannah, to proceed thither. In calm weather, the steamers generally steer their course outside the rocks: the trip is then extremely short and pleasant; but, in winter, when rain and fog are the order of the day, the inland navigation, singular in its kind, is preferred. The country between Charleston and Savannah is everywhere intersected by rivers, which we either ascended or descended, approaching close to the sea-coast, where a number of islands are situated, and form a barrier against the violence of the waves. It was, in fact, a scene full of variety; sometimes we passed unhealthy swamps, then followed the shores of serpentine rivers; again we were surrounded by extensive cotton and rice fields; then a view of fertile islands presented itself; and at last we traversed various bays, where the rivers discharge themselves into the sea. Had the weather been fine, this trip would have afforded me many pleasant recollections; as it was, I had an opportunity of attentively and with deep interest observing the ever-changing scenery, varying from the highest state of cultivation and fertility to the desolation of swamps, with their accessory inanimation. It is on these islands, and all round the coast south of Savannah, that the Sea Island cotton, superior to any other, is cultivated; the length of its threads distinguishes it from ordinary cottons. The cultivation of this particular variety is different from that of the short cotton: the sea air, it is supposed, has also no small influence on the quality. It fetches a much higher price than other cotton.

The steamboat stopped on the following morning at a small town called Beaufort, to land and take on board passengers. Among the number, I observed a middle-aged man, accompanied by a young Negro woman, better dressed than any I had lately seen. Her companion was one of those despicable beings who traffic in human flesh: he had just before bought the unfortunate female from a planter, who, from some caprice or other, had sold her, although brought up in his own family, and a favourite with all its members on account of her honesty and remarkably handsome countenance. Before she left the shore, she bade, oppressed with grief, a tender farewell to her fellow-slaves; and when at length she embraced her husband for the last time, she lost all power, and fell senseless in the arms of her unfeeling master, who kept incessantly repeating his orders to go on board. With the utmost exertion she was able to obey the command, and scarcely had she reached the deck before the steamboat started. Leaning against the side of the boat, she fixed her large black eyes on the home which was gradually disappearing before her, and waved her handkerchief as long as she could see her unhappy husband and the group of friends whom she left behind; but, when the winding of the river concealed from her view the dearest objects on earth, she contemplated in deep silence the waves agitated by the vessel. Presently her native place disappeared altogether, but she remained immoveable in the same attitude. Even on our arrival at Savannah, I observed her eyes fixed on the quarter where Beaufort was situated. Her countenance bore the stamp of perfect resignation, and it was only when her eyes happened to meet those of her new master that her uneasiness became visible. Accustomed to suffer and submit to sacrifices, this unhappy creature was probably no stranger to such trials and heart-rending scenes.

Beside me, on deck, stood a rich planter from the interior of South Carolina. I had in the morning had a long conversation with him on the subject of slavery, and could not help, by way of illustration of this abominable traffic, pointing out to him the case just mentioned. "I do not deny," answered he, very deliberately, "that cases like this sometimes occur; but, for the honour of humanity, they are not frequent. In my neighbourhood, every planter has agreed that, if he has a Negro married to a Negro woman belonging to another, and he wishes to get rid of the Negro or quit the vicinity, he will either offer the slave to the proprietor of the Negro woman, or will himself purchase the latter: in this case, the price is regulated by other planters. People begin," added he, "to show more feeling towards these unfortunate creatures than formerly, so much so, that ill-usage is hardly ever heard of. On the contrary, you will find many proprietors treating their Negroes like their own children, and, partly by salutary admonition, partly by the distribution of religious tracts, endeavouring to make them sensible of simple moral truths, and thus gradually inculcating a deeper and more affectionate love for God and the Bible."

Not far from Beaufort, I saw the palmetto tree growing in great luxuriance: all the banks were covered with it. This southern plant has, when young, a number of excrescences on the trunk, which gradually disappear as it grows up, and is freed from branches. Like Italian fir, the crown of the palmetto is always green. The trunk is of so spongy a nature that a nail driven into it will not hold fast: it is, therefore, unfit for ship-building, but is used as piles in streams or lakes, for which it is particularly adapted. It is not liable to be worm-eaten, neither does it suffer the slightest injury from water. Round the trunk, rings or cracks are formed in the bark; these are said to indicate the age of the tree, each ring signifying a year. The leaves resemble fans, and possess great strength: seats of chairs, hats, baskets, &c. are made of them.

A little farther on, I arrived at a place formerly fortified by the Indians, the ramparts of which were made of oyster-shells. These truly characteristic fortifications were undoubtedly erected long before the arrival of the English in these parts; for history does not mention any occasion for which they were thrown up. The probability is, that they have been constructed by some Indian tribe, to serve as a bulwark against another. One of the redoubts is considerable, of great length, with aisles, and twelve feet in height. Its situation along the shore leads to the inference that it was from this side that attacks were expected. Considered as defences, they certainly possess very little interest; but it is the material of which they are built that attracts the attention of travellers. How many millions of oysters must have perished in order to the erection of these redoubts!

The first view of Savannah produces no very favourable impression, particularly if the traveller is unfortunate enough to alight at an hotel close to the landing-place; but, upon nearer inspection, he cannot avoid pronouncing a fair opinion of the city, namely, that it is far from unpleasant, and that the houses of the inhabitants are ever open to strangers, to whom all the attentions of hospitality and politeness are shown.

Savannah is situated on a ridge of sand, close to a river bearing the same name, which divides the States of South Carolina and Georgia. It is built in a square, with streets perfectly straight, and surrounded by walks, or *boulevards,* shaded by beautiful Pride of India trees. In that part of the walk contiguous to the river, as well as in the one below on the bank itself, all business is transacted, which consists chiefly in cotton shipments to Europe. In this particular spot, nothing is heard but conversations about the article; bales are piled up in every store and at every corner. Whoever visits a merchant's office will find it filled with samples: if the clerks are occupied with correspondence, rest assured the subject is cotton. If the chief of a mercantile house is seen in conversation with any one, be equally sure that he is talking about the price of cotton. But in the interior of the town reigns perfect tranquillity; nothing indicates that on the article of cotton alone depends the prosperity of Savannah. The houses are mostly of wood, and have balconies in the usual southern style. The unpaved streets resemble well-kept high roads.

After heavy rains, or, more properly, drenching showers, it is customary to plough the ground, as in a field, with a view to render it sooner dry. This method of drying streets appeared rather new to a stranger; but certain it is that the object was accomplished with extraordinary rapidity, for the depth of the furrows enabled the sandy soil to imbibe the water much sooner than if it had been left to drain away of itself.

Late in the evening, I again took my departure in a steamer, with the intention of proceeding up the river to Augusta, a distance of about two hundred miles, owing to the continual windings of the river, but which in a direct line would not exceed one hundred and fifty. The character of this stream is exactly similar to all those south of the Potomac; crooked, sometimes winding forward, then turning back round a small projecting point of land, which it often required nearly an hour to double, without gaining, in a straight line, more than a mile. The banks are low, in many places not higher than the surface of the water, and consist exclusively of swamps, in which both bushes and trees grow down to the water's edge, intercepting the prospect of the interior of the country.

The woods appeared covered with a long grey moss, which produced a dismal and desolate effect on the landscape, and reminded man that Death resided in these unhealthy regions. In truth, I perceived but few solitary habitations. The wretched scattered hovels that were visible were occupied only by miserable woodcutters, who seemed to prefer the alternative of death to the horrors of starvation in a healthier climate, or by Negroes, who are less liable to the fevers generated by unhealthy and marshy regions. In the brushwood, near the banks, were myriads of wild ducks and wild turkeys. In summer, I am assured that large snakes and alligators also show themselves on sunny days.

Of all the towns in the Southern States, none, with the exception of New Orleans, has a more agreeable exterior, and inspires the stranger at first with a stronger idea of comfort and wealth than Augusta. Frequent fires have of late years not a little contributed to embellish the town, by the removal of old and the erection of new buildings; but the principal cause of these improvements is to be traced to its active and flourishing trade. The situation of Augusta is in every respect advantageous: on the borders of two cotton-growing States, and lying close to a navigable river, down which produce is sent with the greatest facility to the large exporting towns, Charleston and Savannah, its locality is really enviable. Macon, it is true, divides the interior cotton trade with Augusta; but its share is small when compared with the latter, for Augusta receives produce not only from South Carolina, but from Georgia, wheréas Macon only receives it from the latter State. The cotton stores in Augusta are well worth seeing. These immense buildings, not unlike arsenals at a distance, are planned on a scale which sufficiently shows the extent of the cotton trade. Many of them are spacious enough to contain as many as nine thousand bales. They are built in squares, with an open space in the centre: the sides are formed of stone sheds, roofed with tiles, and open towards the yard.

The houses are of various classes, both in regard to materials and architecture; the greater part, however, are of brick, bearing undeniable evidence of the progress of the art. The streets are capable of many improvements: Augusta may, nevertheless, boast of a thoroughfare called Broad Street, surpassing in width any other in America. Its length is about two miles. When filled with loaded waggons, which is often the case in the winter months, the visiter forgets that he is in the centre of a region but lately a complete desert. Splendid coaches, elegant ladies, or perfumed dandies, are certainly not to be found ; but, notwithstanding the absence of these attributes of a large city, it is still lively. In this street are only to be seen decently dressed women, devoid of all coquetry, speculative merchants, loaded waggons, the size of which exceeded any thing I had as yet seen, close and shrewd farmers, saddle-horses without number, but no equipages. To this catalogue I must not omit to add the noise occasioned by heavy-footed mules, six of which are attached to every loaded cotton waggon, and the peculiar tones with which the Negro, mounted on one of these animals, drives his team. Generally, he has only one rein in the hand, fastened to one of the foremost mules ; but, as this is at times insufficient to give a proper direction to the heavy train, he is continually speaking to his beasts in a manner which they never fail to understand ; and, in order to give a stronger impulse to his words, he adds a few cuts in the air with his whip, which have also a certain meaning, and they are as promptly obeyed as understood.

Opposite to Augusta, in the State of South Carolina, is a small insignificant village, called Hamburg, also possessing a few cotton warehouses: the inhabitants are striving very hard to share the palm with the rich and mighty neighbouring town. Their hopes seem particularly founded on the belief that the now nearly-finished railroad from Charleston, which terminates here, will give new life to their business, to the prejudice of Augusta. How far these expectations will be realized, when the railroad is completed and made available, I am not able to judge; but I cannot help entertaining some doubts on the score of any extraordinary rise of Hamburg, as long as Augusta exists.

A traveller intending to proceed hence by land to New Orleans is earnestly recommended to bid adieu to all comforts on leaving Augusta, and make the necessary preparations for a hard and rough campaign. If he has a wife and children unprovided for, and to whom he has not the means of leaving a suitable legacy, let him by all means be careful to insure his life to the highest amount the offices will take; for the chances of perishing on the road are at the rate of ten to one, calculated according to the following table of casualties:

1. By horses running away.
2. By drowning.
3. By murder.
4. By explosion.

When told in Augusta of the numberless accidents which awaited me on this tour, I could not refrain from laughing, satisfied in my own mind that they were exaggerated, and that I could not possibly have to endure more than I had already encountered during my journey from Norfolk to Charleston; but experience soon taught me to view the latter trip in the light of pleasant and comfortable, when compared with the inconveniences, not to say sufferings, to which a traveller is exposed, when hazarding his person in the woods of Georgia and Alabama. I had hitherto ventured to indulge in invective against the roads in Virginia and both Carolinas: these were now English turnpike-roads, when compared with those I had actually to traverse. I had also complained of the indifference of the stages in the same State: in Alabama I should have deemed myself happy, could I but have got sight of a Virginia stage, instead of the skeleton vehicles which were presented to my view. Too often had I heaped animadversions on the Virginia drivers: in Alabama again, I should have conferred on them the title of real gentlemen. I had even gone so far as to speak in derision and with contempt of the tough, split, and broiled fowls, with which a traveller is regaled at every meal in Virginia, and which are alive five minutes before they are put on the table for consumption: in Alabama, where bacon and sweet potatoes constitute the only delicacies, one of the feathered tribe would have been considered superior to the best Parisian *pateé aux truffes*.

It was towards dusk that I took my place in a narrow, old-fashioned stage, in company with eight passengers, who were proceeding to Macon, a distance of about one hundred and twenty-five miles. Scarcely had we lost sight of Augusta, when a dark, heavy cloud, greeted us with a drenching shower. All the luggage had, in consequence of the great quantity of mail-bags, been thrown carelessly on the top of the stage: let the reader judge of its condition at sunrise on the following morning, when our coach fairly stuck fast in a mud-hole, out of which the soaking wet and mud-covered passengers vainly endeavoured for several successive hours to extricate it. One of them, a foolish landlord, contributed materially to its extrication, and to keep up the spirits of his unfortunate travelling companions, by singing Irish melodies: but, desirous of accompanying his songs by an exhibition on the light fantastic toe, he suddenly slipped, and disappeared in the deep puddle, splashing the bystanders all over with dirty water. Owing to the coolness of the driver, he, however, escaped a watery grave; but, wet as he was, he resumed his seat inside the coach. Having at length obtained assistance from some waggoners, who with difficulty contrived to lift the stage out of the hole, we continued our journey uninterruptedly till evening, when new adventures awaited us. The road, entirely of clay, sadly cut up by the continual transport of cotton, and full of deep holes and furrows, had, besides, numberless roots, stumps, and trunks, of trees, left absolutely untouched by the makers of this highway. Between these, amidst crooked and steep hills, the coachman was obliged to proceed very cautiously; and he was frequently under the necessity of making several turns about the same hill, to avoid coming in contact with these dangerous obstructions, which must infallibly upset the coach. It was on a hill of this kind, where he had probably neglected the usual precaution, that one of the carriage-wheels was unluckily raised by two stumps, high enough to touch the axletree; and, by the violent concussion, the pole, as well as the wheel, was shivered to pieces, and a large hole broken in the bottom of the carriage itself. To me it is still a matter of surprise that none of the passengers were hurt, though I must confess that the confusion was sufficiently great to have produced the most disastrous consequences. To find assistance in the midst of a wild forest, and this too at midnight, was not to be expected. A deliberative council was held, at which it was resolved that we should continue our journey partly on foot, partly on horseback, leaving the coachman to take care of the baggage till the following morning. At daylight we arrived at the much wished-for Macon.

Were I to judge of the little I saw of Georgia, I should say, that the soil of this State did not appear much adapted to the cultivation of cotton; however, from other accounts, it seems that the interior is as fertile as those regions through which I directed my course were poor. Far be it from me to question the correctness of this statement; on the contrary, it is more than probable, considering the large quantities of cotton produced in this State, which are afterwards forwarded for sale to Macon, Augusta, and Savannah. Between Augusta and Macon, nevertheless, the soil is extremely poor, consisting chiefly of sand. I have seldom beheld a wilder picture. No mountains are found; but steep hillocks and heaps of stone in abundance. Between these, in the loose sand, are pines growing close to each other, and a hundred different species of oak. Cultivated fields were hardly ever discernible, and the few scattered ones that we did see bore the appearance of indifferent soil. The houses, which from the road seemed to be at an immense distance from each other, hardly deserved the name of human habitations: had they been without chimneys, I should have been inclined to consider them as sheds for the reception of hogs. Even the inhabitants of these regions had something savage about them: their dress, manners, language, all seemed to partake of the repulsive features of wild nature.

Before arriving at Macon, we passed

through the small towns of Warrenton, Powelton, and Sparta, as well as Milledgeville, the capital of Georgia, situated on a sand-hill, near the River Oconee, and in its present dilapidated state a woful monument of more prosperous days. The town was at this time rather lively and noisy, owing to a land-lottery, organized by the State, then drawing. Georgia had, several years before, bought large tracts of land from the Indians within the territory of the State, which it was now, according to contract, obliged to relinquish. The lots were divided by the State among its citizens in such a manner, that each inhabitant who had resided in Georgia three years after the passing of the act by the Legislature was entitled to a ticket; a married man received an additional ticket, and, if he happened to have children, he obtained a third ticket. Whoever had upon any occasion fought for his country was also presented with a particular ticket. Even gold regions were shared in like manner, and with the same distinctions among the inhabitants: the latter division caused, however, considerable dissatisfaction, it being openly declared that fraud and deception had been practised by an individual who had the management of it. This person was arraigned before the tribunal upon various charges connected with it, but the Court had come to no decision when I left Georgia.

Macon was founded in the year 1823, on a sand-bank near the River Ocmulgee, and counts about three thousand inhabitants. Its excellent locality for purchases of cotton has already had great influence on its increase; so many as eighty thousand bales of this article are annually sent from this place to Savannah, which traffic brings considerable capital into circulation. The environs of Macon retain their pristine features: tall firs rise in every direction, like dismal and impenetrable walls. Here and there may be seen a small piece of land lately cleared; the trees had been so recently felled or burnt that a perpendicular column of smoke rose from the stumps which remained almost to the sky. Amidst these stumps, as if peeping out of the dark wood, were observed a few solitary frame-houses, where some of the townspeople spend their winters and summers. In the town, the buildings, erected at some distance from each other, are also of wood, some two stories, but most of them only one story high, divided into two apartments, of which that fronting the street is used as a store, the other reserved for the family, let it be ever so numerous. In most places recently peopled, the practice of crowding together many persons in the same room is of common occurrence: in houses in the country, particularly in those in the woods, the accommodation of a separate apartment is out of the question; but, in a town with three thousand inhabitants, to find wealthy families living together in one confined room was certainly more than I anticipated. I formed an acquaintance with several of them in very comfortable circumstances, who would in any part of the world have been considered affluent, and yet they lived in a single apartment, beyond the store. The furniture was in harmony with the rest, simple, coarse, and tasteless: the manner of living, too, was simplicity itself. The people are mostly Presbyterians, a sect which forbids every thing bordering on ostentation, and whose principles are not a little conducive to the prevalence of artless and unsophisticated manners: in Macon these seemed to be strictly followed.

The streets are not paved, but covered with light sand, which the least wind raises in volumes, so as to conceal one side of the street from the inhabitants of the other. Like all those in the new Southern States, they form right angles and parallel lines, and are of a width not to be found in older cities. Many of these streets had not yet been named, and were only marked out by the clearing of the wood, and the digging of ditches on the sides: on the map of the town a place had already been assigned to them, as well as to many others, on which were still left the stumps of the trees, which are not a little dangerous to the passenger in the dark. With streets in such a condition, it was not surprising that coaches were very seldom seen: I observed no vehicles in Macon, but a few miserable stages and a couple of country waggons. Most people travelled on horseback; and this rule was observed upon every occasion, whether they were going into the country, or merely to visit a neighbouring friend. The aversion to walking must be either the natural consequence of the heat of the climate, which produces a relaxation of the system, or the effect of indolence, that has insensibly grown into a habit. I shall not stop to decide the question, but only to mention its existence. Saddle-horses were seen whole days standing before the houses, and, when not there, were to be found in sheds in the yards. A merchant could not conclude a bargain with a neighbour, if ever so near, without his horse. A sueing swain would be sure of a rebuff, if he had the temerity to present himself as a pedestrian at the residence of his mistress.

The principal article of commerce in Macon is, as I have before observed, cotton. The bales are forwarded, immediately after purchase, to the two neighbouring seaports, of which Savannah, on account of its proximity, receives the largest supply. The conveyance is effected by means of the rivers, first by the Ocmulgee, on which Macon is situated, afterwards by the Oconee, which joins the Ocmulgee, and forms the large river Alatamaha, down which it is carried as far as Darien. The craft are either long and narrow, or built in the shape of boxes, the bottom of which is made of timber and cork. On these small vessels eight rows of bales are piled up; from four to five hundred constituting a cargo. They float down the stream, and look like moving houses. This method of conveying goods was, however, by some individuals, considered both expensive and tedious: a few of the wealthier and more enterprizing citizens determined to make a trial with steamboats. One was built, by way of experiment, with a flat bottom, to enable her to get over the shoals in the river, at low and high water. This steamer was not finished when I left Macon.

The climate, in these desolate regions, compensates, in some measure, for the pleasures elsewhere so highly valued; which a want of civilization among different classes here precludes. The atmosphere is, during the whole winter, extremely mild and agreeable: in summer the heat is great, without being oppressive, or attended with epidemics, so prevalent near the coast. In the middle of December, the period when I visited Macon, the leaves first began to change colour, a change which I had already witnessed the preceding September in the States of New York and Pennsylvania. Thousands of roses were still in full bloom on terraces before the houses, and here and there I saw flowers in the fields, of which I had been in the habit of taking leave on the appearance of the first autumn day; but in this delightful climate they continue to dispense their fragrance till the arrival of the new year. The surrounding woods were filled with the most odoriferous and enlivening perfumes, and even in certain parts of the town, at sunset, the evening breeze wafted to the pedestrian a delicious odour.

On my return from an excursion to the ruins of a fort, formerly raised against the Indians, a free Negro was shown to me, who, unlike all others of the same race, had not had recourse to beggary after recovering his liberty. It is an incontestable fact, fully authenticated by experience, that a Negro, once a slave, and afterwards set free, from that moment becomes as useless as he has formerly been industrious. I was therefore not a little pleased to form acquaintance with a man so different from the rest, which leaves at least one conclusive evidence on record, that the doctrine so repeatedly advanced, and so revolting to the ideas of the philanthropists, is false, namely, that a Negro is half man and half brute. His name was Solomon Humphries, and he was as well known by all classes a hundred miles round as the governor himself. He kept a kind of grocery store, which yielded a handsome annual profit, and added to an already acquired property of twenty thousand dollars. Known as industrious and prudent, he had greater credit than many an extensive merchant: and there was no individual in Macon, from the richest cotton-dealer to the poorest servant, who did not stop and shake him by the hand. Solomon was married to a woman of colour, drove his own unostentatious carriage, and had a neat and comfortably furnished house, where he often entertained strangers. The principal merchants were not above accepting his invitations to dinner: upon these occasions, they were welcomed with an hospitality and kindness perhaps unexpected from a Negro. Never forgetting his station in life, it was customary with him, when performing the office of host, to wait upon his guests in person; and, although possessing several slaves, he never permitted any of them to stand behind the chairs, or even to approach the table. He made a rule of inviting every stranger coming to the city, and as such I had also the honour of an invitation; I was, however, under the necessity of declining it, having already fixed the period of my departure for Columbus on the following evening. It was with no small mortification that I renounced this pleasure; probably it was the last time in my life that I should have an opportunity of dining with a Negro, as it was the only invitation I ever received.

A little before midnight I was again in the

stage, filled, as usual, with nine travellers, mostly inhabitants of Columbus, returning from Milledgeville, where they had been drawing tickets for lots in the gold region. The conversation turned exclusively on the subject of gold dust and gold bars: calculations of certain incomes, derivable from this source of wealth, were made in the coach, and appeared, at least to them, so clear and infallible, that it would have been easier to convince them that the earth is square, than that they could possibly fail to be possessed, in the course of a few years, of as much of the precious metal as would purchase a kingdom in Europe. I listened for a long time with the greatest attention to these lofty statements and illustrative plans, and was just on the eve of joining the general conversation, with a view to obtain some further information respecting these valuable gold regions, when a very sudden and serious shock at one end of the coach demolished at once all aërial castles and golden dreams, and directed the attention of every one to his personal safety, preparatory to his becoming a Crœsus. The driver, who had probably also been indulging in the same happy dreams, having himself drawn a prize in the golden lottery, had unfortunately missed his way in the dark, and did not discover his error till the carriage was fairly jammed between two old trees, which squeezed the frail vehicle so dreadfully that the axletree was broken in pieces. This accident happened in the middle of a steep hill, down which the coach rolled with no ordinary velocity, so that the horses, once started, could not be stopped, but ran away the moment the accident occurred. Left alone with the fragments of a *ci-devant* stage, we held a consultation as to the best mode of proceeding: at the recommendation of the driver, it was unanimously resolved to await the approach of morning, and take the chance of meeting some waggon, roomy enough to convey ourselves and our luggage to the nearest village, distant about sixteen miles. Without waiting for the break of day, I continued my journey on foot, in company with one of the passengers well acquainted with the road. During this compulsory promenade, I had frequent opportunities of contemplating the wild and uniform appearance of these uncultivated regions. From a soil almost exclusively of sand, rose a close and dark wood, the height of whose trees bespoke venerable age. Here and there the loose and dry sand varied a little; a verdant swamp was seen enveloped in fog, through which drooping cypresses rose like ghosts at a gloomy distance. Nearer to Columbus, the country became more hilly: the Alleghany Mountain chain, which may be called the back-bone of North America, here commences in a long series of sloping hills, above and round which the road winds in various directions.

It was at the foot of one of these hills that I fell in with a gang (as they are called) of slaves, on their march to New Orleans, for sale. The slave-trader had chained them two and two together, and so disposed of them during the few hours in the night allowed for rest after the day's fatigue, that none of them could possibly escape the watchful eyes of the owner or his assistant. A great number of these miserable beings were seated round a large fire, attentively listening to each other's narratives: others were lying in groups, absorbed in profound sleep. At the further extremity, near a tree, was the slave-trader himself, looking sternly at his victims, and now and then roaring to them to be quiet. He was not, however, able to quell the general mirth that prevailed, occasioned by the lively anecdotes related by a young slave, about twenty, to his companions in misfortune: laughter and signs of approbation continued without interruption. Yes, bursts of laughter made the whole wood ring. Who would have supposed that these were slaves, going to a market for sale? Without being perceived, we approached this singular group. They were all without any head-covering, but pretty decently dressed in linen clothes, in my opinion rather too light for winter, but with which they seemed perfectly satisfied. Real joy was expressed in every countenance, and they gave way to fits of laughter, which made their eyes sparkle with tears.

The young speaker related with southern warmth the many vicissitudes he had experienced during his short life, and painted in equally lively colours the happy and unhappy adventures in which he had been engaged. His narrative of an attempt to escape from his owner in South Carolina inspired me with real interest for the young hero: upon several occasions he made the most striking comparisons. It was impossible not to feel compassion, on hearing him describe the severe punishment which followed the unfortunate attempt: even the other slaves, so disposed to be merry, became silent for a moment, horror-struck at the faithful description which he gave of his corporeal sufferings. But this silence continued only for a few minutes: the narrative again became animated, and the audience was not backward in testifying its approbation by loud and reiterated applause.

This short biography was scarcely finished, before a glittering object suddenly made its appearance from the small wood in the swamp, and changed the features of every face, substituting astonishment and curiosity for joy and happiness! The kindled fire spread its pale light over the bushes in the neighbourhood, and between the bald fir-trunks stood a tall, swarthy, and wild-looking figure—it was an Indian of the Creek race, the first of the "Red Men" I had seen in the woods. The strong impression which this meeting produced will not be easily effaced. I had in my subsequent travels frequent opportunities of seeing these sons of the forest, but never did they appear to me so formidable, so noble, so majestic, as this solitary Indian. His head was covered with a kind of red woollen turban, the ends of which hung down on one of his shoulders: on his legs he wore a kind of stockings, made of skins, and his feet were covered by a pair of handsome moccasins. He was wrapped in a blanket, which, nevertheless, did not prevent my seeing his strong, well-proportioned, and athletic figure. His height and martial air (such as a warrior ought to have)—the expression of his countenance—his features—were all noble and grand. Could this really be a savage?

My travelling companion, who had often seen Indians, was not seized with the same degree of admiration as myself, and lost no time in asking him the motive of his sudden appearance. The reply destroyed the illusion as quickly as his person had at first prepossessed me. Whisky was now the only deity he worshipped: for the possession of it he would sell father, children, and country. How much more delighted should I have been, had I seen him raise his tomahawk, and, foaming with rage, demand the blood of the Whites, instead of begging for a compound which, like slow poison, undermined his constitution, enervated the sinewy arm, and made the free hero an object of contempt, commiserated by none. Hardly had he received the wished-for liquor, before he eagerly put the bottle to his mouth, and ran away from us, carrying off the few remaining drops. Unhappy man! His draught was death. In the course of the following day his corpse was found close to a fire in the middle of the wood. Judging from the situation in which his half-consumed body was discovered, he must have fallen asleep in an intoxicated state too near the fire, and been either suffocated or burnt to death.

END OF VOL. I.

LONDON:
F. SHOBERL, JUN., 4, LEICESTER STREET, LEICESTER SQUARE.